GAY AWARENESS

DISCOVERING THE HEART OF THE FATHER
& THE MIND OF CHRIST *on Sexuality*

LANDON SCHOTT
FOREWORD BY Dr. Michael Brown

Gay Awareness Endorsements

"Where there's confusion, there's a crying need for clarity. And since few subjects are as fraught with confusion as the subject of homosexuality, Landon Schott's *Gay Awareness* provides a welcome and much needed voice. This book is a direct, easy-read guide to the many subjects this issue raises, and will leave readers better equipped to discuss same-sex behavior from a biblical perspective."
Joe Dallas
Author and Speaker

"At a time when our culture is being shaped by political correctness and moral cowardice, it is refreshing to have a voice like Landon Schott's shouting in the wilderness. The message of this book is both forcefully prophetic and graciously compassionate—because we need both grace and truth applied to the hot-button issue of homosexuality. This is not a book about hate or condemnation. Landon offers hope to those who struggle with their sexuality, and encouragement to all who minister to the sexually broken."
J. Lee Grady
Former Editor, *Charisma* magazine
Director, The Mordecai Project

"Powerful! Revealing! Filled with both grace and truth! A right now word for one of the most controversial subjects of our time. *Gay Awareness* is written with love and clarity as sharp as any two-edged sword (though sheathed), reminiscent of Jesus's interaction with the woman at the well. A must-read for those who are hurting, confused, and seeking truth! Educational for the church on the true heart of the Father!"
Chris Gilkey
Lead Pastor, Reach Church

"*Gay Awareness: Discovering the Heart of the Father and the Mind of Christ on Sexuality* is a must-read for every Christian. In this provocative book, evangelist Landon Schott tackles the evidence for and against homosexuality from a balanced, unbiased, and biblical perspective. Schott's underlying theme is the importance of lining up our inner life with our outer actions. Dr. Ken Chant, noted author and theologian from Australia, describes it as narrowing the gap between our Standing (in the heavenlies with Christ, for-

given, loved, adopted, all by grace, etc.) and our State (our actual life and struggles on earth, our reactions to life's circumstances, our ethical choices, etc.). In our days of moral relativism it is essential that we reacquaint ourselves with the principles of the Scriptures that are to govern our lives regarding issues of morality and ethical living."
Dr. Alan Bullock
Missionary, Evangelist, and Author

"Everyone is asking questions, and it would be detrimental to the church for them to go unanswered. Homosexuality is a subject that often goes without broach or without being completely understood. For several years I lived that lifestyle without completely understanding the struggle myself. My confusion wasn't broken until Jesus, in His infinite truth and light, set me free. This book addresses the reality of homosexuality in an honest and authoritative voice that will change the dimension with which you understand it. With the truth finally clear in our hearts, we can go forward to have conversations that change our culture and reveal the love of Christ to all the world."
Kegan Wesley
Evangelist and Speaker

"With scholarly skill and biblical clarity, Landon addresses one of the most demanding subjects of our time. Homosexuality is certainly a hot button issue in our culture. With both the heart of a shepherd and voice of a prophet he speaks to the confusion and extremes that swirl around this controversial issue. This book will give hope to those who are struggling and help to those of us who want to minister to others seeking freedom. You will be both challenged and enriched as you read this book and feel the Father's heart!"
Pastor Zane Anderson
Victory Worship Center

"In *Gay Awareness*, Landon taps into scriptural truths and mixes them with compassion to proclaim the truth about the gay agenda. He inspires readers with testimonies of ex-LGBTs and equips them with biblical knowledge they will need to make a loving stand against a rising tide of immorality."
Jennifer LeClaire
Senior Editor, *Charisma* magazine

GAY AWARENESS

DISCOVERING THE HEART OF THE FATHER AND THE MIND OF CHRIST ON SEXUALITY

LANDON SCHOTT

Foreword By
Dr. Michael Brown

Gay Awareness: Discovering the Heart of the Father and the Mind of Christ on Sexuality
© 2016 Landon Schott

Famous Publishing (A Division of The Rev Ministries)
Austin, TX

ISBN: 978-1942306481

DEDICATION

I dedicate this book to my spiritual father and mentor John Paul Jackson (JP). Before I met JP, the Holy Spirit spoke to my spirit and said, "You need him in your life to accomplish your life's assignment." I believe this book is a part of that life assignment. I wouldn't have made it without JP. He taught me about the righteousness of God. He mentored me in the prophetic and challenged me to be a better man in private than I am in public.

JP, you were taken too soon, but I'm so very grateful for every moment I had with you. Thank you for being an amazing spiritual father and teaching me how fathers give and demand nothing in return. Thank you for the father's blessing I get to share with the world in Chapter 14. I love you JP. I miss you greatly.

I want to thank Diane Jackson for sharing John Paul with me and the rest of the world. You are a generous and selfless woman, Diane. Heather and I love and appreciate you.

ACKNOWLEDGMENTS

I would like to thank God for the opportunity to write this book and teach a generation of dedicated Christ followers the heart of the Father and mind of Christ when it comes to sexuality.

I want to thank my beautiful wife, Heather Lynn Schott, for loving me unconditionally and standing by my side as the Lord continues giving me some challenging assignments. You mean the world to me, darling. I love you!

I'm so grateful to Dr. Michael Brown for mentoring me over the last few years. Your influence on my life and this book is second to none. Your unwavering love for homosexuals and the Word of God has had an incredible impact on me. For years I have watched people verbally assault you. In response, you simply turned the other cheek and bled the love of Jesus. You inspire me, sir. Thank you so much for your love, support, and mentorship. (I'm also so honored you agreed to write the foreword for this book. Thank you.)

I want to give honor to my intercessory prayer team. Thank you for standing in the gap for me as I contend for righteousness in this generation. Thank you for daily praying for me. Thank you for praying the heart of the Father and the mind of Christ with me over this book for years. I love you all!

Thank you, Chris Gilkey, Steve Penate, and Dr. Alan Bullock for your prayers, contributions, and insights.

Thank you, Dr. Bullock, for the research you provided for Chapter 3. Thank you, John and the team at BibleHub.com for providing me with an amazing research tool for use with God's holy Word.

I would like to give special thanks to Jim Kochenburger for editing this book, S.C. and Alycia for proofreading, and Justine Hanin for creating the art and cover design. It has been a blessing working with all of you.

Table of Contents

FOREWORD

Landon Schott is a brave young man.

He is sailing into difficult waters—waters marked by spiritual danger that, to the natural mind, offer far more risk than reward—and he is setting his face against the prevailing tide.

Why would a successful leader with a good following tackle such a controversial subject? Why would he address something that is bound to offend many, and perhaps, cost him friends, finances, and favor? In particular, why would he do it when his main audience is young people? It is a cardinal sin among today's youth to fail to celebrate and affirm homosexuality.

The answer is simple: Landon is motivated by love—love for God and love for the gay community—and it is this love that has moved him to write this important, life-changing book. When you really love people, you tell them the truth, regardless of cost or consequence.

Love not only wins, but love also warns. At the same time, when you really love people, you speak the truth with grace, kindness, and compassion, and that's what Landon has done in *Gay Awareness*.

You will find this book to be full of Bible verses, sound biblical reasoning, and hope. You will also find this book to be full of wonderful Jesus-exalting testimonies from people who once identified as gay or lesbian, but now identify as children of God, no longer bound by what enslaved them. This is the power of the gospel!

In January 2005, the Spirit of God spoke to me, saying, "Reach out and resist." He was saying, "Reach out to the gay and lesbian community with compassion; resist gay activism with courage." This book follows these same guidelines. It does not yield an inch to the ideologies and arguments of gay activists and theologians. Instead, it reaches out with compassion to all those who want to follow Jesus, but who struggle with same-sex attraction. If that describes you, then this book has your name on it.

I pray that as you read through the pages of *Gay Awareness* you will determine, by God's grace, to follow the truth wherever it leads. I pray for scales of deception to fall off your eyes with each revelation and insight from the Word. I also pray that God will give you the courage to swim against the tide and go against the grain of our contemporary society, to determine to please the Lord rather than gratify the flesh, and to bow down to Him rather than to conform to the pattern of this age.

Let your identity be found in Jesus—not in your romantic attractions or sexual desires—and in Him you will find everything you could ever want or desire. The Lord will always prove Himself to be more than enough, and He will always give you what you need to live a truly full life.

Some of you may pick up this book in anger, ready to rebut someone you judge to be a homophobe, but as you read, you will not find any homophobia. Instead, you will find the heart of God. Before you know it, you could be on the path to radical transformation in Him!

May you go forward and never look back. You will never have a regret. And one day, hopefully, you'll meet Landon face to face and say, "Thank you for writing this book! It changed my life forever." I assure you that you will not be the first to speak those words to him.

Michael L. Brown, Ph.D.
AskDrBrown.org

I LOVE GAY PEOPLE

It was the summer of 2008. I was watching the number one reality show in America. In it, a billionaire businessman plays boss to a group of excited contestants, or project managers. He gives them ridiculous tasks to manage in order to make the most profit possible. He fires those who fail the worst and kicks them off the show. The show had been popular for a few seasons by then, but that year there was an added twist. Several celebrities were enlisted as the new project managers, and they were all on the show to raise money for their favorite charities.

At the close of the show each week, a different celebrity project manager talked about his or her chosen charity. They talked about charities for wounded veterans with life-altering injuries, charities responsible for humanitarian efforts in poor nations, and more. The celebrities would also share why they had such a heart and passion for their particular charity.

On this specific episode, the project manager was an old '80s rock star who had won the challenge and led her team to victory. As the show wrapped up, the boisterous billionaire host asked her to talk about the charity she had selected to support with funds from the show. The noble cause she had selected was "gay awareness," and the charity was a gay/lesbian-backed organization. I was completely shocked when I heard it. Not because it was 2008 and gay rights and gay marriage weren't mainstream yet, but because, out of all the charities that feed hungry people, clothe children, shelter animals, provide medical care for war torn nations, or save young girls from human trafficking, she had chosen gay awareness. There was no purpose in her choice beyond simply making the world aware of gay people. Things have changed dramatically since 2008.

The world is now very much aware of homosexuality, and America still leads the way in promoting gay "awareness." In fact, gay awareness has swept over our culture like a tidal wave led by Hollywood's influence and fueled by the media.

Later in 2008, pop star Katy Perry released her song, "I Kissed a Girl," and it launched an impressionable generation into bisexual curiosity. The wave of awareness continued to grow. About the same time, movies began pouring out that included plotlines supporting same-sex relationships; just about every TV show started featuring at least one gay character and storyline, and popular TV talk shows amped up their promotion of gay lifestyles. Now, professional athletes win awards not based on their performance on a field/court/track, but for their behavior in the bedroom.

Every time another athlete, celebrity, or TV personality "comes out," the nation seemingly erupts in celebration and gushes support. The most popular magazines feature the star on their covers. The star becomes a top trending subject on Internet search engines. And the most watched prime time talk shows interview him or her. On numerous occasions, even the current president of the United States of America has given nationally broadcast encouragement to gay athletes and celebrities.

Awareness continued to spread spurred on by Lady Gaga's song, "Born This Way," a catchy song that launched to number one in the world. Taking the baton from Katy Perry, who essentially told everyone in the world to kiss a member of the same sex because they just might like it, was usurped by Gaga who basically preached: "Fully give yourself to the homosexual form of sexual lifestyle. You have good reason to—you were born this way."

Month after month and year after year, gay awareness has continued to spread throughout America and the world, and even reached the Supreme Court. On June 26, 2015, the Supreme Court of the United States voted to legalize gay marriage in all fifty states, despite the matter being voted down by the people in most states. We are now very aware.

I want to make sure you are aware of a few other things. I love gay people. I love the gay community. There is no homophobic hate in my entire being. I grew up in Seattle, so I would say I was more aware of the gay community than the majority of Americans. I spent a lot of time in the "Capitol Hill" district, the epicenter for the gay community there. My favorite coffee place was there, I would get my hair cut there, shopped there, and generally spent a lot of time there.

I have always had a heart for the gay community, and been drawn to minister to the people in it. Over the years, a number of my friends struggled with same-sex attraction, and I found myself drawn to them just as people. In high school and junior college, I was into the latest fashion. So every time I wore a daring outfit, others questioned me about my sexuality. It wasn't uncommon. I don't hate anyone, especially those in the gay community.

God loves gay people. God loves people. God loves us so much, He sent His son to die on the cross for us so that we could be restored to relationship with Him. The Bible teaches us God dislikes some behaviors and hates others, but that He loves people. He loves you!

I titled this book *Gay Awareness* because I want you to be aware of God's heart toward you, homosexuality, and those who experience same-sex attraction. In this book I'm going to show you the heart of God and the mind of Christ on sexuality through His words, not through my own or any other man's opinions. I want you to be aware of what the Bible says and what it teaches followers of Christ.

As I spent years praying into this book, it was important for me to know its audience. This book is primarily for the individual who struggles with same-sex attraction, but truly loves God with all his or her heart. This person follows Jesus, but struggles in this area. Secondarily, this book is for the Christ-follower who desires to know what the Bible truly says about homosexuality, and how to show love to family members and friends who struggle with this.

Maybe you've had this attraction as long as you can remember. Maybe you developed it along the way. Regardless of when you started having these feelings, you still have them and they are very real. Your conflict is in managing your attraction to the same sex alongside your fear of the Lord. This becomes excruciating for many people.

Many people pray and ask God to take away their temptation and same-sex desire, but when these don't go away, they give in to them or completely embrace them. Others battle these feelings every day, while believing God for complete deliverance and freedom. If you are praying and battling these feelings, this book is for you! I believe you are going to experience the freedom your heart desires.

If you are a Christ-follower you love God and love people, so it is most likely you have people in your life for whom you care deeply, who struggle with same-sex attraction or claim to be practicing homosexuals. It's a challenge when the God we serve contradicts the actions of the people we love. You want to know how to help those you care about, how to comfort a family member or friend, and how to honor God at the same time. This book will teach you what Scripture says about homosexuality and how to respond to people in different situations with love, grace, and truth.

This is not a book packed with the latest statistics on homosexuality. It is not designed to paint the gay community as a "plague on society." And this is not a scholarly work that will compare first century translations and arguments in the original language (though I will recommend books by brilliant, God-fearing men that deal with homosexuality from a scholarly approach). This is a book on the heart of the Father and the mind of Christ as found in God's Word.

This book may offend some and relieve others, but in it you will not see anywhere written (except here), "You're going to hell!" God is the final judge. And as I will show you in the chapters to come, He knows who His children are. Everyone deserves to be treated with kindness and respect, no matter who they are. I want you to feel respected and safe as you read. I'm not going to yell at you. I'm not going to attack you. I want to show you how much God loves you, and how to respond by loving Him.

Over the years, the church made three primary mistakes in dealing with sexuality and those who struggle with same-sex attraction. The first mistake was to make homosexuality the greatest sin. Homosexual practice is not the greatest sin. Pride is! It's because of pride that Satan and his angels fell from heaven. Pride keeps us from repentance. It also keeps us from a relationship with God. And pride can keep us from entering heaven. This mistake has led to the demonization of people instead of the demonization of devils. When people feel demonized, it keeps them from coming to church. It causes them to not want to be around Christians. The enemy uses this to push them toward unhealthy people and unhealthy places.

The second mistake the church has made is that it has not addressed homosexuality. When this particular issue is unaddressed by the church, it leaves room for many unbiblical opinions and immature conversations to fill in the blanks. Because of a lack of biblical knowledge and the silence of the church, people are confused, left to wonder, and end up making unhealthy decisions that can be very destructive to everyone. Leaving this issue unaddressed helps no one and can end up hurting everyone. Every church must address homosexuality. And every church must use the Bible as its ultimate guide for wisdom, love, and truth.

> ## "Homosexual practice is not the greatest sin. Pride is!"

The third and most harmful mistake many churches have made is to affirm the sinner in his or her practice of homosexuality. It's impossible to affirm what God never affirms. It's impossible to call good what God never called good, and it's impossible to call blessed what God never called blessed. Because of the lack of biblical awareness, many churches have given in to the pressure forged in hell and embraced by man, affirmed homosexual practice, and asserted all that comes with it is blessed by God.

In this book, I'm going to show you that God loves the sinner, but sin separates us from the God of love. As followers of Christ, we must respond with unconditional love to individuals dealing with same-sex attraction, and remain unwavering in our loyalty to God's Word.

I almost titled this book, What the Bible Says About Homosexuality, but I didn't want to sound presumptuous. The reason I contemplated that title is because there are so many Bible verses in this book: over 400 Scripture references, to be exact. I believe the Bible is God's Word. It is the lamp that guides my life. Second Timothy 3:16 says, "All Scripture is God-breathed and is useful for teaching, rebuking, correcting and training in righteousness." Again, I believe the Bible is God's Word. I believe the people and accounts are real. I have faith that it is God's Word.

On a nationally syndicated news show one night, I watched a news anchor interview a well-known pastor from Texas on current events. The pastor used Jonah as an example in his dialogue with the news anchor. At that, the anchor challenged the pastor, saying, "Pastor, isn't that from the Old Testament? Don't we know that story to be more allegorical?" All the while the anchor professed to be a faithful Catholic and believer in Jesus. "What?" I shouted at my TV. He claimed to believe in Jesus. That means he believes a virgin named Mary was impregnated by the Holy Spirit, gave birth to the Son of God, named Jesus, who was (and is) the Savior of the world. Jesus never sinned and he performed countless miracles. Eventually, he was crucified on the cross, rose from the dead three days later, and ascended to heaven. Those who believe all this do so by faith and follow Jesus. So the news anchor believed in all that, but considered the Old Testament to be allegorical? God's Word needs to be taken seriously and treated with sincerity. It's all applicable and beneficial to our walk with the Lord and enables us to live Christ-like lives. Proverbs 30:5-6 says, *"Every word of God is flawless; he is a shield to those who take refuge in him. Do not add to his words, or he will rebuke you and prove you a liar."*

> **"...God loves the sinner, but sin separates us from the God of love."**

♥

Jesus was and is God's Word, loved God's Word, and lived by God's Word. Jesus was the one who said, *"For truly I tell you, until heaven and earth disappear, not the smallest letter, not the least stroke of a pen, will by any means disappear from the Law until everything is accomplished,"* Matthew 5:18. Let there be no confusion: God's Word is always relevant in an evolving culture. God's Word was relevant then, and it's relevant now. This is why Jesus told us, *"Heaven and earth will pass away, but My words will not pass away"* (Mark 13:31). Even when culture changes, God's Word doesn't change. It doesn't adapt to culture, it transcends it. Living according to God's Word (the Bible) is what makes us Christ-followers. If you don't learn, follow, and obey the teachings of the Bible, then you're not an active follower of Christ.

In Ephesians 6, the apostle Paul teaches us how we fight a spiritual battle. The apostle teaches that believers are given the "Sword of the Spirit" (the Word) as a weapon. The sword of the Lord is the Word of God. *"For the word of God is alive and active. Sharper than any double-edged sword, it penetrates even to dividing soul and spirit, joints and marrow; it judges the thoughts and attitudes of the heart"* (Hebrews 4:12). Jesus was well trained with the sword, the Word of God.

> **"...we must respond with unconditional love to individuals dealing with same-sex attraction, and remain unwavering in our loyalty to God's Word."**

When Jesus responded to the temptation of Satan, He did so with God's Word. *"Jesus answered, 'It is written: "Man shall not live on bread alone, but on every word that comes from the mouth of God"'"* (Matthew 4:4). We use the Word of God to cut through every lie, deception, and argument that comes against the body of Christ. If you don't believe the Bible is the true Word of God, how will you overcome anything?

For some people, the obstacle isn't faith in Jesus, but the lack of knowledge about Jesus and passages in the Bible. *"Jesus replied, 'You are in error because you do not know the Scriptures or the power of God'"* (Matthew 22:29). Not knowing what God's Word says is extremely damaging to our relationship with Him. God's Word teaches us right from wrong, good from evil, and the difference between what's holy and what's carnal. Many followers of Jesus have a mixture of beliefs—from biblical to cultural to worldly—that all influence their lives. This mixture creates a lukewarm environment that keeps us from living lives that please the Lord. When the Bible is not the authority, what is? We're left with our own opinions. People let their personal opinions and feelings trump Scripture all the time. All of this taken together leads to false doctrine and compromised lifestyles.

I want to encourage you: please do not skim the many Bible verses you read throughout this book. I have to admit, on more than one occasion, I have been guilty of skimming over quoted Scripture in books, because the verses or passages were so familiar. I promise you, those words are so much more important to read than those I have written.

As I wrote in my spiritual warfare book, *Jezebel: The Witch Is Back,* "Using Scripture to hurt people is witchcraft. God's Word is not meant to hurt people. Satan tried to use God's Word to hurt everyone. The devil will try to use God's Word to bring condemnation. But the Holy Spirit will speak through God's Word to bring conviction to your life. Condemnation brings shame and creates distance between you and God. Conviction brings repentance and draws you closer to God."

I want to challenge you to continue reading this book all the way through. Don't allow any distraction of life or ungodly spirit to keep you from finishing. The enemies of God do not want you to read this book. They do not want you to become equipped as a believer and set free from strongholds in your life. One warning: you will experience attacks and opposition designed to discourage and distract you from finishing this book.

> "God's Word doesn't change. It doesn't adapt to culture, it transcends it."

My prayer is that you will receive conviction from the Holy Spirit as you read this book, and it will bring you to the closest, most intimate place you've ever been with God. As you read, ask the Holy Spirit to speak. Ask the Holy Spirit to come in grace and reveal truth, that you may know the heart of God and live a life that pleases Him. Let's pray together. As with all prayers in this book, I encourage you to read this prayer first, and then speak it out loud with boldness and sincerity. Pray with me below.

Father, I declare you are holy, holy, holy. Jesus, you are holy, holy, holy. Spirit of the living God, you are holy, holy, holy. I pray to you, Father in heaven, in the name of Jesus, and by the power of the Holy Spirit, to speak to me as I read. I ask right now for ears to hear you, a heart to receive you, and a mind to understand you. I declare no spirit but the Holy Spirit has permission to be here or influence me. Every lying and distracting spirit has to LEAVE ME NOW, IN JESUS'S NAME. I pray my heart will align with the heart of the Father, and my mind will align with the mind of Christ. I declare God's Word is the highest authority, and I submit to your Word, God. I pray for peace, clarity, and the power of the Holy Spirit to come over me now in Jesus's name. Speak Lord, I declare, your servant is listening!

THE GOSPEL

As I stated in the last chapter, one of the costliest mistakes the church makes in regard to homosexual practice is to declare it the greatest sin. To make it the greatest sin elevates it above others and leads people to conclude it is worse than their sin.

Unfortunately, it's common for immature Christians to compare themselves favorably to others in order to feel better about themselves. It's the, "at least I'm not as messed up as that person" mentality. This mind-set is incredibly damaging to both the individual who holds it and the people he or she encounters. Our Christianity isn't based on comparing our lives to others, but on comparing our lives to Jesus and the teachings of the Bible. First Corinthians 13:12 says, *"For now we see only a reflection as in a mirror; then we shall see face to face. Now I know in part; then I shall know fully, even as I am fully known."* The Bible is the mirror we use to look at ourselves. It's the reflection of the character of God. We should strive to follow Jesus and emulate Him, not compare ourselves with others.

When I first announced I was writing a book on homosexuality I got an incredible amount of backlash and resistance from non-Christians as well as others who described themselves as Christians. I received many vicious and hate-filled messages that attacked my intentions, ministry, and character. Many people accused me of being homophobic, hateful, ignorant, and judgmental.

One of the most common questions posed to me was, "Why are you writing a book that focuses on this one particular issue?" in attempts to discourage me from writing this book. However, this only encouraged me all the more. The writers were right to a degree. There are many sins the Bible warns us not to commit, and homosexual activity is just one of them. The question is, how do you deal with sin? You deal with sin one issue at a time.

There are thousands of books on the subjects of lying, greed, anger, slander, stealing, and adultery (and the list goes on and on). This book happens to be on the subject of homosexuality.

Sin is an issue not only in the lives of the lost people of the world, but also in the body of Christ. We can't focus on homosexuality and at the same time ignore the sins with which others might struggle. We must deal with our sin. We must confront sin in the church. We must confront the thoughts, attitudes, addictions, and behaviors for which Christ died to set us free. *"How can you say to your brother, 'Let me take the speck out of your eye,' when all the time there is a plank in your own eye?"* (Matthew 7:4). We must take the "plank" out of our own eye! The plank in our own eye is the heterosexual sin of the church. It's time to remove it.

The church has lost its voice to the gay community because of the hypocrisy of those who claim to follow Jesus. The Bible gives clear guidelines for sexuality and the boundaries of morality. I want to address a few of these issues.

It needs to be made clear that *any* form of sex outside of biblical marriage is fornication and sinful in the eyes of the Lord. We get the word, "fornication," from the Greek word, "porneúō," which means, "to commit fornication (sexual immorality).

As I wrote this chapter, my four-year-old daughter interrupted me a few times. The last time she burst into my study and proclaimed, "Dad, I wish I could be a real doctor!" She had been watching an episode of a Mickey Mouse show in which one character was a doctor. I told her, "OK baby, you just need to go to medical school." She replied, "No, Dad, I have to go to a doctor's office and wear a white doctor's coat!" In her four-year-old mind, she believed that going to an office and wearing a doctor's coat made one a doctor. Too many Christians think that going to church and putting on the right persona makes them a Christ-follower! First John 2:6 says, *"Whoever claims to live in him must live as Jesus did."* Christians are posing as Christ-followers while living in sexual sin.

In our society today, it is not uncommon at all for boyfriends and girlfriends to engage in premarital sex. Even if they later decide to get married, they have already been unfaithful to each other with each other because they were unfaithful to God. Even if they "love" each other, they are not married in God's eyes. In His eyes, they are fornicating, and this is sin. This is why He gave us the Scriptures to live by. *"But since sexual immorality is occurring, each man should have sexual relations with his own wife, and each woman with her own husband,"* (1 Corinthians 7:2). It's not uncommon for Christian couples to live together (cohabitate), and then attend church and live as if nothing is wrong. They have kids and raise them together, claim to be disciples of Jesus, but live in sin. We have become so tolerant of our carnal culture that we have lost our reverence for a godly lifestyle.

> ## "Even if they "love" each other, they are not married in God's eyes."

Just about every movie promotes casual sexual relationships. Christian athletes claim to live wholesome lives, wear gold crosses, and thank God in interviews, but get their girlfriends pregnant. All the while, Christians don't seem to care at all. We pick and choose to live by only part of Jesus's instructions.

Many people don't take instructions from the Bible seriously. They consider the Bible to be old-fashioned, outdated, or out of touch with our world today. Parents model sexual sin to their children through their immoral relationships, and teach them by their actions that God's Word is not the highest authority in their lives. Kids quickly learn that if they don't have to obey God's Word when it comes to sex, then why obey it in other areas of life? Sex is designed by God to be enjoyed only between a husband and a wife. Any sexual activity outside of that is a sin against God.

So many people only pretend to follow Christ, and we all pay the price for this. Adultery and divorce are all too common in the lives of Christians. The book of Proverbs is full of warnings for individuals who participate in adultery. A number of verses warn of the consequences of adultery. I cite a few below.

For a prostitute will bring you to poverty, but sleeping with another man's wife will cost you your life. (Proverbs 6:26 NLT)

Proverbs 6:29, *So it is with the man who sleeps with another man's wife. He who embraces her will not go unpunished.* (Proverbs 6:29 NLT)

But the man who commits adultery is an utter fool, for he destroys himself. (Proverbs 6:32 NLT)

This is the way of an adulterous woman: She eats and wipes her mouth and says, "I've done nothing wrong." (Proverbs 30:20 NLT)

My father used to tell me, "The immoral man will lose his health, wealth, and family." He based his advice on a compilation of the sins of David, Solomon, Samson, and many others who suffered greatly because of sexual sin, according to the Bible. The book of James echoes what Moses wrote by the directive of God in the Ten Commandments. *"For he who said, 'You shall not commit adultery,' also said, 'You shall not murder.' If you do not commit adultery but do commit murder, you have become a lawbreaker,"* (James 2:11). It's interesting that adultery is next to murder in the Ten Commandments. Why do you suppose they are linked throughout Scripture? Is it because adultery brings death into a marriage?

". . . **adultery brings death into a marriage.**"

Biblically speaking, marriage is a covenant made unto the Lord by a man and a woman (I will deal with marriage in more detail in Chapter 7.). When a man and woman marry, they vow to love and be sexually faithful to one another as long as they live. Not only does adultery break one's vow to a spouse, but also to God. This is something that cannot be taken lightly. Accurate Christian divorce rates are hard to be certain of, but it's easy to look around your own church and even at your Christian friends and see numerous couples have broken their vows to one another and God, and divorced.

Divorce has become common in the church. People get divorced for many reasons, but short of immorality/adultery, there is no biblical reference for divorce (however, no person should endure an environment of abuse. Abusive relationships require different forms of intervention.). Unfortunately, many couples divorce simply because they fought frequently, drifted apart, got bored, and/or simply decided they had fallen out of love.

It's hard for Christians to make the difficult decision to fight for their marriages when their own pastors and spiritual leaders get divorced without biblical grounds. As a friend of mine posted on his social network page, "When pastors can change wives like they change cars, we can understand why America doesn't take us seriously about marriage." Too many pastors and leaders have struggled with hidden sexual sin, committed adultery, neglected their spouses, ignored their families, and then divorced. On top of that, few leaders step down from ministry to put their families in order after they disobey God's Word. *"If anyone does not know how to manage his own family, how can he take care of God's church?"* (1 Timothy 3:5).

I watched a famous preacher inform his congregation that his wife was leaving him (after his affair), but just like King David fell and rose again, he too would rise from the ashes and remain God's chosen man. Personally, I wouldn't advise comparing yourself to King David when talking about the consequences of immorality. David arranged the death of the husband of the woman with whom he committed adultery. The child born of his adultery died as a result of his sin. King David was never the same after that. There are great consequences to adultery and divorce. Sadly, I continued to watch that pastor inform his church about his sin. As he closed the organist started playing and the majority of those present erupted into praise and support, seemingly unfazed by their pastor's unfaithfulness to his wife and his God. I was incredulous at how that church praised and supported their fallen leader while ignoring what God's Word teaches on adultery and divorce.

Jesus taught on the issue of divorce in Matthew 19:7-9 (NASB): *"They said to Him, 'Why then did Moses command to GIVE HER A CER-*

TIFICATE OF DIVORCE AND SEND HER AWAY?' He said to them, 'Because of your hardness of heart Moses permitted you to divorce your wives; but from the beginning it has not been this way. And I say to you, whoever divorces his wife, except for immorality, and marries another woman commits adultery' " (emphasis added). Jesus explained that from the beginning, a man and woman were to remain married. Hard hearts led people to the sin of divorce.

It's interesting to point out that all the people who divorced in the time of Moses also died in the wilderness because of their rebellion toward God. If you disobey God in the boundaries of your marriage and sex life, all areas of your life are susceptible to disobedience. Jesus gave us an even greater call to purity when He challenged His followers to not only *not* commit adultery and sexual sin in the physical, but to not even engage in the imaginations of lustful thinking. Matthew 5:27-28 (NASB) says, *"You have heard that it was said, 'YOU SHALL NOT COMMIT ADULTERY'; but I say to you that everyone who looks at a woman with lust for her has already committed adultery with her in his heart"* (emphasis added).

My friend Pastor Waylon Sears says, "Lust is any desire that is out of control." Lustful thinking is the domain of pornography. Pornography is one of the most profitable businesses in the world. Annual sales revenue of pornographic material far exceeds the revenue generated by all major sports, combined.[1] And Christians are buying as well. It was a sobering report that showed when a Christian men's purity conference came to a city, sales of pay-per-view pornographic movies at the hotels where the men stayed would skyrocket. Pornography keeps people bound in a false reality of demonic forces. Pornography feeds the lust in the heart of man and is one of the major contributors to failed marriages and divorce.

Malachi 2:16 (NASB) shows us the way God feels about divorce: *" 'For I hate divorce,' Israel, 'and wrong,' hosts. 'So treacherously.' "* God hates divorce! The God of love hates it. It is imperative to know God's heart on the matter.

We were not made for sexual sin. Our lives and DNA were not designed to live a sinful life. First Corinthians 6:13, 18 says, *"You say, 'Food for the stomach and the stomach for food, and God will destroy them both.' The body, however, is not meant for sexual immorality but for the Lord, and the Lord for the body . . . . Flee from sexual immoral-*

ity. *All other sins a person commits are outside the body, but whoever sins sexually, sins against their own body."* When we sin sexually we not only sin against God, but against our own body. We align our lives with the death sin brings. *"For the wages of sin is death, but the gift of God is eternal life in Christ Jesus our Lord"* (Romans 6:23 NLT). The wages of sin is the payment for sin, the earnings of our investment into death.

The book of Genesis records that God created the world. He created the heavens and the earth, and then He created man and woman. The moment God created man in His image and likeness, the devil came to destroy His creation. *"When the woman saw that the fruit of the tree was good for food and pleasing to the eye, and also desirable for gaining wisdom, she took some and ate it"* (Genesis 2:6). When Adam and Eve chose to disobey God and committed the original sin, they brought death onto mankind. Satan tempted Eve and she gave in to it.

When we talk about sin we are talking about, *"Any thought, word, desire, action, or omission of action, contrary to the law of God, or defective when compared with it."* [2] "Sin" is actually a term that means, "missing the mark." The reason the devil wanted Adam and Eve to fall into sin was to create a separation between God and His creation. The devil knows how much God loves us, and that our freewill obedience is the greatest form of worship. The devil knew from experience that if Adam and Eve fell, God would remove them from the Garden of Eden and they would lose the intimate fellowship they enjoyed with God. It is so important to understand that a life of sin will ruin one's intimate relationship with God. You can't serve the God of purity and live a life of immorality. You can't serve two masters.

The devil's entire existence is consumed with destroying man's relationship with God. First John 3:8 says, *"The one who does what is sinful is of the devil, because the devil has been sinning from the beginning."* This is what the devil does. His strategy to get us to sin is to first lead us into temptation. Temptation in itself isn't sin. We know this because Jesus was tempted and never sinned. *"He committed no sin, and no deceit was found in his mouth"* (1 Peter 2:22).

The devil uses the strategy of temptation to get us to fall into sin.

There are three main areas of temptation: the lust of the flesh, the lust of the eyes, and the pride of life. We see this when the devil tempted Eve in the Garden of Eden, and tempted Jesus in the wilderness. These three main temptations all occur when our love for the world exceeds our love for God. They are found in 1 John 2:15-17 (NLT): *"Do not love the world nor the things in the world. If anyone loves the world, the love of the Father is not in him. For all that is in the world, the lust of the flesh and the lust of the eyes and the boastful pride of life, is not from the Father, but is from the world. The world is passing away, and also its lusts; but the one who does the will of God lives forever."*

"You can't serve the God of purity and live a life of immorality."

Again, the three main temptations are the lust of the flesh, lust of the eyes, and the pride of life. Look at how these three temptations relate to Eve first in Genesis 3:4-6: *" 'You will not certainly die,' the serpent said to the woman. 'For God knows that when you eat from it your eyes will be opened, and you will be like God, knowing good and evil.' When the woman saw that the fruit of the tree was good for food and pleasing to the eye, and also desirable for gaining wisdom, she took some and ate it. She also gave some to her husband, who was with her, and he ate it."*

The devil tempted Eve with the exact same temptations of the world listed in 1 John 2:15-17. The lust of the flesh was the temptation of good-looking food. Of all the trees in the garden available to Eve, the devil tempted her to eat from the one from which God had forbidden her to eat. He tempted her to eat from it because it looked good to her flesh. It was pleasing to her eye (the lust of the eyes). It looked good. It was desirable. It appeared innocent. Why wouldn't God want her to have such a good thing? The lust of the eyes appears harmless but its disobedience is deadly.

Finally, the devil used the pride of life and desire for wisdom to be like God: *" 'You will not certainly die,' the serpent said to the woman. 'For God knows that when you eat from it your eyes will be opened, and you will be like God, knowing good and evil' "* (Genesis 3:4-5). The devil told Eve she would be like God. The truth was she was already like God; man was made in the image of God, and woman came from man. What Satan meant was, if she sinned she would be like him—fallen.

In Matthew 4, the Holy Spirit led Jesus into the wilderness for forty days of prayer and fasting. After this, the devil came to tempt Him. He used the same strategy of worldly temptations (1 John) he had used with Eve. Read these verses and then I will compare them.

> 2 After fasting forty days and forty nights, he was hungry. 3 The tempter came to him and said, "If you are the Son of God, tell these stones to become bread." (Matthew 4:2-3)

> 5 Then the devil took him to the holy city and had him stand on the highest point of the temple. 6 "If you are the Son of God," he said, "throw yourself down. For it is written: 'He will command his angels concerning you, and they will lift you up in their hands, so that you will not strike your foot against a stone.' " (Matthew 4:5-6)

> 8 Again, the devil took him to a very high mountain and showed him all the kingdoms of the world and their splendor. 9 "All that I will give you," he said, "if you will bow down and worship me." (Matthew 4:8-9)

We see the lust of the flesh when the devil told Jesus, "tell these stones to become bread" (Matthew 4:3). Again, the devil wanted Jesus to focus on the temporal desires of the flesh.

We see lust of the eyes when the devil took Jesus to a high place and told Him he could give Him everything He saw. If Jesus's eyes had not been on His eternal assignment, the temporal things of this world might have distracted Him. If Jesus compromised with the lust of the eyes and accepted the deal with the devil, He would not have fulfilled His assignment of the cross. Jesus had to stay focused on the things of the Sprit to fulfill His life in the Spirit.

Finally, we see the pride of life when the Devil tempts Jesus to bow down and worship him. There it is again, the greatest sin—the pride of life. Led by the Spirit, Jesus resisted the devil and the devil left Him. Lust for the things of this world, and living a worldly lifestyle consumed with the pride of life, are the greatest forms of temptation. All three primary temptations consist of all worldly temptations. These temporal desires of the flesh have no value in eternity.

Adam and Eve were cast out of the Garden of Eden. We know the Garden of Eden to be a type and shadow of heaven. Genesis 3:23-24 says, *"So the Lord God banished him from the Garden of Eden to work the ground from which he had been taken. After he drove the man out, he placed on the east side of the Garden of Eden cherubim and a flaming sword flashing back and forth to guard the way to the tree of life."* Just as sin was not permitted to remain in the garden, sin won't be permitted in heaven. Sin not only ends in physical death but more alarmingly, in spiritual death.

Like Adam and Eve, we all have sinned. Whether we've sinned sexually or some other way, we have all sinned against God. Romans 3:23-24 says, *"for all have sinned and fall short of the glory of God, and all are justified freely by his grace through the redemption that came by Christ Jesus."* Jesus resisted the devil and his temptations, but Adam and Eve gave in to them. Jesus overcame the devil in the wilderness. Then He triumphed over him once and for all on the cross. Jesus broke the curse of sin and death by offering up His life as a living sacrifice for our sins. Through Jesus, the intimate relationship between God and man was restored.

Romans 3:24-26 (NLT) goes on to say:

24 Yet God, with undeserved kindness, declares that we are righteous. He did this through Christ Jesus when he freed us from the penalty for our sins. 25 For God presented Jesus as the sacrifice for sin. People are made right with God when they believe that Jesus sacrificed his life, shedding his blood. This sacrifice shows that God was being fair when he held back and did not punish those who sinned in times past, 26 for he was looking ahead and including them in what he would do in this present time. God did this to demonstrate his righteousness, for he himself is fair and just, and he declares sinners to be right in his sight when they believe in Jesus.

Our relationship with Jesus is what makes us right with God—nothing else. Faith in Jesus alone makes us right with God.

I want to share the gospel with you. You and I are sinners. We have sinned against God. We have sinned heterosexually, homosexually, and in a variety of different ways. We have all sinned, missed the mark, and missed God. We are all guilty of sin and deserve the punishment for our sin.

Most readers of this book will have areas of sin in their lives, so you probably do as well. There is a log in your eye that is keeping you from seeing God clearly and living a godly life. You might be living a sexually immoral life, bound in the lust of pornography, or broken your vows to your spouse and divorced. It doesn't matter what the area of sin is; you have sinned against God and deserve the consequences of that sin.

But Jesus!

God loved us so much that He sent His Son Jesus to pay the ultimate price—His life for our sin. Romans 5:8 says, *"But God demonstrates his own love for us in this: While we were still sinners, Christ died for us."* The good news of the gospel of Jesus Christ is that while we were dying spiritually (and even physically) as a result of our sin, Jesus took the weight and consequences of our sin and nailed them to the cross. He was the ultimate sacrifice so that you could be restored to relationship with God the Father.

We all need this forgiveness from sin that can only come from Jesus. All it takes is repentance and faith in Jesus. I want to give you an opportunity to get right with God. Ask Him to come into your life. Make Him your Lord, father, and friend. If you want to confess your sins, ask Jesus to forgive you and position you in right standing with God. Then say this prayer:

Prayer of Salvation

Jesus, I need you. Over and over, I fall short of your standards. I fall short of your righteousness. But today I ask you, Jesus, to forgive me of all my sin. I confess my sin is wrong. Jesus, forgive me, cleanse me, wash me, and make me new. Make me a new creation. Help me to resist the devil and his temptations. Jesus, keep me from evil and from sinning against the Father. Holy Spirit, help me, be my comforter. Lead me on paths of righteousness. Disciple me in your holy Word, Lord. I thank you, Father, for your amazing grace. I love you. Amen.

Temptation isn't sin, but giving in to it is. Let's not give in to sin anymore. First Corinthians 10:13 says, *"No temptation has overtaken you except what is common to mankind. And God is faithful; he will not let you be tempted beyond what you can bear. But when you are tempted, he will also provide a way out so that you can endure it."* You don't get to choose what you are tempted with, but you get to choose how you respond to your temptation.

I want to encourage you: you are not your temptation. Don't identify with that with which you are currently tempted. Instead, identify with Jesus who defeated temptation. Jesus taught us how to overcome all temptation. We defeat temptation by responding to it with God's Word. Every time Jesus was tempted, He responded with, "It is written." He knew God and knew God's Word. First John 3:8 says, *"The reason the Son of God appeared was to destroy the devil's work."* Knowing what God's Word says will help you destroy the devil's work in your life.

> **"You don't get to choose what you are tempted with, but you get to choose how you respond to your temptation."**

The purpose of the Great Commission was not merely to get people to make decisions, but to make disciples. A disciple of Jesus follows His teachings and obeys His words.

Billy Graham said, "The cross confronts every person and demands a lifestyle change." Disciples have to make decisions. We must decide to give up everything in our lives, including our sex lives, to follow Jesus in obedience.

Now that the log is out of our own eyes, let's get rid of the speck in the eyes of our brothers and sisters who struggle with the temptations of SSA.

3

IN THE BEGINNING: SEXUAL HISTORY

Where did homosexuality come from? Is it something new? Have we only experienced this new form of sexual revolution in the last hundred years? Did God foresee this shift in our society, or did this catch God off guard as much as it has the church? A great many opinions and hearsay crowd the conversation when it comes to these questions on homosexuality. Many people are misinformed, repeat false information, and form conclusions from opinions rather than facts. As we look at the history of homosexuality briefly from a secular historical prospective, and then more importantly, from a biblical perspective, we will begin to find answers to these questions.

Homosexuality is nothing new. It has existed from nearly the beginning of human history. In a scholarly paper, a mentor of mine, Dr. Alan Bullock, writes:

> The earliest published studies of lesbian activity were written in the early 19th century. Pre-history believes that as far back as 9660 to 5000 BC Mesolithic rock art depicting homosexual intercourse was found in cave walls in Sicily. Other writers post it was first mentioned in the works of Chinese literature around 600 BCW. The first recorded homosexual couple in history is commonly regarded as Khnumhotep and Niankhkhnum, an Egyptian male couple, who lived around the 2400 BC. In Ancient Rome the young male body remained a focus of male sexual attention. All the emperors with the exception of

Claudius took male lovers. Between 1864 and 1880 Karl Heinrich Ulrichs published a series of twelve tracts, which he collectively titled *Research on the Riddle of Man-Manly Love*, and then later there were some places where this lifestyle was (is) freely practiced. Greece was very loose with morality laws and in Medieval France there was a legal category called "enbrotherment."[3]

The Egyptian male couple, Khnumhotep and Niankhkhnum, effectively lived as a legally married couple. History is marked by the influence of homosexuality because men have engaged in it (and in other forms of disobedience to God) since creation.

In the beginning, God created man in His image. Genesis 1:26-28 says:

> *26 Then God said, "Let us make mankind in our image, in our likeness, so that they may rule over the fish in the sea and the birds in the sky, over the livestock and all the wild animals, and over all the creatures that move along the ground." 27 So God created mankind in his own image, in the image of God he created them; male and female he created them. 28 God blessed them and said to them, "Be fruitful and increase in number; fill the earth and subdue it. Rule over the fish in the sea and the birds in the sky and over every living creature that moves on the ground."*

Immediately, the devil came and convinced Eve (the wife God made from Adam) to sin and disobey God. Genesis 3:6 says, *"When the woman saw that the fruit of the tree was good for food and pleasing to the eye, and also desirable for gaining wisdom, she took some and ate it. She also gave some to her husband, who was with her, and he ate it."* Since creation mankind has battled the temptation of the devil and been embroiled in an internal struggle to resist giving in to it. We are torn between obedience to God and His Word and disobedience to them. God forgave Adam and Eve, but still ordered them removed from the garden of paradise. Though Adam and Eve left the garden, the devil and his temptations followed them.

Not long after, in the next chapter of Genesis, Adam and Eve have two sons, Cain and Abel. God warned Cain against temptation, just as He had done for Cain's parents. But Cain followed in the footsteps of his parents and gave in to temptation. He murdered his brother Abel because of disobedience toward God. Genesis 4:6-7 says, *"Then the Lord said to Cain, 'Why are you angry? Why is your face downcast? If you do what is right, will you not be accepted? But if you do not do what is right, sin is crouching at your door; it desires to have you, but you must rule over it.' "* Sin ruled over Cain and he killed his brother.

The sin of the world continued to grow and continued to grieve God. Approximately a thousand years after Adam and Eve were evicted from the garden of paradise, the world gave in to the temptation of the devil and became so evil that God decided to destroy it. Genesis 6:11-12 says, *"Now the earth was corrupt in God's sight and was full of violence. God saw how corrupt the earth had become, for all the people on earth had corrupted their ways."* God called the world corrupt. It was so evil it was fractured spiritually before it was destroyed physically. God had determined to destroy the earth and start over.

God chose a righteous man named Noah to rebuild humanity. God sent violent rains and water to flood the earth and wipe out sinful mankind. God washed the world of sin and left His righteous servants, Noah and his family, to continue to follow Him. God used a rainbow as a sign of His promise to His righteous servants to never completely destroy the earth again. God said, *"I set my rainbow in the clouds, and it will be the sign of the covenant between me and the earth"* (Genesis 9:13).

As Noah and his family repopulated the earth, it didn't take long for the lifestyle of sin to return to mankind. Roughly 500 years after the flood, sin's outcry reached the heavens and grieved the heart of God once again. This time the sin was specifically sexual in nature.

The cities of Sodom and Gomorrah were incredibly wicked—unlike anything the world had ever seen. Genesis 13:13 says, *"Now the people of Sodom were wicked and were sinning greatly against the Lord."* The Bible goes on to give more insight into the evil of Sodom in Genesis 18:20, which says, *"Then the Lord said, 'The outcry against Sodom and Gomorrah is so great and their sin so grievous.' "* This evil was entertained in the city of Sodom until it climaxed in Genesis 19.

The men of the city wanted to have sex with the angels of God who appeared there as men to visit Lot. Genesis 19:4-5 says, *"Before they had gone to bed, all the men from every part of the city of Sodom—both young and old—surrounded the house. They called to Lot, 'Where are the men who came to you tonight? Bring them out to us so that we can have sex with them.' "* Though I will go into more detail on Sodom in the next chapter, know that it was a hub for sexual sin and every other kind of evil. God destroyed the city of Sodom and all who loved her, but the sin wasn't just in Sodom, it was in the hearts of men. It ultimately made its way into every society, and even influenced pagan worship to false gods.

God commanded the Israelites not to follow the ways of the worldly nations. He warned them not to follow their religious practices or sexual sin. Leviticus 18:21-23 says, *"Do not give any of your children to be sacrificed to Molek, for you must not profane the name of your God. I am the Lord. Do not have sexual relations with a man as one does with a woman; that is detestable. Do not have sexual relations with an animal and defile yourself with it. A woman must not present herself to an animal to have sexual relations with it; that is a perversion."* The idolatry of false gods led to sinful lusts and shameful sexual behavior.

God warned the Israelites not to engage in this behavior because it was common for people in surrounding wicked nations. The main god of the surrounding nations was named Baal. As I wrote in my spiritual warfare book, *Jezebel: The Witch Is Back:*

The worship of Baal rejected the holiness set up by Yahweh (God) and encouraged indulgence in every self-pleasing sexual desire as a part of self-worship. Through the worship of Baal came the god Dagon, for Baal was the son of Dagon. Baal, Dagon, Ashtoreth, and Molech combined for the erotic acts of perverted heterosexual relations, homosexual activity, violent sexual acts, body piercing (including genitals), body cutting, and an infatuation with blood (drinking and draining), prostitution, and ceremonial orgies. They were also one of the originators of child sacrifice. Sadly, God's children were participating in all this debauchery and His prophets were being chased off from doing anything about it.

Homosexuality was so prevalent because Baal worship not only encouraged it but required it. Over and over God warned His children not to follow the behavior or gods of worldly nations

From both secular historical writings and the New Testament we know that homosexual practice was common in the Roman empire. Not only did the apostle Paul's writings address homosexual behavior (which we will explore in later chapters), but in 1 Corinthians 6:9-11 (ESV), we get a clear perspective of the sexual activity that was going on in the early church: *"Or do you not know that the unrighteous will not inherit the kingdom of God? Do not be deceived; neither fornicators, nor idolaters, nor adulterers, nor effeminate, nor homosexuals, nor thieves, nor the covetous, nor drunkards, nor revilers, nor swindlers, will inherit the kingdom of God. Such were some of you; but you were washed, but you were sanctified, but you were justified in the name of the Lord Jesus Christ and in the Spirit of our God."* The apostle Paul was writing to an audience that, at least in part, used to live a homosexual lifestyle! In verse 11, Paul says, *"Such were some of you (homosexuals); but you were washed"* (1 Corinthians 6:11, parentheses added).

> **"Homosexuality was so prevalent because Baal worship not only encouraged it but required it."**

Some of Jesus's disciples were gay and practiced homosexuality at some point, but they were washed, purified, and set free from their sin. In the Greek text, the word used for "washed" in 1 Corinthians 6:11 is "apoloúō," which means, "away from" (apó) and "wash" ("loúō"). It literally refers to an *entire* washing—the *complete* removal of sin and its debt.

Paul explains to us that many individuals in our society used to engage in the sin of homosexual practice, but the sin was removed by the blood of Jesus and now they live right in the sight of God. Paul goes on to give New Testament believers a warning similar to the one Moses gave the children of Israel:

1 As for other matters, brothers and sisters, we instructed you how to live in order to please God, as in fact you are living. Now we ask you and urge you in the Lord Jesus to do this more and more. 2 For you know what instructions we gave you by the authority of the Lord Jesus. 3 It is God's will that you should be sanctified: that you should avoid sexual immorality; 4 that each of you should learn to control your own body in a way that is holy not in passionate lust like the pagans, who do not know God. (1 Thessalonians 4:1-4)

The historical context gives us evidence that homosexual behavior has been an ongoing part of society. At times it has been even more common than it is today. For millennia, men have wrestled with conscience as their flesh is tempted with same-sex attraction, but something deep down in their spirit man is grieved, telling them, "This is wrong." Where does that conviction come from? Who put it within us?

This conviction—the moral law of God—has been written on our hearts by God Himself. Romans 2:14-16 (ESV) says, *"For when Gentiles who do not have the Law do instinctively the things of the Law, these, not having the Law, are a law to themselves, in that they show the work of the Law written in their hearts, their conscience bearing witness and their thoughts alternately accusing or else defending them, on the day when, according to my gospel, God will judge the secrets of men through Christ Jesus."*

God's law is written on the collective heart of man. We are aware of this only because the written Word of God (the Bible) tells us so. The conscience of man is only powerful because it bears witness to the written Word of God. As revealed in the Bible, God's heart toward sexuality, and behavior required of us to live a life that pleases Him is so very clear. Let's look specifically at what God's Word clearly says about homosexuality and sexuality.

THE BIG 6
(PART 1: OLD TESTAMENT & THE LAW)

"Well, only six Bible passages even mention homosexuality!" is one of the biggest arguments I frequently hear when engaging with Christ-followers on the topic of homosexuality. This is a common response from those with SSA (same-sex attraction) and those who affirm it. I typically hear this response before even discussing the scriptures themselves. This statement not only cheapens these specific scriptures but the mind-set devalues all Scripture. Second Timothy 3:16 says, *"All Scripture is God-breathed and is useful for teaching, rebuking, correcting and training in righteousness."*

It is true that there are a total of six Bible passages that deal directly with homosexual practice: three verses in the Old Testament, and three in the New Testament. Six passages is a significant amount when it comes to adhering to sound doctrine.

When you think about it, there are other biblical truths we observe that have fewer biblical references. For example, pretty much every believer takes Holy Communion on some sort of regular basis; at least once a year on Christmas or during Holy Week. This is a common Christian practice. But Communion is only mentioned five times in the New Testament. We don't deny taking Communion because there are only five Bible passages that mention it. The truth is, every verse in the Bible is important and we should show reverence to all of them. Even if God only gave us one scripture that contradicted homosexuality, that should be enough for dedicated Christ-followers.

God gave Adam only one instruction in the garden of paradise: *"The Lord God commanded the man, saying, 'From any tree of the garden you may eat freely; but from the tree of the knowledge of good and evil you shall not eat, for in the day that you eat from it you will surely die' "* (Genesis 2:16-17 NASB). Even when man was only given one verse—one command by God—he still disobeyed that command.

> **"...if God only gave us one scripture that contradicted homosexuality, that should be enough for dedicated Christ-followers."**

There are six main scriptures that completely condemn homosexual practice and dozens upon dozens that only support a holy, heterosexual lifestyle. We are going to look at these six main scriptures and some of the controversy and confusion surrounding them. In this chapter, part one of two, we will begin by reviewing the three verses found in the Old Testament.

#1—Genesis 19: The Sin of Sodom

The first mention of homosexual behavior is found in Genesis 19 in the account of the city of Sodom. As previously mentioned in the last chapter, Sodom was a city known for its extreme immorality. We'll look at the story of Sodom in its full context. Again, I encourage you to read this passage thoroughly.

> *1 The two angels arrived at Sodom in the evening, and Lot was sitting in the gateway of the city. When he saw them, he got up to meet them and bowed down with his face to the ground. 2 "My lords," he said, "please turn aside to your servant's house. You can wash your feet and spend the night and then go on your way early in the morning." "No," they answered, "we will spend the night in the square." 3 But he insisted so strongly that they did go with him and entered his house. He prepared a meal for them, baking bread without yeast, and they ate. 4 Before they had gone to bed, all the men from every part of the*

city of Sodom—both young and old—surrounded the house. 5
They called to Lot, "Where are the men who came to you tonight?
Bring them out to us so that we can have sex with them." 6 Lot
went outside to meet them and shut the door behind him
7 and said, "No, my friends. Don't do this wicked thing. 8 Look,
I have two daughters who have never slept with a man. Let
me bring them out to you, and you can do what you like with
them. But don't do anything to these men, for they have come
under the protection of my roof." 9 "Get out of our way," they
replied. "This fellow came here as a foreigner, and now he
wants to play the judge! We'll treat you worse than them." They
kept bringing pressure on Lot and moved forward to break down
the door. 10 But the men inside reached out and pulled Lot back
into the house and shut the door. 11 Then they struck the men
who were at the door of the house, young and old, with blindness
so that they could not find the door. 12 The two men said to Lot,
"Do you have anyone else here—sons-in-law, sons or daughters,
or anyone else in the city who belongs to you? Get them out of
here, 13 because we are going to destroy this place. The outcry
to the Lord against its people is so great that he has sent us to
destroy it." (Genesis 19:1-13)

We must look at this story with fresh eyes and a discerning spirit.
Verse 3 indicates it is late in the evening when Lot, the nephew of
Abraham, insisted the angels (who appeared as men) come with him
to his house. Did Lot know about the wicked behavior of the men of
Sodom and attempt to protect the visitors (angels) from it? That sus-
picion is confirmed in verse 4, when all the men of the city, young and
old, came to Lot's house and asked to have sex with the angels. The
men of the city asked to have sex with men they believed to be from
another town.

Lot attempted to offer his daughters to the men to appease their
sexual appetite (which is horrific). The men of Sodom refused to experience sex with Lot's daughters because they desired to have sex with
men. This proves that this was a particular sexual appetite, and these
men were only interested in what would come to be called sodomy,
which was typical in the city of Sodom.

We get the word "sodomy," which is defined as "anal or oral copulation with a member of the same sex,"[4] from the name of the city of Sodom; a place where such sexual practices were common. The *NASB Bible Dictionary* refers to the sodomite as an "abuser of (that defiles itself) with mankind." Sodomites worked as shrine prostitutes—an expressly forbidden practice. Additionally, the sodomite was not to put his pay into the Temple treasury (Deuteronomy23:18) as such pay was considered "wages of a dog" because of the doglike manner in which he debased himself to earn it.

The Lord destroyed the city of Sodom with burning fire from heaven. This was a foreshadowing example for all time and for all future generations. Genesis 19:24-26 says, *"Then the Lord rained down burning sulfur on Sodom and Gomorrah—from the Lord out of the heavens. Thus he overthrew those cities and the entire plain, destroying all those living in the cities—and also the vegetation in the land. But Lot's wife looked back, and she became a pillar of salt."*

There are two primary arguments that attempt to bring confusion to Genesis 19 in the discussion of homosexuality. The first argument is, the sin of Sodom wasn't about a consenting, monogamous, loving sexual relationship between two individuals of the same sex, but the sin of gang rape. Just think about that for a moment. So, if the men had consensual, monogamous homosexual sex with angels, God would have approved? That is crazy! On top of that, in verse five the men of the town asked for a sexual encounter. They hoped the angels would reciprocate their desire before they turned violent to try and force the sexual encounter.

The second argument used to distract from the focus of Genesis 19 is, the sin of Sodom wasn't sexual sin, but the sin of inhospitality. In 1955, in his book, *Homosexuality and the Western Christian Tradition*, Anglican theologian Dr. Derrick S. Bailey argued for church acceptance of homosexuality, asserting Sodom was destroyed by inhospitality. I first heard this position while watching a news interview between a pastor and a progressive secular columnist from a fringe online magazine. When the pastor brought up the sin of Sodom, the columnist boldly interrupted the pastor to assert, "We all know now that the sin of Sodom was the sin of inhospitality!" The strategy of this argument is to distract from the undeniable reality that Sodom was full of wicked people who had no sexual boundaries, and that their sexual sin was committed through homosexual practice.

Agitators try to base this inhospitality argument on Ezekiel 16:49-50 (ESV): *"Behold, this was the guilt of your sister Sodom: she and her daughters had pride, excess of food, and prosperous ease, but did not aid the poor and needy. They were haughty and did an abomination before me. So I removed them, when I saw it."*

It is true that the people of Sodom committed many kinds of sin, not just one. Romans 1:29 says, *"They have become filled with every kind of wickedness, evil, greed and depravity. They are full of envy, murder, strife, deceit and malice. They are gossips."* Sin gives birth to sin, and when sexual sin rages, a host of other sins come along with it. Every kind of sin grows in a life full of sexual perversion, and though inhospitality could be one of them, it would be one of many. Still, this inhospitality opinion is now widely accepted by so-called "open and affirming believers," and growing in popularity.

The author of the book of Jude gives us a clear understanding of the primary sin that brought about Sodom's destruction. Jude 1:7 says, *"In a similar way, Sodom and Gomorrah and the surrounding towns gave themselves up to sexual immorality and perversion. They serve as an example of those who suffer the punishment of eternal fire."* This is a clear and strong statement about the destiny of those who persist in living an ungodly lifestyle. Jude wrote that Sodom's sins were sexual in nature. Again, Scripture supports this understanding:

4 For if God did not spare angels when they sinned, but sent them to hell, putting them in chains of darkness to be held for judgment; 5 if he did not spare the ancient world when he brought the flood on its ungodly people, but protected Noah, a preacher of righteousness, and seven others; 6 if he condemned the cities of Sodom and Gomorrah by burning them to ashes, and made them an example of what is going to happen to the ungodly; 7 and if he rescued Lot, a righteous man, who was distressed by the depraved conduct of the lawless 8 (for that righteous man, living among them day after day, was tormented in his righteous soul by the lawless deeds he saw and heard)— 9 if this is so, then the Lord knows how to rescue the godly from trials and to hold the unrighteous for punishment on the

day of judgment. 10 This is especially true of those who follow the corrupt desire of the flesh and despise authority.
(2 Peter 2:4-10)

The word "sensual" in 2 Peter 2:7 is "aselgeia" in the Greek. *The Friberg Lexicon* defines this word as "living without any moral restraint *licentiousness, sensuality, lustful indulgence* (2 Corinthians 12.21); especially as indecent and outrageous sexual behavior *debauchery, indecency, flagrant immorality* (Romans 13.13)." This indicates that the people of Sodom lived lives driven by the unbridled, insatiable desire for pleasure and sexual excess, and exercised a total absence of restraint.

If you read Ezekiel 16:50 (and don't stop at verse 49), you will see this Bible verse talks about much greater grievances to God than inhospitality. It says, *"Thus they were haughty and committed abominations before Me. Therefore I removed them when I saw it."*

#2—Leviticus 18: An Abomination

"You shall not lie with a male as with a woman; it is an abomination" (Leviticus 18:22, ESV). It is clear that Scripture forbids men from lying with (having sex with) other men. (The heading over Chapter 18 in the English Standard Version of the Bible is, *"Unlawful Sexual Relations."*) Scripture refers to homosexual sexual acts as an abomination. The Hebrew word used here for "abomination" is "toebah," which means, "something disgusting (morally), i.e. (as noun) an abhorrence; especially idolatry or (concretely) an idol—abominable (custom, thing), abomination." (Note: I'm not calling any reader of this book disgusting. I just wrote the meaning of abomination that the Bible uses to describe homosexual sex.) This form of sexual practice was not accepted by God and was a forbidden behavior for God's children.

It's important to understand that in God's eyes, not all sin is the same. I know immature Christians love to proclaim, "All sin is the same, and if you break one of God's laws you break them all." That sounds good and it sounds scriptural, but is it biblically accurate? No! Naïve believers usually say this by repeating the words of someone else they heard say it, but might also originate from a misunderstanding of James 2:10, which says, *"For whoever keeps the whole law and* yet stumbles at just one point is guilty of breaking all of it." From a biblical perspective, the truth is that if you have broken the law you are a lawbreaker and need forgiveness from Jesus, just like we all do. That is what James 2:10 says. The misperception is that if you break one law, the consequences are the same as if you had broken all the laws.

Many laws had distinctive punishments and consequences. For example, in 1 Samuel 11 and 12, King David committed adultery and arranged for the certain death of Uriah the Hittite (the husband of Bathsheba, the woman with whom he committed adultery). The consequence of this sin was the death of David and Bathsheba's son. Second Samuel 12:14 says, *"Nathan replied, 'The Lord has taken away your sin. You are not going to die. But because by doing this you have shown utter contempt for the Lord, the son born to you will die.' "* The loss of a child is a tragic consequence for a sin of the flesh.

On another occasion David sinned against God by directly disobeying Him. God gave specific instructions on taking a limited census of one branch of the Levites, the Kohathites. Numbers 4:1-3 says, *"The Lord said to Moses and Aaron: "Take a census of the Kohathite branch of the Levites by their clans and families. Count all the men from thirty to fifty years of age who come to serve in the work at the tent of meeting."* Though David knew God's instructions, so did Satan. Satan rose up against Israel and incited David to take a census of all Israel, not just a limited census of the Kohathite branch of the Levites as God had instructed. Second Samuel 24:2-7 says:

> *2 So the king said to Joab and the army commanders with him, "Go throughout the tribes of Israel from Dan to Beersheba and enroll the fighting men, so that I may know how many there are." 3 But Joab replied to the king, "May the LORD your God multiply the troops a hundred times over, and may the eyes of my lord the king see it. But why does my lord the king want to do such a thing?" 4 The king's word, however, overruled Joab and the army commanders; so they left the presence of the king to enroll the fighting men of Israel. 5 After crossing the Jordan, they camped near Aroer, south of the town in the gorge, and then went through Gad and on to Jazer. 6 They went to Gilead and the region of Tahtim Hodshi, and on to Dan Jaan and around toward Sidon. 7 Then they went toward the fortress of Tyre and all the*

towns of the Hivites and Canaanites. Finally, they went on to Beersheba in the Negev of Judah.

God wanted the children of Israel to count on Him, not on themselves. By numbering or counting all of Israel they showed they counted on men, not God, for their strength. The outcome of David's direct disobedience to God caused the greatest negative consequence of his life. First Chronicles 21:13 says, *"David said to Gad, 'I am in deep distress. Let me fall into the hands of the Lord, for his mercy is very great; but do not let me fall into human hands.' "* The result of this sin was that seventy thousand Israelites died. David's disobedience had a catastrophic consequence.

Yes, if you break even one law you are a lawbreaker, but specific sins have specific consequences, and God clearly calls the sin of homosexual practice an abomination—a disgraceful sin toward Him.

> **"By numbering or counting all of Israel they showed they counted on men, not God, for their strength."**

#3—Leviticus 20: The Law

"If a man lies with a male as with a woman, both of them have committed an abomination; they shall surely be put to death; their blood is upon them" (Leviticus 20:13, ESV).

Leviticus is in the middle of the "Law." These were the laws God gave Moses to give to the children of Israel. They were given to people who didn't know, love, honor, or live their lives to please God. These laws were designed to lead the children of Israel to live consecrated lives and separate them from the evil, perverted nations in the new land in which they were living. It is abundantly clear that the Bible condemns sex between men, and the result of this behavior is death.

Since the language used in Bible passages that reference homosexuality is irrefutable by all genuine scholarly standards, the next strategy for those trying to embrace and affirm same-sex sexual activity is to attack the location of certain scripture passages. The argument becomes, "That's the Old Testament and we're not under the law." I have always found interesting exactly when people choose to use this argument. Predictably, they typically use it when they come to a commandment they want to ignore (like tithing)! I never hear this argument used about murder, lying, or bestiality. Isn't that interesting?

Have you ever heard anyone say, "It's OK to have sex with an animal; we're not under the law anymore"? No? Neither have I. When people try to devalue the laws of God to give confidence to the practice of their sin, they prove they lack intimacy with Jesus and understanding of His relationship with the law. God provided the law so that people could live a life in right standing with God. They did this by obeying the law.

Jesus came to complete the law. Matthew 5:17 says, *"Do not think that I have come to abolish the Law or the Prophets; I have not come to abolish them but to fulfill them."* When the children of Israel broke the law and sinned against God, a sacrifice was required in atonement for their sin. In the Garden of Eden, after Adam and Eve sinned, a blood sacrifice was required to cover them. Jesus was the ultimate sacrifice for our sin, and He paid the ultimate price with the shedding of His blood. Colossians 2:14 (NASB) says, *"having canceled out the certificate of debt consisting of decrees against us, which was hostile to us; and He has taken it out of the way, having nailed it to the cross."* So Jesus fulfilled the law by never breaking the law—He never sinned. Then He died on the cross in our place. So we are not under the law but under grace. Romans 6:14 says; *"For sin shall no longer be your master, because you are not under the law, but under grace."* So since we are under grace, sin cannot be our master any longer.

To say, "I'm not under the law" means that you are under grace, and sin is no longer your master. Since there is no biblical evidence that refutes the sexual acts of homosexuality as sin, to be under grace doesn't change the fact that sexual practices of homosexuality are sinful. To live under grace means you live a greater life of conviction than you did under the law. The law required obedience and promised specific punishment for disobedience. Under grace you have been forgiven of your sin and are able to freely obey the commandments and teachings of the Bible.

For example, the law says, *"do not commit adultery"* (Leviticus 18:20). Under grace, Jesus says, *"But I tell you that anyone who looks* at a woman lustfully has already committed adultery with her in his heart" (Matthew 5:28). Do you see what I'm saying? To live under grace takes relationship with Jesus and obedience to the Word of God to the next level.

Another tactic for devaluing the law is to compare the cultural prohibitions on the children of Israel against eating shellfish, wearing mixed patterns, and ceremonial cleansings with the universal sexual prohibition of homosexual practice, incest, and bestiality. God gave the children of Israel certain cultural laws that were to keep them consecrated and separate from pagan nations around them. These cultural laws of the Israelites don't have "jurisdiction" in the New Testament, and Gentiles were and are not required to follow them.

An example of this is found in the book of Acts in an account concerning the apostle Peter. Acts 10:9-15 says:

> 9 About noon the following day as they were on their journey and approaching the city, Peter went up on the roof to pray. 10 He became hungry and wanted something to eat, and while the meal was being prepared, he fell into a trance. 11 He saw heaven opened and something like a large sheet being let down to earth by its four corners. 12 It contained all kinds of four-footed animals, as well as reptiles and birds. 13 Then a voice told him, "Get up, Peter. Kill and eat." 14 "Surely not, Lord!" Peter replied. "I have never eaten anything impure or unclean." 15 The voice spoke to him a second time, "Do not call anything impure that God has made clean."

Another example is of a time when "some men" in the church began forcing Gentile converts to be circumcised. The apostle Paul quickly intervened, asserting physical circumcision was an unnecessary cultural practice for those in the church. Acts 15:1-2 (ESV) says; "Some men came down from Judea and began teaching the brethren, 'Unless you are circumcised according to the custom of Moses, you cannot be saved.' And when Paul and Barnabas had great dissension and debate with them, the brethren determined that Paul and Barnabas and some others of them should go up to Jerusalem to the apostles and elders concerning this issue."

Unlike circumcision, homosexual sexual practices fall under the category of universal prohibitions (those that apply to all people for all time), and are never affirmed in Scripture. All scripture references to homosexual practice condemn it and prohibit it, and never refer to it positively.

There are grave differences between Jewish ceremonial laws and universal prohibitions God gave to all people for all time. Leviticus 18:29-30 says, *"Everyone who does any of these detestable things— such persons must be cut off from their people. Keep my requirements and do not follow any of the detestable customs that were practiced before you came and do not defile yourselves with them. I am the Lord your God."* Chapter 18 states that *all* who broke universal moral pro-hibitions were detestable. God never condemned the Canaanites or other nations for eating shellfish or wearing mixed patterns, but He condemned them for universal sins (including homosexual practice) that He declared wrong and sinful for all people, everywhere, for all time.

It's important to learn the reasons and purposes behind the law before dismissing it. Too many times I've heard Christians talk down and irreverently mock the Old Testament, as if it is beneath them. Well, it wasn't beneath Jesus.

The law was part of the foundation laid for Jesus. The law was important to Jesus, so it should be important to us. Jesus knew the law better than anyone. Jesus and His disciples taught from the Torah (the first five books of the Old Testament) and valued it greatly. People marveled at Jesus's understanding of the law and His authority when teaching it. Luke 4:32 says, *"They were amazed at his teaching, be-cause his words had authority."* When Jesus responded to Satan in the wilderness, He responded with the Old Testament. Matthew 4:4 says, *"Jesus answered, 'It is written: "Man shall not live on bread alone, but on every word that comes from the mouth of God." ' "* This was taken from Deuteronomy 8:3, *"He humbled you, causing you to hunger and then feeding you with manna, which neither you nor your ancestors had known, to teach you that man does not live on bread alone but on every word that comes from the mouth of the Lord."* Every response Jesus gave Satan in Matthew 4 was a response from the Old Testa-ment. In the New Testament, Jesus referenced the Old Testament.

The apostle Peter quoted the law from the Old Testament when he said, *"for it is written: 'Be holy, because I am holy' "* (1 Peter 1:16).

Peter was quoting from the law in Leviticus 11:45: *"I am the LORD, who brought you up out of Egypt to be your God; therefore be holy, because I am holy."* Notice that no one stood up and told Peter: "That's Old Testament! We're not under the law!" In Romans 3:31, Paul taught, *"Do we, then, nullify the law by this faith? Not at all! Rather, we uphold the law."*

When we understand the purpose of the law, it allows us to truly experience the power of the grace of Jesus. Even if we ignore the entire law and the Old Testament, we are still left with the commandments of the New Testament. The New Testament has commandments or requirements for a life of following Jesus. These are not negotiable. Mark 7:7-8 (NASB) says, " *'BUT IN VAIN DO THEY WORSHIP ME, TEACHING AS DOCTRINES THE PRECEPTS OF MEN.'* Neglecting the commandment of God, you hold to the tradition of men." These commandments in the New Testament are all from Jesus. They are His

> **"Even if we ignore the entire law and the Old Testament, we are still left with the commandments of the New Testament."**

instructions for living a Christian life.

Do you remember the Great Commission? It is found in Matthew 28:19-20 (NASB): *"Go therefore and make disciples of all the nations, baptizing them in the name of the Father and the Son and the Holy Spirit, teaching them to observe all that I commanded you; and lo, I am with you always, even to the end of the age."* The Great Commission is not only about making disciples of all nations, but also about teaching them to obey the commandments of God! In the next chapter we'll look at what the New Testament has to say about homosexuality.

THE BIG 6
(PART 2: THE NEW TESTAMENT)

As the saying goes, "Out with the old, in with the new." In this chapter we are going to review the three verses in the New Testament that give an even stronger and clearer understanding of the biblical rejection of homosexual practice.

#4—Romans 1: God's Wrath against Sinful Humanity

In Romans 1, the apostle Paul gives the most defining account of homosexual practice and same-sex relationships.

> *18 For the wrath of God is revealed from heaven against all ungodliness and unrighteousness of men, who by their unrighteousness suppress the truth. 19 For what can be known about God is plain to them, because God has shown it to them. 20 For his invisible attributes, namely, his eternal power and divine nature, have been clearly perceived, ever since the creation of the world, in the things that have been made. So they are without excuse. 21 For although they knew God, they did not honor him as God or give thanks to him, but they became futile in their thinking, and their foolish hearts were darkened. 22 Claiming to be wise, they became fools, 23 and exchanged the glory of the immortal God for images resembling mortal man and birds and animals and creeping things.*

24 Therefore God gave them up in the lusts of their hearts to impurity, to the dishonoring of their bodies among themselves, 25 because they exchanged the truth about God for a lie and worshiped and served the creature rather than the Creator, who is blessed forever! Amen.
26 For this reason God gave them up to dishonorable passions. For their women exchanged natural relations for those that are contrary to nature; 27 and the men likewise gave up natural relations with women and were consumed with passion for one another, men committing shameless acts with men and receiving in themselves the due penalty for their error. 28 And since they did not see fit to acknowledge God, God gave them up to a debased mind to do what ought not to be done. 29 They were filled with all manner of unrighteousness, evil, covetousness, malice. They are full of envy, murder, strife, deceit, maliciousness. They are gossips, 30 slanderers, haters of God, insolent, haughty, boastful, inventors of evil, disobedient to parents, 31 foolish, faithless, heartless, ruthless. 32 Though they know God's righteous decree that those who practice such things deserve to die, they not only do them but give approval to those who practice them. (Romans 1:18-32, ESV)

This is very intense language, and there is little room for theological challenges from a biblical prospective, yet supporters of homosexuality and SSA (same-sex attraction) still try. Let's look at this Bible passage carefully, and then discuss some of the current arguments against it.

My friend Chris Gilkey says, "Bible 101: don't complicate what the Bible makes very clear." Verse 18 gives clear insight on why people have such a hard time taking this Scripture at face value, *"who by their unrighteousness suppress the truth."* The wicked hearts of men blind them from seeing and hearing the obvious truth of sexuality and purity. Because of this, they know God but don't glorify Him. I believe many individuals who claim to be homosexual and Christian know *about* God but *deny* God by their behavior.

Verse 24 goes onto say, *"lusts of their hearts to impurity, to the dishonoring of their bodies among themselves."* This lifestyle of sin is idolatry that leads to sexual sin that leads to the promotion of sexual sin. This describes the world today!

Verse 26 says, *"God gave them up to dishonorable passions"* (*"God gave them over to shameful lusts,"* reads another translation). The sin of homosexual practice is described as shameful. The word, "shameful," comes from the Greek word, "atimia," which means, "disgrace, dishonor; a dishonorable use." The end result of this final state of sin is a debased or reprobate mind. This is a carnal, fleshly mind possessed by those who "make for themselves a God." Carnally minded people love themselves and the lusts of the world more than God. This is a person who no longer fears the Lord.

There are two main arguments from homosexuals and affirming Christians within the context of Romans 1, despite the very clear narrative. This argument is similar to the one used to counter the clear reading of Genesis 19, which identifies the grave sin of Sodom as homosexual intercourse, suggesting instead the grave sin was the attempted gang rape.

Affirmers attempt a similar strategy in Romans 1, using a play on words. The first argument is that the sin Paul refers to in Romans 1 is lust, not homosexual practices between committed, monogamous, and loving partners. This argument implies that sex is only sinful if one lusts. So let's follow this train of thought for a moment. A man can commit adultery, and thus cheat on his wife and sin against His God, but it's not sin if he doesn't lust while doing it? Someone pushing this argument might respond, "but it's different between committed, monogamous, loving partners." Well, no, that is not biblically accurate. Scripture clearly forbids both these sexual activities, whether done by the heterosexual or homosexual. The only difference is those affirming homosexual practice attempt to circumvent the clear meaning of Scripture with a hypothesis that if lust isn't involved, it's not sin. If that was the case, Paul would have just written that, but he didn't. He said the opposite, over and over.

The second argument against Paul's condemnation of homosexual practice focuses on verses 26 and 27. They argue that what Paul writes about men and women giving up "natural" sexual relationships for "unnatural" sexual relationships" applies only to those who engage in homosexual sexual activity, but who were not born homosexual. In other words, it's only sin if homosexuality doesn't come naturally to you. If you were born homosexual and didn't choose the homosexual disposition (the desire chose you), then it would be an unnatural desire to be attracted to the opposite sex.

The Greek word for "natural" here is, "phusikos," which means, "according to nature." This is not your nature, but God's created order (natural order). God's original design is for men and women to naturally come together (divine nature). Natural is what God creates, not what the devil perverts. They call this sin natural so they can commit the sin, defend it, justify it, and encourage others to do the same. This behavior continues into a life of increasing sexual immorality.

> **"Natural is what God creates, not what the devil perverts."**

♥

#5 — 1 Corinthians 6: Sexual Immorality

"Or do you not know that the unrighteous will not inherit the kingdom of God? Do not be deceived: neither the sexually immoral, nor idolaters, nor adulterers, nor men who practice homosexuality, nor thieves, nor the greedy, nor drunkards, nor revilers, nor swindlers will inherit the kingdom of God. And such were some of you. But you were washed, you were sanctified, you were justified in the name of the Lord Jesus Christ and by the Spirit of our God" (1 Corinthians 6:9-11, ESV).

The word homosexual in the Greek is the word "arsenokoites" - sodomites, which means "male-bed, partners/male-partners." This is a clear translation, showing this applies to men in sexual relationships with other men ("practice homosexuality"). Again, the main argument against this Scripture in 1 Corinthians is, "The Bible never addresses the issues of sexual orientation or same-sex marriage, so there's no reason why faithful Christians can't support their gay brothers and sisters in this lifestyle." To assert this is to assert that omnipotent (all-knowing) God didn't understand the sexuality of man and simply missed this one.

The idea that God "back then" really doesn't understand us today is completely absurd. Jesus understood us, but more importantly, He understood the Father. The reason we can't support a homosexual lifestyle for brothers and sisters in Christ is because Jesus never did.

A mentor in my life, Dr. Alan Bullock, said, *"Professing faith in the love and sacrifice of Jesus Christ does not turn this perversion into a virtue no matter how we study these Scriptures and break down each word in the original language."*

> **"Jesus understood us, but more importantly, He understood the Father."**

There are two Greek words behind the translation, "men who practice homosexuality." The first, "malakos," means, "soft." It could well refer to men who dressed like women in order to have sex with other men. It could also refer to the passive partner—the so-called "bottom" in homosexual acts. The second word, "arsenokoites," literally means, "male-bed, partners/male-partners." These two words together clearly speak of men having sex with other men without any reference to pederasty, prostitution, or sexual acts performed in an idolatrous temple.

#6 – 1 Timothy 7: False Teaching

"Desiring to be teachers of the law, without understanding either what they are saying or the things about which they make confident assertions. Now we know that the law is good, if one uses it lawfully, understanding this, that the law is not laid down for the just but for the lawless and disobedient, for the ungodly and sinners, for the unholy and profane, for those who strike their fathers and mothers, for murderers, the sexually immoral, men who practice homosexuality, enslavers, liars, perjurers, and whatever else is contrary to sound doctrine" (1 Timothy 1:7-10, ESV).

It's very interesting that there are six significant scriptures that specifically mention and condemn the practice of homosexuality. The number six in biblical numerics is the number of man, or the number of flesh. Out of these six Scriptures, even the most extreme positions on affirming homosexuality within Christianity admit that none of the scriptures are positive or speak favorably toward it. The Bible is very clear when it comes to the practice of homosexuality. So why do so many people have a hard time accepting it? Because when the truth of God's Word doesn't line up with one's preferences, opinions, or temptations, one is faced with a decision to embrace God's Word or embrace one's temptation. You must reject one of the two. *You must abandon the truth of God when you try to make the Bible agree with you.*

Pray about why you don't see it.
A few years ago I made a comment on my social media page about homosexuality. I don't remember the exact comment, but a gentleman commented on my post and said, "Just don't try to change them" (referring to the gay community). I responded, "A true encounter with Jesus changes everybody!" I then followed him and reviewed his social media page. I soon discovered he was an outspoken, gay-affirming, "practicing" Christian. I later found out that he was a worship pastor at an open and affirming church.

> ## *"You must abandon the truth of God when you try to make the Bible agree with you."*

We began to interact and build a friendship. We had a few phone conversations and continued to get to know each other over the course of a few years, and even had one face-to-face meeting.

On the phone with him one day, I asked him, "When did you lose your conviction?"

"Well, it was after much prayer and what I read in the Word," he said.

"What did you read in the Word?"

"Well, I read Romans 10:13: 'Everyone who calls on the name of the Lord will be saved.' "

"OK," I said. "Well, that Scripture is talking about salvation. And there are a bunch of Scriptures that say if you do certain things you won't enter the kingdom of God. And there is a list of Scriptures that say if you do certain things you will go to heaven. God is the judge. Only He makes those decisions about eternity. My question is, as a

Christ-follower, by which scriptures do you live out your sexuality as a Christ-follower? Which Scriptures back your lifestyle?"

He was silent for about thirty seconds, but finally said, "I don't think there are any."

"Don't you think that's interesting?" I said.

He remained silent, so I continued.

"So, not only do you have to ignore or redefine six Scriptures that condemn homosexuality, you have to overlook every biblical example of marriage and sexuality, which are heterosexual—with strict moral boundaries. Every example God gave us was a man with a woman. Every time He had a plan for a family or marriage union, it was a man with a woman. Do you see that?" I asked.

"I need to pray more about it," he said.

"You need to pray about why you don't see it!"

Not only do you have to reject six clear Scriptures, you have to ignore over 31,000 verses in the Bible in which Jesus, Abraham, Moses, Paul, all the prophets, apostles, disciples universally endorse heterosexuality. Not once—not one time—do any of them endorse homosexuality or same-sex sexual relationships. Not one Scripture in the entire Bible promotes homosexuality. If the Bible doesn't promote homosexuality, how can Christ-followers promote it? We can't! We can love people who struggle with same-sex attraction. We can walk them through the trials and temptations. But we can't promote a lifestyle that God calls sin.

> ## "Not one Scripture in the entire Bible promotes homosexuality."

The reason the Bible doesn't mention committed loving relationships is because you can say "committed, monogamous, and loving partners" in regard to same-sex sexual relationships as many times as you want, but the Word of God doesn't say it, so they are your words, not God's. My spiritual father, John Paul Jackson, used to say, "The conflict begins when we cannot back up what we believe." The homosexual lifestyle opposes the lifestyle of following Jesus. It opposes a godly, biblical lifestyle, and many of the characteristics of the gay lifestyle completely contradict Christianity.

I want to give a word of warning to everyone reading to be careful not to fall into false doctrine taught by corrupt teachers. When individuals set out to "study for themselves" the six Scriptures we just reviewed, typically those individuals have alternative motives, and are looking for anything they can to justify their opinions and lifestyles.

> ## "...we don't use ancient text to commentate on Scripture. We use Scripture to commentate on Scripture!"

Second Timothy 4:3 says, *"For the time will come when people will not put up with sound doctrine. Instead, to suit their own desires, they will gather around them a great number of teachers to say what their itching ears want to hear."* Make sure you're not listening to what you want to hear, but what is biblical, and what you need to hear.

Finally, it's never sound to use secular historical writings and commentaries by worldly philosophers to interpret Scripture. That strategy leads to heresy and false doctrine. The growing trend I'm seeing is homosexual-affirming churches and Christians using first century ancient writings to compose Scripture commentaries sympathetic to their cause rather than following the noble, integrative, and biblical process of allowing the Bible to interpret and create commentary on itself. So again, we don't use ancient text to commentate on Scripture. We use Scripture to commentate on Scripture!

GAY CHRISTIAN CONFLICTS AND CONTRADICTIONS

I've traveled and ministered for years now. And I've declared the words of the prophet Isaiah all around the world: *"Woe to those who call evil good and good evil, who put darkness for light and light for darkness"* (Isaiah 5:20). I believe we are now living in the days of which the prophet spoke. We call good evil and evil good.

Today the world celebrates the homosexual lifestyle and embraces all of its attributes. The world calls it good in contradiction to God's Word, which calls it sinful. For years the world has pushed secular society and the church to embrace the homosexual lifestyle. I want to contrast the homosexual lifestyle and a Bible-based lifestyle, and show the conflict between them. Beyond the sexual act, the homosexual lifestyle is contradictory to the Christ-centered lifestyle. I am not saying someone who lives a gay lifestyle or struggles with SSA cannot be a good person or display godly characteristics. I am saying that the homosexual sexual orientation creates conflict with Christianity. Let me show you.

Note: I again want to express my love for the individuals who make up the gay community. I have a great love for those who struggle with SSA. The purpose of this chapter is to expose the conflicts and barriers between the homosexual lifestyle and the Christ-centered lifestyle.

The Gay Christian

I will never refer to anyone who struggles with SSA as a "gay Christian." If you have faith that Jesus is the Son of God, and you live a life in pursuit of Jesus, you are a Christian. However, there is no biblical context or basis for being a "gay Christian." Even that descriptor places "gay" before "Christian," making the sexual orientation the priority. We don't call people "lying Christians" if they are tempted to lie. We don't call people "stealing Christians" if they cheat on their taxes. We are all Christians, and all of us have temptations and attractions we have to resist.

One of the main strategies of the LGBTQ community and those who affirm homosexuality is to create a pathway of acceptance. It's the "road of least resistance" strategy. Those who want to create compromise in individuals, churches, and denominations ask, "Well, do you believe someone can be gay and a Christian?" Then we have to ask, "What does that mean?" The response is typically, "Someone who has SSA temptations and believes and follows Jesus." Every compassionate Christian is going to say, "Well, of course!" because we all struggle with temptation and have to resist our own personal demons. This is where the pathway begins.

After you accept that someone can be a gay Christian, the next step is to retranslate and manipulate Scripture to validate a homosexual disposition and agenda.

After that, the next step is easy: "Well, if you can be a gay Christian, then why can't you have committed, monogamous sexual relationships?" Though God did say, *"It is not good for the man to be alone"* (Genesis 2:18), it is a manipulation of Scripture to use this as proof of God's support, acceptance, and embrace of homosexuality or gay marriage.

Here is the problem. Nowhere in the Bible does any Scripture support the concept of gay Christians or gay relationships. Scripture only adamantly rejects homosexual practice. The Bible actually shows opposition to the idea of gay Christians or gay relationships. Referring to homosexuals, 1 Corinthians 6:11 says, *"And that is what some of you were. But you were washed."* The Bible doesn't say you should continue to be a homosexual and merely become a gay Christian. It says Christians who had been homosexuals were washed and set free from homosexuality. They had put their faith in Jesus and followed Him. Those who set out to prove they can be gay and Christian are deceived before they begin!

> "Those who set out to prove they can be gay and Christian are deceived before they begin!"

"Pride," The Slogan

As I have previously stated, homosexual practice is not the greatest sin, pride is. But pride is the slogan of the gay community. Pride month, pride week, and prideful lives are celebrated across America. These celebrations pour out into the streets with banners, flyers, and posters that all declare their motto, "Pride!"

Pride is the first characteristic of Satan, and the reason for his fall from grace. Isaiah 14:12 says, *"How you have fallen from heaven, morning star, son of the dawn! You have been cast down to the earth, you who once laid low the nations!"* Satan's pride caused his fall from the heavens, and the Bible warns us that like Satan, our pride will come before our fall.

> "...pride is the slogan of the gay community."

Proverbs 16:18 says, *"Pride goes before destruction."* The pride of man hardens our hearts and keeps us from soft hearts surrendered to the will of God. Pride keeps our hearts and spirits at war with God. James 4:6 says, *"God opposes the proud but gives grace to the humble."* That word, "opposes," is "antitassó" in the Greek, and is a very old military term. It describes the placement of a soldier in a platoon with a specific function; for example, to attack or resist. This military word describes warfare from the tip of a spear. It literally means that the prideful set themselves in complete opposition to God (across the

battlefield) and become challengers of God. The prideful are enemies of God! I believe the greatest sin of homosexuality isn't the sodomy, but pride!

Homosexuals Can't Bear Fruit

It's an undeniable fact that homosexual relationships cannot bear natural fruit (reproduce, conceive children). Genetically, they cannot produce children because their sexual relationships defy God's natural order. Genesis 1:28 says, *"God blessed them and said to them, 'Be fruitful and increase in number; fill the earth and subdue it.'"* God's first instruction to Adam and Eve was to reproduce. Just as the plants and animals were created to reproduce after their own kind, so was man created to do so. Homosexual relationships are not blessed by God, and are not in order with his divine nature, so they have no capacity for the blessing of reproduction.

Some people argue, "Some heterosexuals can't have children!" That is very true. Many couples struggle to have children. The Bible gives many references to barren women like Sara, Hanna, and others. The difference is, those women received a miracle from God, their wombs were opened, and through heterosexual intercourse they were able to conceive and have children, thus producing offspring (fruit).

Best friends of my wife and I were unable to have children for years. The doctors told them it wasn't possible for them, and that they should look into adoption. After a season of prayer and seeking God, they felt the Lord place it on their hearts to go ahead in faith and make a baby room in their house. They obeyed the leading of the Lord and just a few weeks later they were pregnant! They now have two beautiful girls. It was a miracle!

These miracles don't take place in the lives of homosexual couples. They can adopt, but they don't get the honor and blessing of joining their DNA with God's miracle of creation. The homosexual lifestyle defies creation, so it cannot participate in creating new life. This is why the Bible tells us we are known by our fruit—literally—our children (our fruit) bear our DNA. Matthew 12:33 says, *"Make a tree good and its fruit will be good, or make a tree bad and its fruit will be bad, for a tree is recognized by its fruit."*

The kingdom of God multiplies. What God blesses multiplies, and homosexual unions cannot multiply because they are not under the blessing of the Lord. They emulate this blessing, but never experience it. Matthew 21:43 says, *"Therefore I tell you that the kingdom of God will be taken away from you and given to a people who will produce its fruit."*

> ### "The homosexual lifestyle defies creation, so it cannot participate in creating new life."

Throughout Scripture we are warned to pay attention to what doesn't produce fruit in our lives. *"Every tree that does not bear good fruit is cut down and thrown into the fire. Thus, by their fruit you will recognize them. Not everyone who says to me, 'Lord, Lord,' will enter the kingdom of heaven, but only he who does the will of my Father who is in heaven. Many will say to me on that day, 'Lord, Lord, did we not prophesy in your name, and in your name drive out demons and perform many miracles?' Then I will tell them plainly, 'I never knew you. Away from me, you evildoers!' "* (Matthew 7:19-23).

We are spiritually known by the spiritual fruit we produce. So what causes us to not produce fruit, natural and spiritual? Living for the world! *"And the one on whom seed was sown among the thorns, this is the man who hears the word, and the worry of the world and the deceitfulness of wealth choke the word, and it becomes unfruitful"* (Matthew 13:22, NASB). The gay lifestyle completely embraces this worldly nature.

Open and Affirming

The first time I heard the phrase, "open and affirming," I thought to myself, *That's odd. What are we open to and what are we affirming?* I soon found out.

I want to be very clear that the house of God is a place for everyone to come to as they are, but no church should affirm any form of sin, let alone the sin of homosexual practice. We can't affirm what

God never affirms. Jesus never shunned any sinner. He loved every single one of them, but he never affirmed any of their sin—not once! He loved the individual, but confronted his or her sin. An example of this is Jesus's interaction with the paralyzed man after He healed him: *"Later Jesus found him at the temple and said to him, 'See, you are well again. Stop sinning or something even worse may happen to you'"* (John 5:14 NLT).

"We can't affirm what God never affirms."

Many Christians have great compassion for people who struggle with SSA, and desperately want to help them. They want to comfort them and help ease their burden. But they soon discover the truth that you cannot remove a burden that isn't yours to carry. God is there and ready to help the SSA struggler if he or she is willing to give it to God. When you try to help individuals with SSA temptations by affirming their lifestyle you can do more damage than good. You can do eternal damage. *"Though they know God's righteous decree that those who practice such things deserve to die, they not only do them but give approval to those who practice them"* (Romans 1:32, ESV). You can't give approval of or affirm this sin, for by doing so you would not only encourage sin but participate in it.

Anna's Story

Anna grew up in a detached home. Her father was in the military and not around much at all. Her mom was a good homemaker, and filled the void left by Anna's absent father as well as she could. When Anna's father was home he wasn't happy, and he and her mom would fight more often than not. Her parents went to church off and on, and Anna always considered herself a Christian.

One day, she stumbled upon her dad's pornographic magazines. She was mortified. She went to her mom in an outrage and demanded to know why her dad had such disgusting magazines in their home. Even at a young age she recognized the material was degrading (she felt degraded even seeing them) and knew they weren't right. Her mom, tired of fighting her father, encouraged Anna to confront her dad.

Anna did just that.

With the same confidence she had used in confronting her mom, she confronted her dad, demanding he explain himself. Her dad snatched the magazines out of her hand faster than she could blink and said, "All men are pigs. Stay out of my stuff!" It was over just like that.

Her dad had the final say and no one was able to stand up to him. Anna and her mom felt powerless. This was a defining moment in Anna's mind and heart. What is a woman but an inferior being to an abusive, controlling, perverted man? Women are left to contend with pornography, sex abuse, affairs, verbal abuse, and divorce, because of men and what they do, she concluded. If all men were pigs—as her dad had raged—she didn't want anything to do with them! She was embittered and began feeling drawn to gay culture where men would not abuse, control, or use her.

Anna found herself in a college classroom, with an instructor bent on "opening" her mind. It was really just a way for the enemy to grab hold of her feelings and exploit her own desire to be free from God.

Anna carried an offended spirit, so rebellion came easy. Sex, drugs, drinking, and extreme tattoos were the norm. She found herself in a lifestyle that offered all of that, with the added bonus of being celebrated as a social and spiritual outcast. Over time, she couldn't pull away. The problem wasn't with attraction; that was just the flesh. The problem was in the segregation and celebration.

She followed her instructor's advice. Maybe sexuality wasn't a choice after all, she thought. Men are pigs, and the whole homosexual culture is above reproach. No one could question her choices. She safely hid behind the walls of "equality." The only problem was, God was able to get through that wall, and so were conviction, guilt, and shame. So Anna drowned all that out with drugs, more drinking, more anger, and great pride. Her plan was to dive deeper into homosexual society and get lost in love, lust, and acceptance. It was "us against the world"!

Anna developed a relationship with an Hispanic girl who was very masculine and in a gang. None of the other girls would mess with her. Anna played the nurturing wife role and her girlfriend played the macho provider, "tough guy" role. But it wasn't all an act. There were serious feelings between them—serious codependent, self-sacrificing, perverted feelings of love. It never was about sex. It was about connection, safety, commitment, and satisfying a deep void inside.

All the while she was pulling further and further from God, and the void she felt grew massive. Anna and her girlfriend moved in with each other and began a long-term intimate relationship, girlfriend and girlfriend. If gay marriage had been legal at the time, they would have married. The relationship was as serious as it gets, they felt. They were pretending to be married and lived in a trailer together. Anna brought her girlfriend home to her mom on the holidays and to family events. They even planned to start a family together.

Anna was open about being gay. She worked with a man named John who was always nice to her and well aware of her sexual orientation, but he had a crush on her. Anna approached John one day and asked if he would be willing to get her pregnant so she could raise a child with her girlfriend. John was more than willing to participate in Anna's plan.

What Anna didn't plan on was her girlfriend becoming so violent and abusive. Her alcoholic rages grew increasingly common and more and more out of control. One night, Anna found herself bleeding with a busted up face after her girlfriend attacked her. It was mentally and emotionally tormenting for Anna. She couldn't take it anymore.

Anna was numb all the time. She started cutting herself just to feel something—anything. Anna's arms were completely carved up with razor marks. One night, she cut too deep. Blood poured from her arms, so she decided to lie down on the floor of her trailer. Anna went in and out of consciousness, but when she woke up the next day, she was in the hospital.

Anna left her girlfriend and moved in with John. She tried to take time to get healthy, but it was a long journey. Eventually, Anna got pregnant by John. She thought that since they were pregnant they should probably get married. Anna was playing house again.

At the same time, she still battled demonic attacks. Anxiety, fear, and depression were destroying her life. Anna had a panic attack every time her phone rang. She feared driving and even doing basic life activities. It got so bad that she finally couldn't leave her house. She was *completely tormented by demonic spirits.*

One day, her brother visited her and she couldn't get over how happy he was. She knew he did missions work in other countries and lived a bold, adventurous life, but she couldn't get over how much joy he had.

"Why are you so happy?" she asked him.

"Sister," he replied, "you just need Jesus!"

That was weird for her to hear. Anna always thought of herself as a Christian, so she thought she already had Jesus in her heart.

"Just come to church with me and you will find out why I'm so happy," her brother continued.

Intrigued by his challenge, Anna accepted his invitation and joined him for a midweek service at his church. As they walked up the steps to his church, her brother leaned toward her and whispered, "Get ready to feel a wall of Jesus when you walk through those doors!" She was nervous but excited.

She walked into the lobby of the church and felt absolutely nothing. She immediately started to cry. She sat in the back row as everyone else in the church lifted their hands and sang songs of joy. She just sat there and wept. Everyone can feel God but me, she thought. She sat there and cried uncontrollably. At that moment the pastor called out to her brother and said, "Bring your sister up here to the front." She went with him. The pastor took Anna by the hand and said, "Jesus has come to you!" The pastor had a word of knowledge and began to tell Anna practically her entire life's story. Anna couldn't believe what was happening. The pastor then started declaring over her, "Never the same. You will never be the same!" He said this over and over.

The pastor was right, Anna was never the same.

She fell in love with Jesus that day. Anna never missed a service from that week on. She fell in love with God's house, herself, and finally, her husband. She lived a gay lifestyle for six years, but has served God faithfully for over ten years now. Anna hears God's voice and is raising her three kids in the presence of God. God is teaching her how to be a better wife and mother every day. Anna got her life back when she fully surrendered it to God. Find a portion of her testimony in her own words below.

Anna's Own Words

I was a lost, lonely girl who fell headlong into drugs, alcohol, self-mutilation, multiple suicide attempts . . . and finally, God's grace. I was lucky, because God loved me enough not to let me die on that bathroom floor. I had a mother who never gave in to my perversion and stood firm against "tolerance." I had (and have) a God who called to my heart. In spite of me, God sent me a man who showed me patience. He would restore in me my desire for motherhood, and hold my hand until I could stand in defense of womanhood and biblical marriage. I am not healed completely from what "gay" did to me. I don't know what will become of my sister who is now legally married to a woman, or what will come of our family if she succeeds in her plans to have children with her "wife." But I am certain that my flesh will not win out over my spirit, that any "desires" that come up will not again become a lifestyle, and that God is not done with me.

One of the things that stood out to me about Anna's story was something she said to me. She said, "Landon, my mom was a Christian and she was so kind and loving to me and my girlfriend, but she refused to affirm my sin. She always referred to my girlfriend as my "friend." If my mom had ever given in and affirmed my lifestyle, I would probably still be in it today."

Tolerance

Tolerance is defined as *"a fair, objective, and permissive attitude toward those whose opinions, beliefs, practices, racial or ethnic origins . . . differ from one's own; freedom from bigotry."* Here is the problem with the foundation of tolerance. It indirectly implies that two belief systems are equal in value. It places a value on the homosexual lifestyle equivalent to the Bible-based lifestyle. In my spiritual warfare book, *Jezebel: The Witch Is Back*, I wrote: "The purpose was not for Jezebel's god to answer by fire, but to get him on the same stage as the true God. Jezebel will force her way onto the stage because she wants Baal to be on the same altar as God." The Bible teaches us to confront sin, not to tolerate it. Revelation 2:20-22 (ESV) says, *"But I have this against you, that you tolerate the woman Jezebel, who calls herself a prophetess, and she teaches and leads My bond-servants astray so that they commit acts of immorality and eat things sacrificed to idols. I gave her time to repent, and she does not want to repent of her immorality. Behold, I will throw her on a bed of sickness, and those who commit adultery with her into great tribulation, unless they repent of her deeds."*

I do find it interesting that the gay community demands tolerance from every part of society, but offers little to no tolerance of anyone who disagrees with them. If a baker refuses to make a cake for a wedding, he or she gets entangled in lawsuits and court orders. Does that sound like tolerance? If a sportscaster doesn't agree with promoting the sexual orientation of a gay athlete, he or she gets fired. If you don't accept the homosexual lifestyle, you are portrayed as ignorant. The truth is the only people they demand to be tolerant are those who disagree with the homosexual lifestyle.

The Bible shows us that God will not tolerate blatant sin—heterosexual or homosexual. First Corinthians 5:1-2 says, *"It is actually reported that there is sexual immorality among you, and of a kind that even pagans do not tolerate: A man is sleeping with his father's wife. And you are proud! Shouldn't you rather have gone into mourning and have put out of your fellowship the man who has been doing this?"*

Acceptance vs. Repentance

The final stage of tolerance and affirmation is acceptance. The gay community encourages people to accept and embrace who they are, but the Bible teaches us to deny who we are and be like Jesus. Matthew 16:24 says, *"Then Jesus said to his disciples, 'Whoever wants to be my disciple must deny themselves and take up their cross and follow me.'"*

We have clearly seen the Bible emphatically, on all accounts, refer to homosexuality as sinful. We are taught in the Bible not to accept sin, but to repent from it. Second Corinthians 12:21 says, *"I am afraid that when I come again my God will humble me before you, and I will be grieved over many who have sinned earlier and have not repent-*

ed of the impurity, sexual sin and debauchery in which they have in-
dulged." Jesus, John, Peter, Moses, the prophets, and all the apostles
preached a repentance from sin, not an acceptance of it.

Sexual Confusion

People often use "confused" to describe their debate over their sexuality or sexual orientation. They experience uncertainty over their
feelings, desires, and attractions, and this leaves them in a state of
confusion. 1 Corinthians 14:33 (ESV) says, *"For God is not a God of
confusion but of peace."* The King James translation says, *"God is not
the author of confusion."* If God is not confused, and He has already
made you in His perfect image and likeness, then where is this confusion coming from? Who is behind it?

Remember Satan in the garden. He immediately caused Eve to
question God's Word and brought her into a state of confusion. This is
what he does. He is the author and originator of confusion. Like Eve,
Satan taunts those who struggle with SSA and encourages them to act
on it, to give in to it, and to embrace it. Satan is behind every confused
thought, feeling, and temptation. God is a God of purity, clarity, and a
sound mind. Second Timothy 1:7 (ESV) says, *"For God hath not given
us the spirit of fear; but of power, and of love, and of a sound mind."*

The Rainbow Flag

It's quite interesting that the gay community has adopted a rainbow
flag as its logo. They have taken a sign of God's covenant promise as
their banner. This was the sign of covenant right after God judged and
destroyed the earth.

I have a great love in my heart for the city of San Francisco. The
Lord started putting that city on my heart a few years ago. I often go
to that city and just walk the streets and pray. I always visit the Castro District (gay district), which was one of the birthplaces of the gay
rights movement in America. The Castro District sits on a hill over-
looking the city of San Francisco. In the middle of the district is a giant
rainbow flag that flies over the city.

As I prayed on one trip I went over to the giant flag, laid both my hands on it and began to declare that righteousness would rule and reign in the city. As I prayed this I saw a vision. I saw the flag high in the sky, but I saw the rainbow of God hang higher in the sky. I heard the Spirit of God whisper to me, "My rainbow waves higher." Genesis 9:13 says, *"I have set my rainbow in the clouds, and it will be the sign of the covenant between me and the earth."*

This is where discerning Christians need to pay attention. The gay community is using the sign of the covenant after God's judgment of the earth as their banner! This is prideful action, and it taunts the grace of God. This in itself is a very dangerous act. As we previously reviewed, pride comes before destruction. They are waiving a banner of destruction, asking God for more judgment. Knowingly or unknowingly, this is what is happening, spiritually. (I will address the issue of the rainbow flag in detail in Chapter 12, along with the additional revelation God gave me on the rainbow.)

Parades

The gay community is known for their parades of pride, featuring dancing in the streets while wearing sexually explicit outfits and costumes to celebrate their sexuality. The marches are always held in highly populated areas so the world can see that they are gay and proud of it. The Bible references this kind of behavior. Isaiah 3:9 says, *"The look on their faces testifies against them; they parade their sin like Sodom; they do not hide it. Woe to them! They have brought disaster upon themselves."*

As we saw in Chapters 2 and 3, the inhabitants of the city of Sodom were known for parading their sin for all to see. They celebrated their sexuality. They celebrated their sin. It was that behavior that got God's "attention." Their parading was a sound like false worship that reached heaven. Genesis 18:20 says, *"Then the LORD said, 'The outcry against Sodom and Gomorrah is so great and their sin so grievous.' "* This kind of parading reaches beyond the packed streets. It passes neighborhoods and cities and reaches the heavens. It gets the attention of God.

Gay Is the New Civil Rights Movement (Slavery)

Not long ago, I discussed life, ministry, and the spiritual condition of America with pastor friends. As most ministers do, we discussed where we felt the nation was, spiritually. The topic of homosexuality and the church came up and one of the ministers said, "I just don't want to be on the wrong side of history on this, like many Christians were on slavery." His point of view surprised me. How has standing on the Word of God ever put anyone on the wrong side of history? This "wrong side of history" phrase and philosophy have been spoon-fed to the church to try to frighten us into wavering from a biblical foundation. The problem with the statement is, to be on the right side of history can put you on the wrong side of eternity.

The related "Gay is the New Civil Rights" strategy to attach the sexual rights movement to the civil rights movement is also very popular in our culture. To compare slavery to the mistreatment of the homosexual community is one of the most offensively extreme comparisons I've ever heard. How do you compare hundreds of years of forced labor, rape, murder, and every kind of human rights injustice known to man with the sexual orientation of the homosexual community? You can't choose the pigmentation of your skin. It is completely out of your control. God chooses that. But you can choose your sexual actions. The two are not comparable.

> **"...to be on the right side of history can put you on the wrong side of eternity."**

The homosexual community and those affirming of SSA have chosen the comparison for two reasons. First, they would like to believe that being gay, like being African American, is completely out of their control. For the sake of argument, I agree that you can't choose the temptations that come to you, but you can choose how to respond to them. Being African American isn't a temptation, it's a skin color.

Second, the gay community identifies with the discrimination they have experienced over the years to the discrimination of the African-American community. Again, the two are not comparable. Without a doubt, evil atrocities have happened to individuals in the gay community, but besides the ongoing genocide of abortion, there is nothing in our nation's history that compares to the generations of barbarism known as slavery.

I follow many outspoken professed "gay Christians" on social media. Almost daily, they post about racial injustice and equality. Every time a national story arouses racial tension, they are the first to post and comment about it, not because they care so much about the well-being of the African-American community in our country, but to use the civil rights movement as their vehicle to advance their agenda.

I would like to respond to that minister's comment about not wanting to be on the wrong side of history on the issue of homosexuality and the church. He was implying that white men, ministers, and Christians generally approved of slavery and used biblical references to support their corrupt stance. Remember what Paul told Timothy: *"For the time will come when people will not put up with sound doctrine. Instead, to suit their own desires, they will gather around them a great number of teachers to say what their itching ears want to hear"* (2 Timothy 4:3). I believe men twist Scripture to support the wicked desires of their hearts. Those motivated by evil twisted Scripture to use and abuse people of color.

Even if you want to take the standpoint that the Bible doesn't outlaw all slavery, it does outlaw the type of slavery perpetrated in our nation. The Bible gave clear instructions that evil slave owners who posed as Christians did not obey: *"And masters, treat your slaves in the same way. Do not threaten them, since you know that he who is both their Master and yours is in heaven, and there is no favoritism with him"* (Ephesians 6:9). Colossians 4:1 says, *"Masters, provide your slaves with what is right and fair, because you know that you also have a Master in heaven."* Slavery as practiced in our nation, was never the will of God.

I believe the slave owners and traders were the ones originally on the wrong side of history. If we give in to affirming homosexuality, we will again be on the wrong side. God didn't desire for His children (the Israelites) to be slaves. That's why He used Moses to deliver them out of slavery in Egypt. Exodus 3:7-10 says:

7 The Lord said, "I have indeed seen the misery of my people in Egypt. I have heard them crying out because of their slave drivers, and I am concerned about their suffering. 8 So I have come down to rescue them from the hand of the Egyptians and to bring them up out of that land into a good and spacious land, a land flowing with milk and honey—the home of the Canaanites, Hittites, Amorites, Perizzites, Hivites and Jebusites. 9 And now the cry of the Israelites has reached me, and I have seen the way the Egyptians are oppressing them. 10 So now, go. I am sending you to Pharaoh to bring my people the Israelites out of Egypt."

God's heart was for His people to live in freedom, not slavery. But even after they were delivered out of Egypt into the Promised Land, His people still desired a man to rule over them, and not submit to their God.

God warned them that if they did not trust Him, they would again be slaves and servants. First Samuel 8:10-18 says:

10 Samuel told all the words of the Lord to the people who were asking him for a king. 11 He said, "This is what the king who will reign over you will claim as his rights: He will take your sons and make them serve with his chariots and horses, and they will run in front of his chariots. 12 Some he will assign to be commanders of thousands and commanders of fifties, and others to plow his ground and reap his harvest, and still others to make weapons of war and equipment for his chariots. 13 He will take your daughters to be perfumers and cooks and bakers. 14 He will take the best of your fields and vineyards and olive groves and give them to his attendants. 15 He will take a tenth of your grain and of your vintage and give it to his officials and attendants. 16 Your male and female servants and the best of your cattle and donkeys he will take for his own use. 17 He will take a tenth of your flocks, and you yourselves will become his slaves. 18 When that day comes, you will cry out for relief from the king you have chosen, but the Lord will not answer you in that day."

God warned Israel that he didn't desire them to be slaves, but every time they rebelled against God they ended up in slavery.

The Bible also relates slavery to sin. Romans 6:17 says, *"But thanks be to God that, though you used to be slaves to sin, you have come to obey from your heart the pattern of teaching that has now claimed your allegiance."* Slavery relates to a life of sin. The heart of God isn't sin or slavery for His people, but freedom and righteousness.

Slavery isn't the heart of God. Freedom is. Luke 4:18 says, *"The Spirit of the Lord is on me, because he has anointed me to proclaim good news to the poor. He has sent me to proclaim freedom for the prisoners and recovery of sight for the blind, to set the oppressed free."* Over and over throughout Scripture, we see the theme of freedom. God's desire is for His people to live free and obey Him freely. Gay is not the new Civil Rights Movement, and the body of Christ needs to become dead to sin, blind to color, and alive in Christ.

> **"Gay is not the new Civil Rights Movement, and the body of Christ needs to become dead to sin, blind to color, and alive in Christ."**

Love Wins

During the summer of 2015, the biggest news in America was the Supreme Court ruling on marriage. As the decision by the nation's highest court came down effectively legalizing gay marriage across America, the hashtag #LoveWins flooded the Internet. The White House was lit up like a rainbow, along with buildings all over the country. People changed their social media profile pictures to display a rainbow over their faces. The social media company, Twitter, even automatically embedded a rainbow heart into every post, using the hashtag #Love-Wins. The contradiction is, love already won! Jesus displayed His love for us when He died on the cross. No sexual orientation can compare to the love He showed on that day on the cross at Calvary.

Bullying

No one should be treated unkindly or mistreated anytime, anywhere. All people from all walks of life deserve to be treated with dignity and respect. The gay community loves to use the word "bullying" to force Christians to not disagree with them. The gay community has adopted the disposition of the bullied, so they advocate for those bullied anywhere in attempts to make it look like there are even more of them. This is the "strength in numbers" strategy. More than anything, the greatest display of bullying in America is done on a daily basis by the secular media. Anything that has to do with God, morality, or righteousness is slandered, mocked, and rejected. If you disagree with a lifestyle of homosexual practice and quote the Bible, you are charged with being a hateful bigot, and can even lose your job or reputation. The bullied have become the bullies, and you better not cross them.

There are a few contradictions between this adopted identity of the gay community and Christianity. First, Christians are the most bullied and persecuted people group on the planet. According to Open Doors USA, over 100 million Christians are currently being persecuted worldwide.[5] More Christians were martyred (killed for their faith) in the twentieth century than in all previous centuries combined! No other people group in the world besides the Jews has experienced anything like this. Jesus warned us that we would be persecuted because of our faith in Him and His teaching. *"Blessed are those who are persecuted because of righteousness, for theirs is the kingdom of heaven"* (Matthew 5:10).

> ## "The bullied have become the bullies, and you better not cross them."

Second, not only are we going to be persecuted, but Jesus gave us clear instructions on how to respond to this, and it was not to cry, "Bully!" Matthew 5:39 says, *"But I tell you, do not resist an evil person. If anyone slaps you on the right cheek, turn to them the other cheek also."* When we respond to our bullies and persecutors in a Christ-like way, we honor Jesus in doing so. Jesus told us not to be sorrowful, but to rejoice in our sufferings. *"Blessed are those who have been persecuted for the sake of righteousness, for theirs is the kingdom of heaven. Blessed are you when people insult you and persecute you, and falsely say all kinds of evil against you because of Me. Rejoice and be glad, for your reward in heaven is great; for in the same way they persecuted the prophets who were before you"* (Matthew 5:10-12 ESV).

Queen James Bible

There is an actual "Bible" called *The Queen James Bible* (QJB) put together by a group of "gay Christians." They actually rewrote every Scripture that references homosexuality. Yes, this is real. They say on their website, *"The Queen James Bible seeks to resolve interpretive ambiguity in the Bible as it pertains to homosexuality: We edited those eight verses in a way that makes homophobic interpretations impossible."* The authors of the QJB edited the King James Bible to prevent what they call "homophobic misinterpretation." They edited alright, but they didn't translate it! In the Amazon description of the QJB it says, *"You can't choose your sexuality, but you can choose Jesus. Now you can choose a Bible, too."* Before the QJB, gay people had no Bible to teach them. But now they do! Could you imagine if a group of people retranslated a Bible and took out every Scripture about lying, stealing, murder, or any other sin? If you don't like what the Bible says, don't worry, we will make a Bible that takes out the passages you don't like. I want to point out a specific Bible passage the editors of the QJB forgot to change. Revelation 22:18-19 says, *"I warn everyone who hears the words of the prophecy of this book: if anyone adds to them, God will add to him the plagues described in this book, and if anyone takes away from the words of the book of this prophecy, God will take away his share in the tree of life and in the holy city, which are described in this book."* We should take very seriously these words of Jesus.

Gay Marriage

When it comes to the homosexual lifestyle and Christianity, the greatest conflict is over the topic of gay marriage. It's such a major contradiction, I've dedicated the next chapter to it.

John Paul Jackson said, *"We have to love in the midst of the con-flict."* Despite these conflicts, I love the gay community and those who struggle with SSA, but not nearly as much as God does!

GAY MARRIAGE: "I DON'T"

Gay marriage has been at the very heart of the debate on homosexuality and its conflict with Christianity. The gay community has made it clear that they want civil unions or legal relationships that protect their human rights and interests when it comes to taxes, health care matters, and inheritances. The gay rights movement has demanded equality. But can they ever be equal? The answer is, no.

Homosexuals can wear rings, cut cakes, and say, "I do," but despite all the festivity, gay marriage will never be equal to traditional marriage because man cannot redefine what he never originally defined. God defined marriage, not man.

God created man, woman, and marriage in that order. He set up the requirements and He set the boundaries. This is God's original design. *"But at the beginning of creation God made them male and female. For this reason a man will leave his father and mother and be united to his wife, and the two will become one flesh. So they are no longer two, but one flesh. Therefore what God has joined together, let no one separate"* (Mark 10:6–9). Everything you need to know and understand about marriage is found in this verse.

Keep in mind, Jesus was speaking in Mark 10. This is important for a number of reasons. First, proponents of gay marriage like to point out, "Jesus never talked about gay marriage." This is only true in the sense that Jesus never said the phrase, "gay marriage." That doesn't mean He didn't address the subject. If activities Jesus never talked about were understood to be automatically approved by God, then kidnapping, bestiality, and arson would all be OK, because Jesus never mentioned them, either. Do you see what I'm saying? Of course those things aren't OK! Just because a particular sin is not specifically mentioned does not mean it is approved biblical behavior.

> "...gay marriage will never be equal to traditional marriage because man cannot redefine what he never originally defined."

When people say Jesus never talked about homosexuality, my response is, "EXACTLY! It must not be His plan and purpose for your life!"

Piers Morgan brought this very argument up to a mentor of mine, Dr. Michael Brown, in an interview on CNN. The liberal host challenged Dr. Brown, saying, "Give me one verse where Jesus says anything about gay or being gay."

"I won't just give you one, I'll give you three!" Dr. Brown responded. "In Matthew 5, the Sermon on the Mount, Jesus said that He didn't come to abolish the Torah but to fulfill it. And in the Sermon on the Mount, He takes the moral laws of the Torah to a higher level—including laws of sexual morality. The second is in Matthew 15 where Jesus said all sexual acts done outside traditional marriage defile the human being. The Greek word for sexual immorality is "porneia," and it speaks of all sexual acts outside of marriage. The third is in Matthew 19, where Jesus explained that from the beginning, God's intent for marriage was one man and one woman joined together for life." Piers Morgan didn't have much to say after Dr. Brown's biblical response. Jesus's only teaching on traditional marriage automatically contradicts gay marriage.

Gender Roles and God's Design

Back to Mark 10. Jesus pointed out from the beginning that God made male and female. Once again, Jesus references the Old Testament with confidence. He's quoting from Genesis 2. This implies distinct gender roles and differences. God created both men and women with distinct, strategic, and purposeful characteristics and attributes. He made the man and woman to complement each other spiritually, emotionally, and physically.

> *18 The Lord God said, "It is not good for the man to be alone. I will make a helper suitable for him." 19 Now the Lord God had formed out of the ground all the wild animals and all the birds in the sky. He brought them to the man to see what he would name them; and whatever the man called each living creature, that was its name. 20 So the man gave names to all the livestock, the birds in the sky and all the wild animals. But for Adam no suitable helper was found. 21 So the Lord God caused the man to fall into a deep sleep; and while he was sleeping, he took one of the man's ribs and then closed up the place with flesh. 22 Then the Lord God made a woman from the rib he had taken out of the man, and he brought her to the man. 23 The man said, "This is now bone of my bones and flesh of my flesh; she shall be called 'woman,' for she was taken out of man." 24 That is why a man leaves his father and mother and is united to his wife, and they become one flesh. 25 Adam and his wife were both naked, and they felt no shame."*
> (Genesis 2:18-25)

Look at what God's Word says and pay particular attention to verse 20, *"But for Adam no suitable helper was found."* The only thing that God determined would meet man's needs was a woman. It wasn't good for man to "be alone," so God brought him a woman, not a man. In the Bible, every time God brought a helper, helpmate, or soul mate to a man as a marriage partner, He always brought a woman. I want to say that again. Every biblical example in which God brings a marriage together involves a man and woman.

We see a great example of this in Genesis 24. Abraham was old and his son, Isaac, had no wife. Abraham asked his servant to go find his son a wife. While his servant prayed to God and asked God to lead him to Isaac's wife, Rebecca came right into the picture. In the Bible, when God leads men into their destiny of marriage, the relationships are always heterosexual.

In Mark 10:7, Jesus goes on to say, *"For this reason a man will leave his father and mother and be united to his wife."* Once again, these are clearly defined gender-specific roles: father, mother, wife, and husband. There are no alternative genders. Even in death and separation, the Bible still only brings us back to these options. These gender roles are crucial to the family structure and makeup of society.

> **"Every biblical example in which God brings a marriage together involves a man and woman."**

♥

Throughout Scripture, men are charged to be strong and courageous. *"Have I not commanded you? Be strong and courageous. Do not be afraid; do not be discouraged, for the Lord your God will be with you wherever you go"* (Joshua 1:9). Men are taught to serve and protect their families, while contending for the will of God. Women are taught to be strong as well, but *"to be submissive to their husbands as unto the Lord"* (Ephesians 5:22).

Gender roles are being demolished in our society. The image of God in the image of gender is being destroyed. Companies are removing gender-specific phrases like "Sir" and "Ma'am" from the workplace. Gender-specific bathrooms are being replaced with unisex bathrooms. Social media offers countless gender options to choose from. Why is all of this happening? Are we evolving as a society, or just growing darker in a reprobate mind toward the original design of God's creation?

Gender roles were created by God, not man. God teaches us what those roles entail. He calls us as sons and daughters. If it didn't matter, why did He create the distinction? First Timothy 4:6-7 says, *"If you point these things out to the brothers and sisters, you will be a good minister of Christ Jesus, nourished on the truths of the faith and of the good teaching that you have followed. Have nothing to do with godless myths and old wives' tales; rather, train yourself to be godly."* This Scripture is gender-specific because men and women have unique and distinct callings of God on their lives.

No man could have done what Queen Esther did for her people. In the book of Esther a wicked man named Haman was bent on destroying all the Jews. If not for Esther, the genealogy of Christ would have been wiped out. There would have been no line of David to Jesus. God wouldn't let that happen. He sent a woman on an assignment that only she could do. Thank God, Queen Esther embraced her gender role and walked out the call of God on her life. Men and women both need to embrace their gender-specific roles and walk out the plan and purpose God has for their lives.

The Bible gives us more examples of men and women living godly lives as husbands and wives. *"Wives, submit yourselves to your husbands, as is fitting in the Lord. Husbands, love your wives and do not be harsh with them. Children, obey your parents in everything, for this pleases the Lord. Fathers, do not embitter your children, or they will become discouraged"* (Colossians 3:18-21). We see another example in 1 Peter 3:1-7:

> *1 Wives, in the same way submit yourselves to your own husbands so that, if any of them do not believe the word, they may be won over without words by the behavior of their wives, 2 when they see the purity and reverence of your lives. 3 Your beauty should not come from outward adornment, such as elaborate hairstyles and the wearing of gold jewelry or fine clothes. 4 Rather, it should be that of your inner self, the unfading beauty of a gentle and quiet spirit, which is of great worth in God's sight. 5 For this is the way the holy women of the past who put their hope in God used to adorn themselves. They submitted themselves to their own husbands, 6 like Sarah, who obeyed Abraham and called him her lord. You are her daughters if you do what is right and do not give way to fear. 7 Husbands, in the same way be considerate as you live with your wives, and treat them with respect as the weaker partner and as heirs with you of the gracious gift of life, so that nothing will hinder your prayers.*

These are all instructions for men and women and husbands and wives to obey. There are no instructions for a husband and husband or wife and wife to obey.

In a gay marriage, who is the husband and who is the wife? Who submits to whom? In a lesbian relationship, there is no father. Fathers have a key role to play in raising healthy children. There are no biblical instructions for gay marriage because it was never God's plan.

> **"There are no biblical instructions for gay marriage because it was never God's plan."**

Understanding One Flesh

The next instruction and insight we get for marriage is found in Mark 10:8: *"and the two will become one flesh. So they are no longer two, but one flesh."* All same-sex sexual relationships and behavior are forbidden. In all cases in the Bible they are rejected. In traditional heterosexual marriage, sexual activity is embraced and promoted within biblical boundaries.

Genesis 1:28 says, *"God blessed them; and God said to them, 'Be fruitful and multiply, and fill the earth.' "* In the bounds of marriage, the sexual relationship is celebrated and encouraged. The apostle Paul taught more about this in 1 Corinthians 7:1-5:

> *1 Now for the matters you wrote about: "It is good for a man not to have sexual relations with a woman." 2 But since sexual immorality is occurring, each man should have sexual relations with his own wife, and each woman with her own husband. 3 The husband should fulfill his marital duty to his wife, and likewise the wife to her husband. 4 The wife does not have authority over her own body but yields it to her husband. In the same way, the husband does not have authority over his own body but yields it to his wife. 5 Do not deprive each other except perhaps by mutual consent and for a time, so that you may devote yourselves to prayer. Then come together again so that Satan will not tempt you because of your lack of self-control.*

Within biblical heterosexual marriage, men and women are encouraged to give themselves to each other as designed by God. This is a beautiful thing because it is designed to reflect God. Ephesians 5:22-33 (NASB) says:

> *22 Wives, be subject to your own husbands, as to the Lord. 23 For the husband is the head of the wife, as Christ also is the head of the church, He Himself being the Savior of the body. 24 But as the church is subject to Christ, so also the wives ought to be to their husbands in everything. 25 Husbands, love your wives, just as Christ also loved the church and gave Himself up for her, 26 so that He might sanctify her, having cleansed her by the washing of water with the word, 27 that He might present to Himself the church in all her glory, having no spot or wrinkle or any such thing; but that she would be holy and blameless. 28 So husbands ought also to love their own wives as their own bodies. He who loves his own wife loves himself; 29 for no one ever hated his own flesh, but nourishes and cherishes it, just as Christ also does the church, 30 because we are members of His body. 31 FOR THIS REASON A MAN SHALL LEAVE HIS FATHER AND MOTHER AND SHALL BE JOINED TO HIS WIFE, AND THE TWO SHALL BECOME ONE FLESH. 32 This mystery is great; but I am speaking with reference to Christ and the church. 33 Nevertheless, each individual among you also is to love his own wife even as himself, and the wife must see to it that she respects her husband.*

This Scripture in Ephesians reflects Mark 10 and Genesis 2, which essentially say the same thing: the two shall become *"one flesh."* "One flesh," in the Greek, conveys "to be glued unto, by which it signifies the union by marriage, which is between man and wife, as though they were glued together. They who were two become one as it were: and this word flesh is figuratively taken for the whole man, or the body, after the manner of the Hebrews.[6] This is so important. Woman was created from man (Genesis 2:21-23). God brought Eve (woman) out of Adam (man). To become one flesh means for men and women to go back into that from which they were taken. Only men and women can become one flesh because woman was made from man. Men and women are biologically designed to come together, physically. Only men and women complement one another physically, emotionally, sexually, and spiritually. Marriage was only created for one man and one woman to become one flesh.

The Trinity of Marriage

Ephesians 5:32 speaks of marriage as a *"profound mystery."* The mystery isn't about the question of men marrying men or women marrying women, but about marriage being holy because it reflects the trinity of God. Genesis 1:26 says, *"Then God said, 'Let us make mankind in our image, in our likeness.' "* The Trinity is made up of Father God, His Son Jesus and the Spirit of God, the Holy Spirit. Just as God is Father, Son, and Holy Spirit, we are body, soul, and spirit. Marriage reflects this holy trinity because it is made up of three in one: man, woman, and God make a marriage. This is why it's so damaging for any relationship—homosexual or heterosexual—to be sexual without the boundaries of marriage, because God is not at the center of it.

> "Only men and women can become one flesh because woman was made from man."

It's impossible for God to join the sexual union of a homosexual relationship because He doesn't ordain or approve of homosexual marriage. First Corinthians 6:15-17 says, *"Do you not know that your bodies are members of Christ himself? Shall I then take the members of Christ and unite them with a prostitute? Never! Do you not know that he who unites himself with a prostitute is one with her in body? For it is said, 'The two will become one flesh.' But whoever is united with the Lord is one with him in spirit."* To unite sexually with a prostitute or someone else outside the boundaries of biblical, traditional, God-ordained marriage means you must leave your relationship and unity with Jesus to do it! All sexual relationships outside of traditional, biblical marriage are sinful according to the teachings of Jesus. You have to reject your relationship with Jesus to enter into sexual relationships He doesn't bless.

Mark 10:9 says, *"Therefore what God has joined together, let no one separate."* God designed marriage to be between a man and woman. Scripture declares, "Let no one try to separate it!" Gay marriage attempts to separate what God created, and it will not succeed. Gay marriage is now legal in America, but it's not lawful in the kingdom of God. As Christians, we are not just citizens of a nation on earth, but of heaven, and we adhere to God's commands and His government. This is one of the hardest parts of ministering to individuals with SSA. Many of them worry about whether they can ever be attracted to members of the opposite sex. They wonder if they will ever be able to sexually satisfy their husbands or wives. These are very real, serious issues that our friends with SSA deal with on a daily basis.

Chad had the same daily fears. Here is his story.

> **"Gay marriage is now legal in America, but it's not lawful in the kingdom of God."**

Chad's Story

Chad grew up in a pastor's home. He was a very outgoing and creative kid. Chad loved the arts: singing, dancing, acting, and music. He was very talented in all of them. He grew up performing in his dad's church. Ministry put a strain on Chad's parents' marriage. When Chad was still a child, his mom and dad got a divorce. Chad went to live with his mom, and it limited his involvement in church.

One night, at a friend's sleepover, the boy who had gone to sleep next to Chad started to play with his penis. Chad was terrified! He just pretended he was asleep. After that night, this began to happen on a regular basis, but Chad no longer pretended he was asleep. Chad fell in with a group of boys who fondled one another's genitals. This continued off and on throughout junior and senior high school.

Chad's behavior became more and more effeminate. He was the star of the musical at the high school, and had a hidden relationship with some boys. He had to keep it quiet because his dad and conservative family would freak out if they ever found out. Chad kept it hidden and continued to pursue a career in theater. He tried out for the FOX hit show, "So You Think You Can Dance." He made it on TV, and doors began opening for him. Still, he remained "in the closet" with his sexual orientation.

One evening, Chad was out all night partying with some friends at a club. He had just graduated high school, but was still underage. He didn't know that his family was desperately trying to contact him. His dad had a heart attack and was in critical condition in the hospital, and no one in his family was able to reach him until the next day.

The close-knit family knew something was off with Chad. When they confronted him about where he had been and who he was with, he admitted to underage drinking but kept his sexuality secret. Chad knew it had been a close call and realized he was playing with fire.

Chad's dad wasn't a pastor at the time, and Chad wasn't going to church. He knew he needed to be in church, so he found a local church with a good youth ministry. He ended up going to a Monday night prayer service. He had never seen teenagers as spiritually on fire as those at that meeting. Throughout the prayer meeting the young people knelt before God and cried out for Him to touch their generation. Chad felt the presence of God and knew he had found a church home. Chad was soon fully engaged in his new church. He led worship for the youth, and got involved in leadership. He even played drums and sometimes sang on Sunday morning. Chad had never been so in love with Jesus.

Despite his newfound church, Chad still struggled greatly with sexual temptation and attraction to boys. He worked for a national coffee chain that encourages homosexuality, and had many gay coworkers. Due to his effeminate qualities, Chad's coworkers constantly asked him if he was gay. He got so tired of it. Chad began to let his guard down.

His prayer time and Bible reading became nearly nonexistent. He soon found himself scrolling through his social media accounts, looking at old friends from old places. His friends from high school had "come out" publicly about their homosexuality. He started having conversations with some of these boys and the temptation grew stronger and stronger. One boy in particular enticed Chad. Chad's compromise continued to grow deeper.

Online flirting turned into face-to-face meetings, and soon Chad had fallen back into homosexual activity, and a same-sex sexual relationship. Chad would drive a few hours away to visit his boyfriend during the week, but return home on the weekend to lead worship at church. Chad became numb at church, and could no longer feel the presence of God. Chad was living a double life, and his ability to manage both lives finally came to an end.

Once again his dad suffered a health emergency, and they had him rushed to the ER. The family rallied around to support him, but Chad was nowhere to be found. His family called and called, but no one could reached or find Chad. When his cousin finally reached him, Chad raced to the hospital as fast as he could make the three hour drive from his boyfriend's house.

When Chad finally got to the hospital, his dad was in recovery, and he joined his family and his pastor there. There would be no more hiding. Chad had a meeting with his family and told them he was gay. He told them that for years he had tried to resist the temptation to be gay, and every time it just came back even stronger. Chad told his family he was moving away to live with his boyfriend. His father begged him not to go. He told him, "I love you, son. I'm here for you. We will get through this as a family, no matter what it takes." But Chad had made up his mind. He was done talking. That day, he left his parents' house to go live a publicly gay life. Chad looked into his rearview mirror and saw his dad running after the car with tears streaming down his face. Chad kept driving.

When Chad got to his boyfriend's place, his gay friends celebrated. The story of a pastor's kid who left his family in the dust was an epic win for the gay community. Chad was a hero to his new circle of friends. After a while, the party died down and Chad was finally able to face the reality of what he had done. Chad might have stopped praying, but his dad, family, and church had not. Youth church members he used to lead in worship watched as he posted pictures of himself with his boyfriend on his social media page. However, Chad's youth church was a praying youth church.

One night, at a prayer meeting, a student stood in for prayer as Chad. The entire youth church laid hands on the student, and went to spiritual war for him. They began declaring that God would convict, speak, and lead Chad back to a life of purity. That night, Chad awoke suddenly from a deep sleep. He looked over and saw his boyfriend asleep in the bed. He went to the bathroom, looked in the mirror, and said out loud, *"What am I doing here?"* Something was different. He knew what he was doing wasn't right. He missed the presence of God, and hadn't felt it in a very long time. The next morning, Chad called his dad and told him what happened. His dad began to cry and said, *"Come home, my son. Just come home!"*

Chad sat his boyfriend down and told him he was sorry, but their relationship wasn't OK, and he had been running from God. Chad told his boyfriend this wasn't his real identity, and that he had to move home and live for God. Then, for the first time ever, Chad asked his ex-boyfriend if he could pray for him, and then he did.

Chad moved home and couldn't wait for church. As he worshiped that Sunday he felt what he described as *"a wave of redemption"* pour over his entire body. Chad felt the Lord tell him to get baptized again that Sunday. God had spoken the very same thing to his pastor. Chad submitted himself to restoration, and has been fully restored to life and ministry. He leads worship at his church and is very involved with the youth ministry.

Chad married a beautiful girl he met in church, and they are truly in love. Interestingly enough, the girl he married was in the prayer meeting years prior, when they laid hands on the student who stood in for Chad!

Isn't God amazing? Chad told me, *"I know who I am with and without God. I want to be with God."* Chad has to guard his mind and thoughts like every man, but he told me, *"If I stay close to God, it's not a struggle!"*

God gave Chad a love and attraction to his wife, and they are happily married and serving God today. But what about the individuals with SSA who haven't had a breakthrough yet? What about the ones who have prayed and prayed but are still only attracted to the same sex? What option do they have?

Since gay marriage and sexual relationships are not an option for Christ-followers who live a Bible-based lifestyle, the only other option is celibacy. First Corinthians 7:25-26 says, *"Now about virgins: I have no command from the Lord, but I give a judgment as one who by the Lord's mercy is trustworthy. Because of the present crisis, I think that it is good for a man to remain as he is."* First Corinthians 7:32-35 says, *"I would like you to be free from concern. An unmarried man is concerned about the Lord's affairs—how he can please the Lord. But a* married man is concerned about the affairs of this world—how he can please his wife—and his interests are divided. An unmarried woman or virgin is concerned about the Lord's affairs: Her aim is to be devoted to the Lord in both body and spirit. But a married woman is concerned about the affairs of this world—how she can please her husband. I am saying this for your own good, not to restrict you, but that you may live in a right way in undivided devotion to the Lord." Every Christian who is not committed to biblical marriage should practice celibacy and living a life devoted to Christ.

> ## "God chose an earthly father and mother for his Son as the best for Jesus's life because it is the best example for our lives."

We can't willfully, with a clear conscience, say "I do" to gay marriage when God has clearly said, "I don't." When God chose to send His own Son Jesus into the world, He chose to do it through the example of traditional marriage and heterosexuality. Even though Mary was impregnated by the Holy Spirit (Matthew 1:18), God chose an earthly father and mother for his Son as the best for Jesus's life because it is the best example for our lives.

LOVE SPEECH

As an outspoken minister on the topic of homosexuality and SSA from a biblical foundation, one question I hear frequently is, "If two people love each other, why can't they be together?" Individuals genuinely confused about what the Bible truly teaches about love sincerely ask this question. I've already addressed why you can't be a Bible-based follower of Jesus and participate in or support gay marriage. In this chapter we are going to explore love.

Who created love? Who defined love? God did! God *is* love. First John 4:8 says, *"Whoever does not love does not know God, because God is love."* Similar to gay marriage, man can't redefine love because God originally defined love. You might be surprised to see how God's definition of love is radically different from how our secular society and even Christians use the word. The world has strayed so far from the heart of God that the worldly definition of love now contradicts God's, and has become the opposite in its definition. Now the world calls hate speech what God calls love speech. Let's look how God describes love.

"I love Jesus. It's not that complicated!" Many followers of Christ believe because they *feel* like they love God, they truly do. What happens when your love for God and your love of the things of the world begin to conflict with each other? You are forced to choose which you love more (Matthew 6:24).

What do you love? How do you personally use the word? We love our family, friends, and people who are close to us. Do you use love to describe your favorite movie or restaurant? Do you use it to describe your favorite outfit or song? How about using love to describe your favorite pop star or celebrity you never met?

Let's step back and look at this. There is a good chance you use the same word to describe your love for movies, music, food, and fashion as you use for your love for God. Does this seem odd to you? It should. We desperately need to clarify this very broad definition of love. How do you define love? How did you come up with your definition? Most people quote a song or poem or describe an emotion or feeling. We must understand love. If we don't understand love we don't understand God, because God *is* love.

Love Isn't

God is love but He doesn't love everything. Let's start with what love is not and what we're taught not to love. We're not supposed to love sinful pleasure. Second Timothy 3:4-5 says, *"treacherous, rash, conceited, lovers of pleasure rather than lovers of God—having a form of godliness but denying its power. Have nothing to do with such people."* We're not supposed to love ourselves over others. Second Timothy 3:1-2 says, *"But mark this: There will be terrible times in the last days. People will be lovers of themselves, lovers of money, boastful, proud, abusive, disobedient to their parents, ungrateful, unholy."* The Bible also teaches us not to love the things of this world. First John 2:15 says, *"Do not love the world or anything in the world. If anyone loves the world, love for the Father is not in them."* Finally, we're taught to not love evil or sinful behavior. Romans 12:9 says, *"Love must be sincere. Hate what is evil; cling to what is good."* In order to love what God loves, we can't love what God hates. God's description of love is vastly different from ours. God doesn't attribute love for everything. He is very precise in how He uses the word and what it entails. In 1 Corinthians 13, we find God's definition of love.

Love Is

> *1 If I speak in the tongues of men or of angels, but do not have love, I am only a resounding gong or a clanging cymbal. 2 If I have the gift of prophecy and can fathom all mysteries and all*

knowledge, and if I have a faith that can move mountains, but do not have love, I am nothing. 3 If I give all I possess to the poor and give over my body to hardship that I may boast, but do not have love, I gain nothing. 4 Love is patient, love is kind. It does not envy, it does not boast, it is not proud. 5 It does not dishonor others, it is not self-seeking, it is not easily an gered, it keeps no record of wrongs. 6 Love does not delight in evil but rejoices with the truth. 7 It always protects, always trusts, always hopes, always perseveres. 8 Love never fails. But where there are prophecies, they will cease; where there are tongues, they will be stilled; where there is knowledge, it will pass away. 9 For we know in part and we prophesy in part, 10 but when completeness comes, what is in part disappears. 11 When I was a child, I talked like a child, I thought like a child, I reasoned like a child. When I became a man, I put the ways of childhood behind me. 12 For now we see only a reflection as in a mirror; then we shall see face to face. Now I know in part; then I shall know fully, even as I am fully known. 13 And now these three remain: faith, hope and love. But the greatest of these is love. (1 Corinthians 13:1-13)

At age sixteen I memorized this chapter. Over my fifteen years of ministry, I've had every one of my student leaders in every ministry I've pastored memorize it as well. It's imperative to know how God defines love.

I want to point out a few things that stand out to me in God's definition of love. Notice that God's definition of love has nothing to do with sex! The world, along with the homosexual community, refers to the highest level of love as a sexual experience, but that's not even mentioned in God's description. In 1 Corinthians 13, God describes love as patient, kind, never jealous or envious, never boastful, proud, or rude. None of these descriptions are sexual. This means that with God's love, Christians with SSA can have meaningful relationships without sin through sex. Proverbs 18:24 says, *"But there is a friend who sticks closer than a brother."* Friendships can be full of God's love without sexual sin.

As we have covered thoroughly, the Bible calls homosexual activity sin, evil, and an abomination, whether it refers to men having sex with men, and women having sex with women. All accounts of homosexual practice are negative. And the Bible rejects homosexual practice as godly behavior.

"...God's definition of love has nothing to do with sex!"

Look closely at verse 6. It says, *"Love does not delight in evil but rejoices with the truth."* This is very important. Love can't delight in evil. Homosexual practice is described as evil in the Bible, so it can't be love. Biblically speaking, love can't exist in evil, so love can't exist in sexual relationships between homosexuals.

If it's not love, then what is it? Romans 1:27 says, *"In the same way the men also abandoned natural relations with women and were inflamed with lust for one another. Men committed shameful acts with other men, and received in themselves the due penalty for their error."* The apostle Paul called it lust. Lust feels like love, but it's imperfect love. It's not love as God intended.

"Biblically speaking, love can't exist in evil, so love can't exist in sexual relationships between homosexuals."

The two main types of love in the Bible are "phileo" and "agapao." Phileo is the "love of impulse, friendship, affection, or feeling." Agapao is the "love of esteem, regard, perfect love, or love of choice." Phileo is the love of friendship versus the love of God. It is the love of impulse versus perfect love. It is the love of feeling versus the love of choice. The majority of things we say we love involve phileo love—impulse feelings.

God's love isn't impulsive, it's intentional—it's a choice. I'm so glad Jesus chose to obey the Father and chose to die on the cross for us when He didn't feel like it. Matthew 26:39 says, *"Going a little farther, he fell with his face to the ground and prayed, 'My Father, if it is possible, may this cup be taken from me. Yet not as I will, but as you will.' "* Jesus loved us so much He chose to do what He didn't feel like doing, and expressed love in action. That's how much Jesus loves you!

God loves you so much that He chose to send His Son Jesus to earth to save you. He watched Jesus suffer brutality, endure torture, and then experience a horrific death on the cross as He paid the highest price and made the ultimate sacrifice for our sin. John 3:16 says, *"For God so loved the world that he gave his one and only Son, that whoever believes in him shall not perish but have eternal life."* I love how Romans 8:38-39 describes God's love for us:

> *38-39 So, what do you think? With God on our side like this, how can we lose? If God didn't hesitate to put everything on the line for us, embracing our condition and exposing himself to the worst by sending his own Son, is there anything else he wouldn't gladly and freely do for us? And who would dare tangle with God by messing with one of God's chosen? Who would dare even to point a finger? The One who died for us—who was raised to life for us!—is in the presence of God at this very moment sticking up for us. Do you think anyone is going to be able to drive a wedge between us and Christ's love for us? There is no way! Not trouble, not hard times, not hatred, not hunger, not homelessness, not bullying threats, not backstabbing, not even the worst sins listed in Scripture: They kill us in cold blood because they hate you. We're sitting ducks; they pick us off one by one. None of this fazes us because Jesus loves us. I'm absolutely convinced that nothing—nothing living or dead, angelic or demonic, today or tomorrow, high or low, thinkable or unthinkable—absolutely nothing can get between us and God's love because of the way that Jesus our Master has embraced us.* (Romans 8:38-39, MSG)

God's love is all you need. It's enough. You don't need perverted feelings of lust to fulfill you because they don't. Lust will never satisfy. It can't satisfy you because it's imperfect. Only the love of Jesus can satisfy you.

Karter's Story

Confusion and chaos became the primary themes in Karter's life when his parents divorced when he was three years old. Growing up, he had only limited interaction with his dad, so he lacked a strong father role model. Karter was very outspoken and very outgoing as a child. He was also a very attractive young man, and people were drawn to him.

In elementary school, Karter's confusion continued to grow. On the playground and in the bathroom, other children began to touch his private parts, both boys and girls. This happened regularly.

In the fourth grade the sexual encounters escalated. In the middle of the night at a birthday party sleepover, two older boys held Karter down to the bed while two other boys molested him. Karter was humiliated and embarrassed, so he didn't tell anyone. He was scared. He thought maybe he was supposed to let that kind of thing happen. Confusion dominated his thoughts.

Karter didn't know what he liked when it came to boys and girls, but he liked what he knew. Karter desired love, and he thought what he was experiencing might be what it felt like to love. After the molestation, Karter felt a change within him. He had never been attracted to boys before, but he started to feel this and same-sex desires.

Karter became addicted to attention. He became very flamboyant in every part of his life. From the latest fashion to makeup, he always pushed the cultural envelope.

Karter had a very strained relationship with his dad. He learned to use his dad's abandonment to his advantage. His dad didn't have a lot of time, but he had a lot of money, so he became little more than Karter's cash machine. With money and style and friends, Karter became the life of the party. He was open to anything to distract him from his true reality. Karter's identity continued to evolve through his confusion, and he began to seek out boys to perform sexual acts on him. Karter just wanted to feel love.

One day, his mom found gay porn on his computer, so she asked him about it. He told her, "I was just researching stuff—it was disgusting." She bought his lies. His SSA desires continued to grow.

With a fake ID in hand, Karter began to frequent gay clubs. Every "relationship" he engaged in was heavily physical. He needed to feel something—anything. Deep inside, he knew every sexual encounter he had was wrong, but he did not know what "right" was. This pattern continued. Karter hooked up with more guys than he could remember, and he felt disgusted with himself every time. He had everything he could want in life, so why did he feel so empty? He cried himself to sleep every night, for though he had more "relationships" than he had time for, he still didn't have love.

Karter never went to church, and he didn't know God. But as he lay in bed one night he prayed out loud, "God, if you're real, show me. But I'm gay. Can you still save me?" (He would later say that at the time, he simply cried out without realizing he had prayed.) Karter started going to church with his mom. He went in the hope someone would see he needed help, and help him. He went for about a year, but no one reached out to him or befriended him—not one. Just as he was about to conclude he was done with church, he was invited to attend a church service led by a traveling minister with a powerful ministry. He decided to go.

He arrived at the service and it looked like a concert, though there was something different about it. He didn't know what it was, but there just seemed to be a different kind of atmosphere there. He felt tremendous peace in the room. He saw hundreds of young people worship and praise God with incredible passion. He didn't know what they had, but he wanted it.

He watched and listened as a dozen young people, in turn, grabbed a microphone and shared their testimonies. Some had battled with addictions and sexual sin. Others had undergone abortions, attempted suicide, and even lived a homosexual lifestyle. He couldn't believe his ears. The students shared how God had transformed their lives.

Karter ran to the front and prayed, "God, you did it for them . . . so do it for me!" As he lifted his hands at that altar, he described a sensation like liquid love being poured all over him. He began to cry the hardest he had ever cried in his entire life. But it wasn't a sad cry, it was a refreshing cry, a cleansing cry . . . a freedom cry. He wasn't sure how long he stayed at the altar, but it felt like hours. When he got up he thought, "This is what I've been looking for. I don't have to escape my reality. Jesus is my reality!" Karter fell in love with Jesus that day, and fell out of lust with his old lifestyle.

He later shared his story with the traveling minister. The minister invited Karter to allow him to disciple him, and to travel with him. This seemed to be exactly what he needed and had always sought. Karter jumped at the opportunity and joined the minister, even entering his process of purity.

Falling in love with Jesus meant saying yes to God and no to the temptations, the devil, and his own lustful desires. Karter had to learn how to renew his mind and take ungodly thoughts captive. The devil and his tempting spirit tried to tell Karter every day, "This won't last," but Karter made a choice to love God and follow Jesus. Every time the enemy would lie to Karter about his sexual identity, he would hear God speak to him and say, "Choose me over the tree" (referring to the tree in the Garden of Eden). Every day, Karter chooses to love God and serve him. Karter knows what real love is . . . love is a choice.

Today, Karter travels around the world ministering the gospel of the power of Jesus. God uses him in a supernatural way to display the heart of the Father and mind of Christ. Karter has dedicated his life to making Jesus famous!

Love Is Obedience

God loves you! The homosexual, the heterosexual, the sinner, the redeemed—He loves us all. In sin or in righteousness, He loves us. God has proven His great love for us. The question isn't whether God love us. The question is, do we love Him? You can't love God with phileo love and agapao love at the same time. You can't love God and serve Him when you "feel" like it, and then "choose" to not serve Him. Romans 6:16 says, *"Don't you know that when you offer yourselves to someone as obedient slaves, you are slaves of the one you obey."* If you really love God, you make the choice to obey Him.

Jesus had a hard conversation with His disciple Peter in which He questioned Peter's love for Him. Peter had just denied Him three times. This was the same Peter who, not long before this, had declared his unwavering love for Jesus (Mark 14), emphatically declaring he would never deny Jesus. But then he did . . . three times. John 21:15-17 (ESV) gives an account of Jesus's confrontation of Peter:

15 So when they had finished breakfast, Jesus said to Simon Peter, "Simon, son of John, do you love Me more than these?" He said to Him, "Yes, Lord; You know that I love You." He said to him, "Tend My lambs." 16 He said to him again a second time, "Simon, son of John, do you love Me?" He said to Him, "Yes, Lord; You know that I love You." He said to him, "Shepherd My sheep." 17 He said to him the third time, "Simon, son of John, do you love Me?" Peter was grieved because He said to him the third time, "Do you love Me?" And he said to Him, "Lord, You know all things; You know that I love You." Jesus said to him, "Tend My sheep."

Jesus asked Peter, "Do you really love me?" He was asking Peter if he loved Him just when he felt like it, or all the time, only when it was easy, or even when it was hard. Jesus was asking Peter, do you "agapao" me? Do you choose to love me and follow me? We know the name Peter means "rock," and that Peter was a part of establishing the New Testament church, built on the cornerstone of Jesus. I believe this is a prophetic picture of what Jesus is asking the church today. Church, do you "agapao" me? Do you love me? If you love me, you will choose to express your love with obedience. John 14:15 says, *"If you love me, keep my commands."* The true evidence of love for God is obedience to His commands.

> ## "The true evidence of love for God is obedience to His commands."

Second Timothy 2:12 says, *"If we endure, we will also reign with him. If we disown him, he will also disown us."* Many believers read the story of Peter's denial of Jesus and say to themselves, *I would never do that.* But how do you know?

Sometimes, we can become so familiar with Scripture that we miss crucial parts. For example, look at the familiar verse, Luke 9:26:

"Whoever is ashamed of me and my words, the Son of Man will be ashamed of them when he comes in his glory and in the glory of the

Father and of the holy angels." For most people, the emphasis is on Jesus, and being ashamed of Him. If we are ashamed of Him now, He will be ashamed of us when He comes in His glory. They overlook what Jesus says about being ashamed of His *words*. His words are the teachings of the Bible. If we are ashamed of them, Jesus said He will be ashamed of us. We must obey the words of Jesus on sexual purity. We can't ignore His teachings on traditional marriage. We can't be ashamed of what the Bible clearly teaches.

We must be obedient as followers of Christ. To deny Jesus is not about denying His existence, it's about denying His words and teachings. If you deny a holy lifestyle and affirm homosexual practice, you deny the words of Jesus. John 14:21 says, *"Whoever has my commands and keeps them is the one who loves me. The one who loves me will be loved by my Father, and I too will love them and show myself to them."* As dedicated Christ-followers, we don't get to live how we want. We don't get to love how we want. We live for God and love like God.

Those who claim to be gay and Christian, and those who affirm a homosexual Christian lifestyle, disobey God's commands and the teachings of Jesus. This isn't love. Gay-affirming Christians describe the climax of love as sex, but God declares it to be obedience. You lived in disobedience before you followed Jesus, but that is not how you are supposed to live now.

> *1 As for you, you were dead in your transgressions and sins, 2 in which you used to live when you followed the ways of this world and of the ruler of the kingdom of the air, the spirit who is now at work in those who are disobedient. 3 All of us also lived among them at one time, gratifying the cravings of our flesh and following its desires and thoughts. Like the rest, we were by nature deserving of wrath. 4 But because of his great love for us, God, who is rich in mercy, 5 made us alive with Christ even when we were dead in transgressions —it is by grace you have been saved. (Ephesians 2:1-5)*

Love can't be about sexual preference. It must be about biblical obedience. We have many definitions of love, but God defines love simply as *obedience*. Luke 6:46-48 (NASB) says, *"Why do you call Me, 'Lord,*

Lord,' and do not do what I say? Everyone who comes to Me and hears My words and acts on them, I will show you whom he is like: he is like a man building a house, who dug deep and laid a foundation on the rock; and when a flood occurred, the torrent burst against that house and could not shake it, because it had been well built."* A relationship built on Jesus can only be built on obedience to His word. Hebrews 5:9 says, *"And, once made perfect, he became the source of eternal salvation for all who obey him."* Our salvation is found in our faith in and obedience to Jesus!

> **"Love can't be about sexual preference.
> It must be about biblical obedience."**

This theme and solid biblical evidence for it continue throughout the Bible. First John 2:3-6 (NASB) says, *"By this we know that we have come to know Him, if we keep His commandments. The one who says, 'I have come to know Him,' and does not keep His commandments, is a liar, and the truth is not in him; but whoever keeps His word, in him the love of God has truly been perfected. By this we know that we are in Him: the one who says he abides in Him ought himself to walk in the same manner as He walked."*

Obedience is love answering to love. It's our love responding to God's love. John 14:23-24 says, *"Jesus replied, 'Anyone who loves me will obey my teaching. My Father will love them, and we will come to them and make our home with them. 24 Anyone who does not love me will not obey my teaching. These words you hear are not my own; they belong to the Father who sent me.' "*

The Greatest Commandment

After rising from the dead, but before He ascended to heaven, Jesus gave us the Great Commission. In Matthew 28:19-20 (NASB), Jesus says, *"Go therefore and make disciples of all the nations, baptizing them in the name of the Father and the Son and the Holy Spirit, 20 teaching them to obey all that I commanded you; and lo, I am with you always, even to the end of the age."* The Great Commission is the great mission or main assignment for all of Jesus's faithful followers: you, me, and all yet to come. It has two parts. First, we are charged with discipling people in all nations. Second, we are to teach them to obey all His commands. To be a disciple of Jesus, we need to obey His commands. To obey His commands, we need to know His commandments. Out of all the commandments and teachings of Jesus, He said one was greatest: to love God. In Matthew 22:36-38 we read: *" 'Teacher, which is the greatest commandment in the Law?' Jesus replied: ' "Love the Lord your God with all your heart and with all your soul and with all your mind." This is the first and greatest commandment.' "* To love God with everything you have is the greatest assignment of Christ-followers. To love God with all your heart means nothing is comparable to Him, and you're willing to abandon anything for Him. This is true Christianity. Matthew 16:24 says, *"Then Jesus said to his disciples, 'Whoever wants to be my disciple must deny themselves and take up their cross and follow me.' "* That's why the love chapter ends with, *"And now these three remain: faith, hope and love. But the greatest of these is love"* (1 Corinthians 13:13). The love of God and your love for Him need to be the greatest focuses of your life.

"Obedience is love answering to love."

As Christ-followers we are to live crucified lives, in passionate pursuit of Jesus. The gay community teaches you to accept yourself and follow your heart. Jesus taught His disciples to deny themselves and follow Him. To know His love is to obey Him, and to obey Him is to love Him.

The Place of Perfect Love

The cross was the place of perfect obedience. When we fully submit to the Lordship of Jesus, our obedience begins to look like the love of God! Obedience is the place where love is perfected. John 15:10 says, *"If you keep my commands, you will remain in my love, just as I* have kept my Father's commands and remain in his love." Some people don't want to remain in God's love because they choose to live in disobedience. God's love isn't contingent on our actions, but His presence is. Consider the Garden of Eden, and how Adam and Eve allowed evil and sin into their lives. If you welcome evil and sin into your life, you will be removed from the presence of God.

Revelation 2:4 says, *"Yet I hold this against you: You have forsaken the love you had at first."* Some people forsake the love of God by continuing to live in the sin from which Jesus died to save them. First John 2:3-6 is a heavy scripture. It says, *"By this we know that we have come to know Him, if we keep His commandments. The one who says, 'I have come to know Him,' and does not keep His commandments, is a liar, and the truth is not in him; but whoever keeps His word, in him the love of God has truly been perfected. By this we know that we are in Him: the one who says he abides in Him ought himself to walk in the same manner as He walked"* (1 John 2:3-6 NASB).

Many people who deal with SSA and similar temptations are terrified they will deal with it the rest of their lives. If this is your fear, I want you to know God loves you. If you love Him, that's all that matters. That's all you need. First John 4:18 says, *"There is no fear in love. But perfect love drives out fear, because fear has to do with punishment. The one who fears is not made perfect in love."* There is no fear in love. God loves you with everything He has, and when you love Him with everything in you, there is nothing you can't overcome, with Him.

When we love God we have nothing to fear. This should get you excited—not about what you don't have in your life, but about what God has in store for you. First Corinthians 2:9 says, *"However, as it is written: 'What no eye has seen, what no ear has heard, and what no human mind has conceived'—the things God has prepared for those who love him."*

God's Word has always been love speech toward us. The devil is the one who uses hate speech. The devil hates God, so he hates what God loves most . . . you!

THE DEMONIC

As I prepared to write this book, I spent a few years reading and researching self-proclaimed gay-affirming Christian authors and teachers. I read numerous books that are popular in the "gay Christian" community to learn their evolving liberal biblical stance on sexuality and faith. Many of these books are very similar in their approach. They state over and over, "the Bible doesn't address loving, monogamous same-sex relationships, and Jesus never addressed homosexuality." Their strategy is that if they say it enough times it will magically become true. In this book, we have already covered these topics and know both these statements to not only be completely false, biblically, but deceptive and misleading as well.

As I read those books and listened to those teachers, I noticed a very troubling pattern. Not one of the gay-affirming faith teachers ever mentioned Satan (the devil), demons, or the demonic. Not one time did they mention any of this! This is not a coincidence or accident. It is purposeful and strategically orchestrated by Satan himself.

I told you this wasn't going to be a statistics book, so in keeping with my word I won't list the staggering statistics on the disproportionately high percentage of people in the homosexual community who struggle with drug addiction, alcoholism, promiscuity, depression, sexually transmitted diseases, and suicide. All of these issues are absolutely demonic. Who is behind these evils and the evil of the world? Satan, of course! No one hates the gay community and all humanity more than the devil.

You would think somewhere within their teachings, gay faith teachers would talk about the greatest enemy to the church they belong to: Satan. Why won't these authors mention the demonic strongholds within the gay community? These gay-affirming teachers won't mention the demonic because they are influenced by demons. First Timothy 4:1 tells us, *"The Spirit clearly says that in later times some will abandon the faith and follow deceiving spirits and things taught by demons."* In this chapter I will show you how faith related to homosexuality is not the faith in Jesus we know as true Christianity, but Satanism. In this chapter I'm going to say what most won't or don't want to say; homosexual practice is demonic!

> ## "No one hates the gay community and all humanity more than the devil."

It's Spiritual

Please hear me correctly. I did not say all people who struggle with SSA are demonic or possessed by demons. I am simply going to show you that the spirit behind homosexual practice is designed by the devil and influenced by demons. All lifestyles that encourage a life of sin and destructive physical and/or spiritual behavior are influenced by the demonic. The drug addict who hurts people and relationships is influenced by demons. The parent who leaves his or her family for a sexual affair is influenced by the demonic. The greedy businessperson who lies and cheats and takes advantage of the naïve for another dollar is influenced by the demonic.

Anytime you let the devil influence your thoughts and behavior, it's demonic. In fact, once Jesus rebuked Peter for sin and called him. Matthew 16:23 says, *"Jesus turned and said to Peter, 'Get behind me, Satan! You are a stumbling block to me; you do not have in mind the concerns of God, but merely human concerns.' "* Jesus was quick to rebuke His closest disciple when Peter's thoughts became influenced by the demonic.

Gay-affirming faith teachers and authors are not the only ones who don't mention or believe in Satan or hell. According to a Christian research company, 79 percent of Americans believe in God, while only 27 percent believe in the devil or hell. E.W. Kenyon said, "God is, Satan is, sin is." We must not ignore this truth as we follow after Jesus. I find it interesting that every time something bad happens to humanity, humanity questions the existence of God. When bad things happen, it doesn't disprove the existence of God, it proves the existence of the devil! I love what R.C. Sproul Jr. says: "Why do bad things happen to good people? That only happened once and he (Jesus) signed up for it." We must be spiritually mature and acknowledge that we are in a spiritual war and must be trained to engage in spiritual warfare. Ephesians 6:12 says, *"For our struggle is not against flesh and blood, but against the rulers, against the authorities, against the powers of this dark world and against the spiritual forces of evil in the heavenly realms."* We were made in the image of God. Satan hates God and all that mirrors Him. Satan derives his hate for us from his hate for God. It's not personal, it's spiritual.

"It's not personal, it's spiritual."

The Real Enemy

Depending on the translation you read, the Bible mentions Satan around fifty times, and the devil is mentioned just over thirty times. Demons and demonic activity have hundreds of references. Satan's role in everything, including sex, is to pervert and destroy the beauty, order, and creation of God. John 10:10 says, *"The thief comes only to steal and kill and destroy; I have come that they may have life, and have it to the full."* God is the God of all creation, and the devil does not have the power to destroy the Creator, so he settles for destroying His creation (mankind). First Peter 5:8 (NIV1984) says, *"Be self-controlled and alert. Your enemy the devil prowls around like a roaring lion looking for someone to devour."*

The three main characteristics of Satan are pride, lying, and deception. Satan's pride caused his fall from grace and his excommunication from heaven. Isaiah 14:12 says, *"How you have fallen from heaven, morning star, son of the dawn! You have been cast down to the earth, you who once laid low the nations!"* Satan's lies are formed from his proud heart. The Bible refers to him as the father of lies. John 8:44 says, *"You belong to your father, the devil, and you want to carry out your father's desires. He was a murderer from the beginning, not holding to the truth, for there is no truth in him. When he lies, he speaks his native language, for he is a liar and the father of lies."* From the beginning of time, we see this characteristic as the devil interacts with the woman God created, Eve. The purpose of Satan's lies is to deceive and confuse the followers of God, trapping them in sin. First Corinthians 14:33 (KJV) says, *"For God is not the author of confusion, but of peace."* In his book, *Knowing the Doctrines of the Bible*, Myer Pearlman says this about Satan: "Satan opposes God's work, hinders the Gospel, possesses, blinds, deceives and snares the wicked. He afflicts and tempts the saints of God." [7]

It's important to note that someone saying, "God told me" or, "I prayed about it," will never override Scripture! As I have now stated a few times, out of the 31,102 verses in the Bible, not one supports a homosexual lifestyle in any way—not one. If you are still looking for a scripture that supports homosexuality you need to close your Holy Bible and open *The Satanic Bible*!

The Church of Satan and the Satanic Bible

"Satanism condones any type of sexual activity which properly satisfies your individual desires be it heterosexual, homosexual, bisexual, or even asexual, if you choose. Satanism also sanctions any fetish or deviation which will enhance your sex life, so long as it involves no one who does not wish to be involved." [8]

Satan's existence is consumed with a mission; to defy and mock God, to defy His order of creation, and to mock His governing orders. Everything Satan does is designed to mock the holiness of God. The Church of Satan follows this agenda. The Church of Satan reverses the order of the Lord's Prayer, saying it backward as they begin their services, to defy God. God says love; the Church of Satan says hate.

God says heterosexual relationships; the Church of Satan says homo-sexual relationships. God says monogamous marriage between a man and woman; the Church of Satan says polygamous and sexually open relationships. God gave the Ten Commandments; the Church of Satan established their version, called the Nine Tenets, shown below.

1. *Satan represents indulgence instead of abstinence!*
2. *Satan represents vital existence instead of spiritual pipe dreams!*
3. *Satan represents undefiled wisdom instead of hypocritical self-deceit!*
4. *Satan represents kindness to those who deserve it instead of love wasted!*
5. *Satan represents vengeance instead of turning the other cheek!*
6. *Satan represents man as just another animal, sometimes better, more often worse than those that walk on all-fours, who, because of his "divine spiritual and intellectual development," has become the most vicious animal of all!*
7. *Satan represents all of the so-called sins, as they all lead to physical, mental, or emotional gratification!*
8. *Satan has been the best friend the Church has ever had, as He has kept it in business all these years!*
9. *When walking in open territory, bother no one. If someone bothers you, ask him to stop. If he does not stop, destroy him.* [9]

Satanism fully supports the gay lifestyle because it contradicts the teachings of the Bible and Satan contradicts God. In fact, you will find many passages in *The Satanic Bible* that contradict the Holy Bible, and encourage every sexual sin and desire with which the devil tempts you. See a few more passages from *The Satanic Bible* below.

Each person must decide for himself what form of sexual activity best suits his individual needs. [10]
Satanism ENCOURAGES any form of sexual expression you may desire so long as it hurts no one else. [11]
If all parties involved are mature adults who willingly take full responsibility for their actions and voluntarily engages in a giv-

en of sexual expression—even if it is generally considered taboo—then there is no reason for them to repress their sexual
inclinations . . . . you have no cause to suppress your sexual
preferences.[12]

It is important to point out here that spiritual love and sexual
love can, but do not necessarily, go hand in hand. [13]

Unless we emancipate ourselves from the ridiculous sexual
standards of our present society, including the so-called sexual
revolution, the neuroses caused by those stifling regulations
will persist. Adherence to the sensible and humanistic new
morality can grow up healthy and without the devastating
moral encumbrances of our existing sick society. [14]

The Satanist realizes that if he is to be a sexual connoisseur
(and free from sexual guilt) he cannot be stifled by the so-
called sexual revolutionist any more that he can by the prudery
of his guilt-ridden society. [15]

That last verse from *The Satanic Bible* reminds me of a powerful proverb on the adulterous woman. Proverbs 30:20 says, *"This is the way
of an adulterous woman: She eats and wipes her mouth and says, 'I've
done nothing wrong.' "* Again and again *The Satanic Bible* tells its readers that there is nothing wrong with giving in to your natural sexual
desires. The Bible tells us to resist the sexual desires of the flesh. Romans 13:13-14 (NASB) says, *"Let us behave properly as in the day, not
in carousing and drunkenness, not in sexual promiscuity and sensuality, not in strife and jealousy. But put on the Lord Jesus Christ, and make
no provision for the flesh in regard to its lusts."*

The "gay Christian" lifestyle aligns better with the Church of Satan's teachings than biblical teachings of Christianity. Satanism teaches, "Do what you want. Do what feels right. Embrace your desires."
Bible-based Christianity teaches the opposite on all accounts. Satanism is a religion of sexual indulgence (immorality). Sexual indulgence
is sinful. First Corinthians 6:13, 18 (ESV) says, *"The body, however, is
not meant for sexual immorality but for the Lord, and the Lord for the
body . . . . Flee from sexual immorality. All other sins a person commits
are outside the body, but whoever sins sexually, sins against their own
body."*

The devil understands how important sexual purity is to God, which is why he works so hard to destroy it. The devil knows how destructive sexual sin is to God's people. Look at this verse from a Bible account of a false prophet and leader named Balaam: "They were the ones who followed Balaam's advice and enticed the Israelites to be unfaithful to the LORD in the Peor incident, so that a plague struck the LORD's people" (Numbers 31:16).

Balaam knew that if the people began to sin sexually, it would cause a rift in their relationship with God. Balaam told an enemy of Israel the way to defeat God's chosen people was from the inside out, through sexual perversion. And that is exactly what happened! In Numbers 25:1-3 (NLT), we read, *"While the Israelites were camped at Acacia Grove, some of the men defiled themselves by having sexual relations with local Moabite women. These women invited them to attend sacrifices to their gods, so the Israelites feasted with them and worshiped the gods of Moab. In this way, Israel joined in the worship of Baal of Peor, causing the LORD's anger to blaze against his people."* Balaam introduced God's people to the compromise of sexual sin that led to idolatry. The Israelites gave their bodies to sexual sin, and that meant their hearts didn't belong to the Lord.

The Antichrist Spirit

This demonic spirit of perversion in the form of homosexuality is all a part of an end time, anti-Bible, anti-holy, anti-Jesus spirit. The world embraces homosexuality and sexual sin like the satanic church does. An antichrist spirit has positioned the culture for the Antichrist. Revelation 13:12-14 (ESV) tells us:

12 He exercises all the authority of the first beast in his presence. And he makes the earth and those who dwell in it to worship the first beast, whose fatal wound was healed. 13 He performs great signs, so that he even makes fire come down out of heaven to the earth in the presence of men. 14 And he deceives those who dwell on the earth because of the signs which it was given him to perform in the presence of the beast, telling those who dwell on the earth to make an image to the beast who had the wound of the sword and has come to life.

The Antichrist will deceive many because deceiving spirits have gone out before him.

This antichrist spirit is at work in the world today, and this spirit is fueling the seductive, perverted display of sexuality that dominates our society. This anti-Jesus spirit is pushing a perversion agenda in Hollywood, the media, and politics. You can't get away from it, no matter how badly you want to. Every time another athlete or entertainer comes out as being gay, he or she gets awards and praise from elected government officials in the highest offices, the media, and Hollywood. This is all driven by an antichrist spirit.

Recently, while scrolling through the Internet search engine I use, on just the home page, I counted nineteen articles supporting homosexuality. The national news supports and promotes it; collectively, the country's largest Fortune 500 companies donate countless of millions of dollars to gay awareness and promotions. Just about every store you shop in now supports homosexuality. Children's shows are changing story lines to prepare children to open up to same-sex parents. This is all the spirit of the antichrist, which is the spirit of the world! First Corinthians 2:12 (ESV) says, *"Now we have received, not the spirit of the world, but the spirit which is of God."*

> **"If the satanic church promotes homosexuality, and the world celebrates it, what makes you think God's people and God's house would support it?"**

Here is my question: If the satanic church promotes homosexuality, and the world celebrates it, what makes you think God's people and God's house would support it? E.W. Kenyon said, "The man of iniquity is united with Satan as the believer is united with God." I have wondered at times, *If the Church can't resist homosexuality from overtaking the church now, how will they one day resist the mark of the beast from the Antichrist?* The antichrist spirit is the spirit of the world. This is why we are instructed to not love the things of the world (1 John 2:15).

We are in a spiritual war. Galatians 5:19-21 says, *"The acts of the flesh are obvious: sexual immorality, impurity and debauchery; idola-*

try and witchcraft; hatred, discord, jealousy, fits of rage, selfish ambition, dissensions, factions and envy; drunkenness, orgies, and the like. I warn you, as I did before, that those who live like this will not inherit the kingdom of God." This is the battle between the flesh and the spirit, and the battle is won by the one you feed most.

Liz's Story

Liz was a fun, outgoing, energetic little girl. Raised by a single mom, she grew up not knowing who her dad was because her mom wasn't even sure. Her mom did her best to raise five kids by herself. Still, Liz's home life was chaotic to say the least. Many different men circulated in and out of the home when she was little. These men would take her three older brothers to see prostitutes before they were even thirteen years old. The prostitutes taught them sexual acts, and then they would return home to practice them on Liz. She was just six years old when they molested her the first time.

Liz was a severely neglected child. The only peace she had was when her mom put her on the bus to Sunday school on Sunday morning. But eventually, some boys on the bus touched her inappropriately on the ride to church (for they too were from abusive, dysfunctional homes). Liz didn't feel safe going to church any longer.

The sexual abuse continued into her preteens. Her brothers, family members, and neighbors molested her on a regular basis. She always felt as if she had done something wrong to deserve all that happened to her. No one protected or looked out for Liz. She had to look out for herself.

Liz quickly learned that guys wanted only one thing. She became sexually promiscuous in her teenage years. At age nineteen, she became pregnant and had her own daughter. Even as a young mother, she continued down the path of fun at all cost, pleasure-seeking, and carefree sexual experimentation.

She hung out with a certain group of people. She became attracted to one of the girls in the group called "Squeaky." She was rough and tough and rode a Harley Davidson motorcycle. Squeaky was publicly out with her homosexuality. Liz identified with Squeaky and was infatuated with her confidence. These feelings caught Liz off guard. How could she be gay when she had a daughter?

Squeaky always used masculine words toward Liz. She would say, "Come over here, studly!" These words and attention drew Liz towards Squeaky. She was hypnotized by her, but not confident enough to act on her developing feelings. But then one day, it suddenly seemed to make perfect sense. None of her relationships with boyfriends had ever worked out or lasted very long, so maybe she should give girls a try, she reasoned. Her sexual perversion and desires began to transition toward women, and further away from men.

Liz always felt this spiritual war around her. She knew about God from her days in Sunday school class, and was always drawn to His peace, but at the same time the demonic spirit of death followed her and wouldn't leave her alone. She constantly felt a war of light and darkness swirling all around her. Then the war began to manifest physically.

When Liz was in her early twenties, she took her daughter to an amusement park. They rode a wild ride that dropped riders from ten stories up. When the ride got to the top, just before the drop, the safety bar came loose and opened completely up. The ride dropped and she began to fall out of the ride. Liz heard a voice of comfort say out loud, "She's not yours yet!" Just then the bar came crashing down on its own, locking back into place. Liz had to get eight stitches that day, and nearly lost her life. The spiritual battle was real, but she was losing the fight.

Liz started to frequent gay bars. One night, she met a girl. After a night of drinking, they went back to her place and she had her first lesbian encounter. From that moment on, Liz gained a confidence she had never felt before. She came out to her daughter, friends, and family, and embraced her life as a homosexual. Liz got a manly job in engineering where two older lesbians worked. They mentored Liz on how to be gay. She moved in with a girlfriend, and the two of them had a lesbian relationship that lasted six years.

When things began getting stale in her life, Liz met a girl online and moved across the country with her daughter to live with her new lesbian partner. For nine more years, Liz embraced the gay lifestyle. But down deep, something inside her never felt at peace. In her decades of living a lesbian lifestyle, Liz never for a moment believed God was OK with her lifestyle. In fact, she knew it was wrong. But inwardly she raged against God for allowing all the horrible things that had happened to her. Where was God when she needed Him? She determined in her heart that living a lesbian lifestyle was a way to get back at Him for all the pain she had endured. At the same time, it was eating away at her. Liz would often find herself looking in the mirror, asking, "What are you doing?"

Just as Liz was on the verge of softening her heart toward God, out of nowhere, she got a message from her old friend, Squeaky. She hadn't been in contact with Squeaky for almost ten years. She felt instantly intoxicated by the desire to be with her.. Squeaky was the one that got away; the one she felt the strongest desire for, but lacked the courage to act on it at the time. She thought this might be their second chance.

Squeaky invited her on a camping trip, and the seduction began. The first night, as the women flirted while sitting around the campfire, Liz heard a voice. It was not the voice of comfort she had heard before. This was the voice of seduction. She heard this voice say out loud, "If you'll deny God, you will have her." Liz was instantly sick to her stomach. She refused to deny God in her heart, and the sexual temptation she felt toward Squeaky immediately left her.

When she got home from the camping trip, something was different. She took her Bible to work with her that week and started reading. One of her Christian coworkers saw her reading and asked if she could pray for Liz. When the lady began to pray over Liz, she felt peace like she did as a child at church. She felt God for the first time in a long time. Liz was confused. She felt the war inside her heart was coming to a head.

She was at home one day when she prayed to God out loud: "If you don't want me to be gay, you're going to have to show me why!" She opened her Bible to read and happened to start in Romans 1. She read Paul's words that clearly showed God rejected the homosexual lifestyle. She read about people abandoning the truth of God for a lie. She prayed out loud again: "God, I need you to show me. What is my purpose?"

That week, she met the man who cleaned the carpets at the apartment complex she managed at the time. He was so kind and full of life. As they talked, the man told her he was also a pastor. She couldn't believe it! She had just started talking to God again, and now she had met a pastor! The pastor befriended Liz. He showed her the love of God and she never felt judged by him. Though Liz tried to start arguments about the Bible with the carpet-cleaning pastor, he was unwaveringly nice to her.

Liz started to regularly attend the pastor's Bible study, and began to feel the peace of God every time she went. At one service, the pastor gave an opportunity for people to give their lives to the Lord. Liz thought her heart would beat out of her chest! She was so nervous. With everything in her she wanted to give her life to the Lord, but was afraid. The spiritual battle raged, and she felt demonic entanglements just wouldn't let her go. Liz didn't take the pastor up on the invitation and left the Bible study feeling defeated.

She got to her house, but had no peace. She knew if she didn't get right with God that very moment she might never again have the opportunity. Right there in her living room she cried out to God: "I'm gay, but God, please don't take your presence from me!" she shouted. In that moment she felt a huge shift. Something had suddenly changed. She continued to pray and asked Jesus to forgive her of her sins and to be Lord of her life. In that moment, the demonic stronghold she had felt from childhood was gone. She didn't feel the spirit of death hanging over her. Instead, she felt the peace of God within her. Liz noticed her lustful attraction to women was absolutely gone.

Liz still didn't know who she was. But she got ahold of Christian books on renewing the mind and the identity of Christ and made steady progress. She never missed a Bible study. Eventually, she was part of a Bible study group that became a church plant. She began to change the music she listened to, and put out her final cigarette on the way to be water baptized. She found that Jesus was enough, and that He fulfilled all her needs.

Liz has lived a victorious Christian lifestyle for over fifteen years now. She plays on the worship team at the church, and runs the children's ministry. She is now a grandmother, and she tells her story of freedom and deliverance around the nation.

War in the Spirit

We all participate in spiritual battle. Whether you realize it or not, you are a part of it. If you're not aware that you are involved in spiritual warfare, you are surely not fighting spiritually. We must begin to wage spiritual war according to God's Word. Second Corinthians 10:3-5 (NASB) says: *"For though we walk in the flesh, we do not war according to the flesh, for the weapons of our warfare are not of the flesh, but divinely powerful for the destruction of fortresses. We are destroying speculations and every lofty thing raised up against the knowledge of God, and we are taking every thought captive to the obedience of Christ."* We battle spiritually by aligning our thoughts with the Word of God. Listen, feeling sorry for our friends with SSA doesn't help them fight their spiritual battle. Encouraging them to accept and embrace SSA (to give in to demonic temptation) certainly doesn't help them. The best thing we can do is encourage them to stand on God's Word in faith. James 4:7 says, *"Submit yourselves, then, to God. Resist the devil, and he will flee from you."*

> **"This is the battle between the flesh and the spirit, and the battle is won by the one you feed most."**

I love what my wife says about flesh and temptation. She says, "If you feed it, it will live!" Galatians 5:16-17 (NASB) says, "But I say, walk by the Spirit, and you will not carry out the desire of the flesh. For the flesh sets its desire against the Spirit, and the Spirit against the flesh; for these are in opposition to one another, so that you may not do the things that you please." If you give in to the demonic desires of the flesh, they will remain alive and even grow stronger in your life. This is the battle between the flesh and the Spirit.

I want to take a moment and allow you who are in the battle between the flesh and the Spirit to find rest. You have been fighting, but you are tired. Jesus said, *"Come to me, all you who are weary and burdened, and I will give you rest"* (Matthew 11:28). The greatest prayer of spiritual warfare is to declare Jesus to be the highest authority, and to ask Him to fight your battle. Pray the prayer below out loud.

Prayer

"Father I come to you in Jesus's name and ask for your help. I need you right now. I feel weak. But your Word says that in my weakness you show yourself strong in my life. So I ask for you to give me your strength. Jesus, I declare your name is the highest name and carries the greatest authority. I declare . . . the Lord rebuke you spirit of death, spirit of perversion, spirit of depression, all witchcraft and anxiety— you must leave IN JESUS'S NAME! I declare that I will not submit to any spirit but the Holy Spirit of God. Come, Holy Spirit. Give me your sweet peace. Comfort my soul. Give me rest in your love. I receive this now in Jesus's name. Amen.

Demonic spirits always operate in deception. Again, 1 Timothy 4:1 tells us, "The Spirit clearly says that in later times some will abandon the faith and follow deceiving spirits and things taught by demons." The devil and his demons work in deception. If we expose his deception, it limits his power and influence. Let's ask God to continue to expose these deceiving spirits in the body of Christ and in our lives.

DECEPTION

The strategy of deception operates in stealth. Deception doesn't want to be detected. It is often difficult to recognize you are deceived until it's too late. The longer the enemy can keep you in deception, the longer he can keep you from your purpose and destiny. And his ultimate goal is to keep you separated from God for all eternity.

One of the names the Bible attributes to the devil is, "deceiver of the world." Revelation 12:9 (NASB) says, *"And the great dragon was thrown down, the serpent of old who is called the devil and Satan, who deceives the whole world; he was thrown down to the earth, and his angels were thrown down with him."* Deception is his domain. He doesn't have the power of God, so he works to deceive through his dark thoughts.

The danger of deception is that when you are deceived, you truly believe you are right. The majority of individuals who affirm homosexuality and SSA truly believe they are right. They believe they are acting in love and compassion. But they aren't seeing clearly through the eyes of God's Word. Their vision is distorted through deceiving spirits.

Deception always sees the sins and faults of others, but rarely sees its own sin. Proverbs 14:12 says, *"There is a way that appears to be right, but in the end it leads to death."* Deception sounds like, "I'm just going with my heart!" You might be going with your heart, but the Bible warns about the deception in our hearts. The prophet Jeremiah warned about trusting our hearts: "The heart is deceitful above all things and beyond cure. Who can understand it?" (Jeremiah 17:9). It's very dangerous to trust your heart. This is why we must search our hearts to see the hidden areas of deception in our lives. After he experienced a great deal of his own self-deception, King David prayed, *"Search me, God, and know my heart; test me and know my anxious thoughts"* (Psalm 139:23). Deception makes it about your life and your happiness rather than living a life that pleases the Lord. Ephesians 5:10 says, *"And find out what pleases the Lord."*

Before he was apostle Paul, he was known as Saul, a zealous Jewish leader who thought he was doing the work of the Lord by imprisoning and overseeing the persecution of Christians. In Acts we read, *"Meanwhile, Saul was still breathing out murderous threats against the Lord's disciples. He went to the high priest and asked him for letters to the synagogues in Damascus, so that if he found any there who belonged to the Way, whether men or women, he might take them as prisoners to Jerusalem. As he neared Damascus on his journey, suddenly a light from heaven flashed around him. He fell to the ground and heard a voice say to him, 'Saul, Saul, why do you persecute me?' 'Who are you, Lord?' Saul asked. 'I am Jesus, whom you are persecuting,' he replied"* (Acts 9:1-5). Paul thought he was serving God and doing the right thing, but he discovered he was a persecutor of righteousness. He had scales on his eyes. He had fallen into deception.

If deception remains undetected and unchallenged, you live your life, lead ministries, and adopt doctrines that are contrary to the biblical teachings of the Word of God.

Deception Spreads

As I have mentioned, I have a number of friendships with individuals who profess to be practicing gay Christians. Some of them are involved in different areas of ministry. On one occasion, while I was traveling and ministering, I got a text message from a gay minister who saw that I would be in his area. He invited me to come to their service after I was done ministering that morning. I accepted his invitation and brought a pastor friend with me to the service. They were a self-proclaimed Spirit-filled gay church. I was very curious to see what their service was like.

We walked in and worship started. I lifted my hands and worshiped God like I would anywhere else. As I worshiped I felt the presence of God. This surprised me! I asked the Lord, "Why do I feel your presence in a gay church?" I heard the Lord whisper to me, "You will always feel my presence when you worship me." I continued to worship as the pastor started exhorting. He used a prayer language and spoke in tongues. He did it very dramatically, in a way that didn't fit with the flow and tone of the service. It was just weird. I got the idea he might be trying to show me, "Look, we are gay and Spirit-filled, too!"

I was confused. I asked the Lord, "How is he speaking in tongues?" I heard the Lord say to my spirit, "It's the same deceiving spirit that works in false prophecy." The clarification helped me process the moment. Then the thought came to me that God never took Satan's gifts from him when He removed him from heaven. And then Romans 11:29 came to mind, *"for God's gifts and his call are irrevocable"* (without repentance). Someone can receive a spiritual gift from God and still walk away from Him and into deception. The service continued (as well as the unbiblical behavior).

At one point, a lady stood up and gave a prophetic word in tongues that was very generic and only served to interrupt the service. Now, I'm a prophetic minister, so operating in the spiritual gifts in order is very important to me. After her prophetic word in tongues, she then interpreted it. Paul gave us instructions that we need to have order in prophetic ministry. First Corinthians 14:27 says, *"If anyone speaks in a tongue, two—or at the most three—should speak, one at a time, and someone must interpret."* This was another indication that not only had this ministry been deceived on sexuality, but also spirituality. Deception will bleed over into every area of your life, not just your sexuality.

Did God Really Say?

The first step in Satan's deception is to get you to doubt what God said. Genesis 3:1-5 says:

> *1 Now the serpent was more crafty than any of the wild animals the LORD God had made. He said to the woman, "Did God really say, 'You must not eat from any tree in the garden'?" 2 The woman said to the serpent, 'We may eat fruit from the*

trees in the garden, 3 but God did say, 'You must not eat fruit from the tree that is in the middle of the garden, and you must not touch it, or you will die.' " 4 "You will not surely die," the serpent said to the woman. 5 "For God knows that when you eat of it your eyes will be opened, and you will be like God, knowing good and evil."

"Deception will bleed over into every area of your life, not just your sexuality."

Pay attention to verse 1. The serpent (the devil) said, "Did God really say?" The answer was clear, yes! That is what God said in Genesis 2:15-17, *"The Lord God took the man and put him in the Garden of Eden to work it and take care of it. And the Lord God commanded the man, 'You are free to eat from any tree in the garden; but you must not eat from the tree of the knowledge of good and evil, for when you eat from it you will certainly die.' "* Satan had Eve on the pathway to sin and death, not when she ate the forbidden fruit, but when he got her to doubt what God said. This scripture teaches us that from the beginning of time, Satan lied and deceived mankind into questioning God's Word though it was so abundantly clear.

"The first step in Satan's deception is to get you to doubt what God said."

After questioning God's Word, deception continues in what you want to hear. Genesis 3:5 says, *"For God knows that when you eat from it your eyes will be opened, and you will be like God, knowing good and evil."* The devil continued with Eve, telling her what her flesh wanted to hear. You don't have to pray about clear Scripture. If you pray about it and don't feel conviction, you are in deception. Second Timothy 4:3 says, *"For the time will come when people will not put up with sound doctrine. Instead, to suit their own desires, they will gath-*

er around them a great number of teachers to say what their itching ears want to hear." The devil led Eve astray. Second Corinthians 11:3 says, *"But I am afraid that just as Eve was deceived by the serpent's cunning, your minds may somehow be led astray from your sincere and pure devotion to Christ."*

Not only does Satan directly lie about Scripture, but he deceitfully manipulates it by misusing it. Let's read the interaction Jesus had with Satan when Jesus was led into the wilderness for forty days of prayer and fasting.

> **"If you pray about it and don't feel conviction, you are in deception."**

1 Then Jesus was led by the Spirit into the wilderness to be tempted by the devil. 2 After fasting forty days and forty nights, he was hungry. 3 The tempter came to him and said, "If you are the Son of God, tell these stones to become bread." 4 Jesus answered, "It is written: 'Man shall not live on bread alone, but on every word that comes from the mouth of God.' " 5 Then the devil took him to the holy city and had him stand on the highest point of the temple. 6 "If you are the Son of God," he said, "throw yourself down. For it is written: " 'He will command his angels concerning you, and they will lift you up in their hands, so that you will not strike your foot against a stone." 7 Jesus answered him, "It is also written: 'Do not put the Lord your God to the test.' " 8 Again, the devil took him to a very high mountain and showed him all the kingdoms of the world and their splendor. 9 "All this I will give you," he said, "if you will bow down and worship me." 10 Jesus said to him, "Away from me, Satan! For it is written: 'Worship the Lord your God, and serve him only.' " (Matthew 4:1-10)

False Teachings and Manipulation

Through deception, Satan uses Scripture to manipulate people. As I wrote in my spiritual warfare book, *Jezebel: The Witch Is Back*, "Using Scripture to manipulate people is witchcraft." [16] Satan used these Old Testament references to try to manipulate Jesus to disobey God's Word and serve and worship him. The devil uses the same strategy through false, gay-affirming faith teachers to manipulate Bible verses to question God's clear word, while embracing radical, biblically unfounded teachings. Some of these false teachings include: David and Jonathan were gay, Ruth and Naomi were lesbian lovers, the centurion and his servant were gay lovers, you can practice homosexuality and affirm SSA and still be a true follower of Christ, and the list goes on and on.

Let's go back to Genesis 3. In verse 5, Satan attempts to reason with Eve after lying to her. He claimed she just didn't understand and was ignorant of God's real intentions. The devil attempted to reason his claims to make God appear unjust and unfair. Isn't this the same strategy he uses today to convince Christians that follow Jesus from a Bible-based perspective to abandon sound doctrine and embrace a new philosophy based on equality? It is! They say, "It is simply unfair that some people struggle with SSA, so since it is unfair, it must not be from God." This is the lie of the enemy that the devil gave to Eve, and is giving to Christians with SSA. People are tempted first. Then after they yield to temptation, they try to justify it.

Another danger of deception is that the deceived becomes the deceiver. Adam wasn't innocent, either. Adam gave in to Eve's deception and let her deception become his own. Genesis 3:6 says, *"When the woman saw that the fruit of the tree was good for food and pleasing to the eye, and also desirable for gaining wisdom, she took some and ate it. She also gave some to her husband, who was with her, and he ate it."* Even if you're not gay and don't personally experience SSA, if you support a lifestyle that does, then like Adam, you allow the deception of others to become your own. Ephesians 5:6-7 says, *"Let no one deceive you with empty words, for because of such things God's wrath comes on those who are disobedient. Therefore do not be partners with them."*

Deception will never allow you to be honest with yourself because as we read in Proverbs and Psalms, we want to hear what our flesh wants to hear. So when someone tells you that you can be gay and a Christian, or in a sexual, loving, monogamous same-sex relationship, you believe it. You want to hold on to John 3:16 and Romans 10:13, but ignore the many other verses that bring the clear perspective of discipleship in following Jesus. This deception continues to grow in the lives of believers through false teaching.

> ### "People are tempted first. Then after they yield to temptation, they try to justify it."

It's no coincidence that so many Bible verses warn us of false teaching in relation to immorality. Second Peter 2:2 says, *"Many will follow their evil teaching and shameful immorality. And because of these teachers, the way of truth will be slandered."* In the book of Galatians, the apostle Paul wrote, *"Evidently some people are throwing you into confusion and are trying to pervert the gospel of Christ. But even if we or an angel from heaven should preach a gospel other than the one we preached to you, let them be under God's curse!"* (Galatians 1:7-8). These are strong words when it comes to false teaching on morality we cannot take lightly. Second Peter 2:1-3 says, *"But there were also false prophets among the people, just as there will be false teachers among you. They will secretly introduce destructive heresies, even denying the sovereign Lord who bought them—bringing swift destruction on themselves. Many will follow their depraved conduct and will bring the way of truth into disrepute. In their greed these teachers will exploit you with fabricated stories. Their condemnation has long been hanging over them, and their destruction has not been sleeping."*

You might be thinking, *Can't we just love everyone?* We can, but we already dealt with love, remember? We have to love God *first* through obedience, and *then* it will be reflected in our interactions with others. The Bible warns us that we cannot let false teaching that defies sound doctrine continue to be taught in our presence or sphere of influence because it can deceive and destroy people's lives. I've listed a few scriptures below on how to respond to false teachings.

3 If anyone advocates a different doctrine and does not agree with sound words, those of our Lord Jesus Christ, and with the doctrine conforming to godliness, 4 he is conceited and understands nothing; but he has a morbid interest in controversial questions and disputes about words, out of which arise envy, strife, abusive language, evil suspicions. (1 Timothy 6:3-4, ESV)

9 He must hold firmly to the trustworthy message as it has been taught, so that he can encourage others by sound doctrine and refute those who oppose it. (Titus 1:9)

20 O Timothy, guard what has been entrusted to you, avoiding worldly and empty chatter and the opposing arguments of what is falsely called knowledge 21 which some have professed and thus gone astray from the faith. (1 Timothy 6:20-21, NASB)

13 This saying is true. Therefore rebuke them sharply, so that they will be sound in the faith 14 and will pay no attention to Jewish myths or to the merely human commands of those who reject the truth. 15 To the pure, all things are pure, but to those who are corrupted and do not believe, nothing is pure. In fact, both their minds and consciences are corrupted. 16 They claim to know God, but by their actions they deny him. They are detestable, disobedient and unfit for doing anything good. (Titus 1:13-16)

Heaven and Hell

Like I said in the beginning of this chapter, many people don't know they are deceived. They don't know they're living in sin. They don't realize they are on the pathway to destruction. Matthew 7:13-14 says, *"Enter through the narrow gate. For wide is the gate and broad is the road that leads to destruction, and many enter through it. But small is the gate and narrow the road that leads to life, and only a few find it."*

This brings us to a critical question: Do practicing gay people go to heaven? I will say that one of the greatest deceptions in the world today is that if you are a good person you will go to heaven. Most people believe that there are many ways to God. But we are not most people. We are dedicated followers of Christ who desire to worship God in the Spirit and in truth. We must look at what the Bible says about heaven and hell.

I decided to list Scriptures that refer to those who will go to heaven and enter the kingdom of God, and those who will not. Read them below and see for yourself what the Bible says. Read with caution. Ask the Holy Spirit for His conviction as you read.

Will Not Inherit the Kingdom of God / Will Not Go to Heaven

8 On the contrary, you yourselves wrong and defraud. You do this even to your brethren. 9 Or do you not know that the unrighteous will not inherit the kingdom of God? Do not be deceived; neither fornicators, nor idolaters, nor adulterers, nor effeminate, nor homosexuals, 10 nor thieves, nor the covetous, nor drunkards, nor revilers, nor swindlers, will inherit the kingdom of God. (1 Corinthians 6:8-10, NASB)

19 The acts of the flesh are obvious: sexual immorality, impurity and debauchery; 20 idolatry and witchcraft; hatred, discord, jealousy, fits of rage, selfish ambition, dissensions, factions 21 and envy; drunkenness, orgies, and the like. I warn you, as I did before, that those who live like this will not inherit the kingdom of God. (Galatians 5:19-21)

For of this you can be sure: No immoral, impure or greedy person—such a person is an idolater—has any inheritance in the kingdom of Christ and of God. (Ephesians 5:5)

(Jesus speaking) 29 If your right eye makes you to stumble, tear it out and throw it from you; for it is better for you to lose one of the parts of your body, than for your whole body to be thrown into hell. 30 If your right hand makes you stumble, cut it off and throw it from you; for it is better for you to lose one of the parts of your body, than for your whole body to go into hell. (Matthew 5:29-30, NASB)

But the cowardly, the unbelieving, the vile, the murderers, the sexually immoral, those who practice magic arts, the idolaters and all liars —they will be consigned to the fiery lake of burning sulfur. This is the second death. (Revelation 21:8)

(Jesus speaking) 14 Blessed are those who wash their robes, that they may have the right to the tree of life and may go through the gates into the city. 15 Outside are the dogs, those who practice magic arts, the sexually immoral, the murderers, the idolaters and everyone who loves and practices falsehood. (Revelation 22:14-15)

13 The sea gave up the dead that were in it, and death and Hades gave up the dead that were in them, and each person was judged according to what they had done. 14 Then death and Hades were thrown into the lake of fire. The lake of fire is the second death. 15 Anyone whose name was not found written in the book of life was thrown into the lake of fire. (Revelation 20:13-15)

9 Or do you not know that the unrighteous will not inherit the kingdom of God? Do not be deceived: neither the sexually immoral, nor idolaters, nor adulterers, nor men who practice homosexuality, 10 nor thieves, nor the greedy, nor drunkards, nor revilers, nor swindlers will inherit the kingdom of God. 11 And such were some of you. But you were washed, you were sanctified, you were justified in the name of the Lord Jesus Christ and by the Spirit of our God. (1 Corinthians 6:9-11, ESV)

(Jesus speaking) Not everyone who says to Me, "Lord, Lord," will enter the kingdom of heaven, but he who does the will of My Father who is in heaven will enter. 22 Many will say to Me on that day, "Lord, Lord, did we not prophesy in Your name, and in Your name cast out demons, and in Your name perform many miracles?" 23 "And then I will declare to them, 'I never knew you; DEPART FROM ME, YOU WHO PRACTICE LAWLESSNESS.' " (Matthew 7:21-23, NASB)

Will Inherit the Kingdom of God / Will Go to Heaven

For God so loved the world that he gave his one and only Son, that whoever believes in him shall not perish but have eternal life. (John 3:16)

9 If you declare with your mouth, "Jesus is Lord," and believe in your heart that God raised him from the dead, you will be saved. 10 For it is with your heart that you believe and are justified, and it is with your mouth that you profess your faith and are saved. 11 As Scripture says, "Anyone who believes in him will never be put to shame." 12 For there is no difference between Jew and Gentile—the same Lord is Lord of all and richly blesses all who call on him, 13 for, Everyone who calls on the name of the Lord will be saved. (Romans 10:9-13)

Jesus said to her, "I am the resurrection and the life. The one who believes in me will live, even though they die." (John 11:25)

Whoever believes in him is not condemned, but whoever does not believe stands condemned already because they have not believed in the name of God's one and only Son. (John 3:18)

Whoever believes in the Son has eternal life, but whoever rejects the Son will not see life, for God's wrath remains on them. (John 3:36)

50 I am not seeking glory for myself; but there is one who seeks it, and he is the judge. 51 Very truly I tell you, whoever obeys my word will never see death. (John 8:50-51)

3 Blessed are the poor in spirit, for theirs is the kingdom of heaven . . . . 10 Blessed are those who have been persecuted for the sake of righteousness, for theirs is the kingdom of heaven. (Matthew 5:3, 10 NASB)

And, once made perfect, he (Jesus) became the source of eternal salvation for all who obey him. (Hebrews 5:9, parentheses

added)
10 At that time many will turn away from the faith and will betray and hate each other, 11 and many false prophets will appear and deceive many people. 12 Because of the increase of wickedness, the love of most will grow cold, 13 but the one who stands firm to the end will be saved. (Matthew 24:10-13)

"Very truly I tell you, whoever obeys my Word will never see death." (John 8:51)

"Why do you ask me about what is good?" Jesus replied. "There is only One who is good. If you want to enter life, keep the commandments". . . . 25 When the disciples heard this, they were greatly astonished and asked, "Who then can be saved?" 26 Jesus looked at them and said, "With man this is impossible, but with God all things are possible." (Matthew 19:17, 25-26)

10 At that time many will turn away from the faith and will betray and hate each other, 11 and many false prophets will appear and deceive many people. 12 Because of the increase of wickedness, the love of most will grow cold, 13 but the one who stands firm to the end will be saved. (Matthew 24:10-13)

As you have just seen, there are quite a few Scriptures that state if you live in a certain manner, you will not go to heaven. You also saw the list of Scriptures that state if you live in another manner, you will go to heaven. God is the judge, and He has the final say. Let's read one more verse. Second Timothy 2:19 says, *"Nevertheless, God's solid foundation stands firm, sealed with this inscription: 'The Lord knows those who are his,' and, 'Everyone who confesses the name of the Lord must turn away from wickedness.' "* It is imperative that once we have encountered God that we turn from our wicked ways and the deceitfulness of sin.

I want to make this incredibly clear: If you have believed in your heart and confessed with your mouth that Jesus is Lord, and are following Him (not continuing to live a sinful life), YOU ARE SAVED AND GOING TO HEAVEN. No matter what temptations you face, you are saved. We have all sinned; the heterosexual, the homosexual, and everyone in-between. We have all fallen short of God's glory (Romans 3:23). We all will continue to make mistakes and stumble in our pursuit of a life that fully reflects Jesus. The danger is when people wrongly think that because they said a prayer one time (though they never submitted their lives to God), that they are in no danger of eternal judgment. The danger is when they continue to willfully choose to live a sinful life after experiencing the mercy of God. The gospel is that Jesus, full of grace, came to save us from a life of sin. His grace didn't give us a license to sin. That is not the good news of Jesus Christ. That is another gospel, which is deception. I call it "graception," the deception of a false grace.

Note: This may be a good moment to reread those Scriptures on heaven and hell carefully, and reflect on your life. Ask the Holy Spirit to reveal to you areas in which you may be unknowingly deceived.

GRACEPTION

I have had a heart for the gay community and individuals who struggle with SSA all my adult life. You might know that my wife and I have hosted some international faith-based talk shows and a few years ago, launched our own online TV network called REVtv, aimed at a youth and young adult audience, with the goal of making Jesus famous through media. For years I've wanted to do a show that ministered to those with SSA by telling the stories of young people who came out of lives of homosexual practice to live Bible-based lives, pursuing Jesus. Nothing is more powerful than a testimony of grace and redemption.

I shared the vision for this ministry project show with individuals willing to invest in it. I reached out at the time to one of the nation's largest ministries to the gay community. I didn't want to just do a show on homosexuality, but wanted to be able to recommend a ministry to the audience that was already equipped to minister to them after the episodes aired.

It took almost a year to get a meeting with the president of this national ex-gay Christian ministry, but I finally succeeded. I decided to look this man up online and read about him before our meeting. As I watched his videos I felt a strong discernment from the Holy Spirit telling my spirit he was not free or living in victory. "This guy needs deliverance," I said out loud.

I was still excited when it came time for the meeting because a show like the one I envisioned could truly minister to people. As I talked with the man I began to share my heart and ideas for the show.

I noticed he was very resistant throughout the first part of the conversation. "Landon," he said, "you are using some terms and phrases we don't use around here."

"Like what?"

"Well you're using terms like 'spiritual warfare' and 'confrontation,' and we don't really promote homosexuality or heterosexuality. We promote holiness."

"Well, that's good," I said. "I do, too. But let me ask you this question: What does your ministry do when people continue to knowingly choose to sin? In Matthew 18, Jesus teaches about biblical separation of relationships if individuals continue to sin and refuse to repent."

"Well," he said, "there is a difference between good news and good advice."

What? I couldn't believe what I just heard! My spiritual discernment went from cautious to code red! "So, who determines what's good news and what's good advice?" I asked.

He replied, "Well, that's where grace comes in."

At that moment I knew I could never partner with that ministry on anything. Not six months later, that ministry closed its doors and recanted its stance on biblical sexuality. They claimed their attempts to change people were a complete failure. They became a gay-affirming nonprofit, and publicly stated (falsely) that none of the people they ministered to ever experienced change. Since then, many organizations and ministries have found substantial evidence that that many people did change. Stories in this book are from people who experienced freedom through that ministry. It might be that many people did experience true grace and freedom—just not the president of the ministry.

True Biblical Grace

The grace of God is beautiful. It's profound to experience the authentic grace of God. The word "grace" appears 277 times in modern translations of the Bible. It is a key principle and major theme in the Word of God. We are saved by grace through faith. Ephesians 2:4-10 (ESV) says:

4 But God, being rich in mercy, because of His great love with which He loved us, 5 even when we were dead in our transgres-

sions, made us alive together with Christ (by grace you have been saved), 6 and raised us up with Him, and seated us with Him in the heavenly places in Christ Jesus, 7 so that in the ages to come He might show the surpassing riches of His grace in kindness toward us in Christ Jesus. 8 For by grace you have been saved through faith; and that not of yourselves, it is the gift of God; 9 not as a result of works, so that no one may boast. 10 For we are His workmanship, created in Christ Jesus for good works, which God prepared beforehand so that we would walk in them.

In the Greek text, the word for "grace" is "charis," which, in the context of our salvation, speaks of God's kindness toward us. It speaks of His unmerited favor—His attitude to do good to us. It refers to God *freely extending* Himself (*His favor*), *reaching* (*inclining*) to people because He is *disposed* to bless (be near) them. Theologian A.M. Hunter said, "Grace is free, forgiving, love of Christ to sinners."

The truth is, we're all in need of the marvelous grace of God in our lives. We were all dead in our sin until we encountered the grace of Jesus. Acts 15:11 says, *"We believe it is through the grace of our Lord Jesus that we are saved, just as they are."* This grace only comes as a free gift through faith in Jesus.

As New Testament followers of Jesus, we understand that even though the laws of the Old Testament are good and beneficial to us, we are not saved by keeping them. We are saved by grace and taught by Jesus to obey His commands. John 1:17 says, *"For the law was given through Moses; grace and truth came through Jesus Christ."*

Grace has become a very popular topic in mainstream Christianity. It must be one of the most preached about, written about, and sung about topics in the church today. What a wonderful topic it is. But many teachers are only teaching grace and forgetting truth. We must understand that grace without truth is deception.

Grace and Truth

The full understanding of grace can only be found in Jesus. Grace is not a person, but Jesus was all man and all God. Jesus was full of grace, but also full of truth. John 1:14 says, *"The Word became flesh and made his dwelling among us. We have seen his glory, the glory of the one and only Son, who came from the Father, full of grace and truth."* Jesus was grace and He was truth. Presenting the gospel of Jesus as grace without truth is deception. Presenting the truth of Jesus without grace becomes legalism.

The grace of God teaches that all sinners are welcome at the feet of Jesus. His precious blood has redeemed all of us. The truth of God teaches us that encountering grace produces a spiritual renewal that results in a lifestyle change. Not overnight, but like any healthy tree, it will begin to bear fruit in season.

> **"We must understand that grace without truth is deception."**

Jesus is the truth. John 14:6 says, *"Jesus answered, 'I am the way and the truth and the life. No one comes to the Father except through me.' "* When you walk with Jesus you do not live in the old life of sin and sinful behavior. Ephesians 4:19-21 says, *"Having lost all sensitivity, they have given themselves over to sensuality so as to indulge in every kind of impurity, and they are full of greed. That, however, is not the way of life you learned when you heard about Christ and were taught in him in accordance with the truth that is in Jesus."* Living in impurity is not the way of grace because it's not the way of truth. Grace teaches us to resist sin. Titus 2:11-12 says, *"For the grace of God has appeared that offers salvation to all people. It teaches us to say 'No' to ungodliness and worldly passions, and to live self-controlled, upright and godly lives in this present age."*

A False Grace

A new grace is taught today that is *not* the grace of Jesus. It is what I call *graception*. Graception is extreme. It is an unbiblical grace that leaves out the truth of Jesus and encourages sinful sexuality. The Bible warned us of this day of graception. Jude 1:4 says, *"For certain individuals whose condemnation was written about long ago have secretly slipped in among you. They are ungodly people, who pervert the grace of our God into a license for immorality and deny Jesus Christ our only Sovereign and Lord."* Did you read that? Grace teaching or understanding that encourages or approves of immorality is not of God and not true grace. Paul warns that these teachers and those who love this false teaching delight in wickedness. Second Thessalonians 2:12 says, *"And so that all will be condemned who have not believed the truth but have delighted in wickedness."* People who love sinful sexuality will always oppose the truth of Jesus and the Word of God.

Graception teaches that you don't need to repent. You are already saved and forgiven. This is a form of heresy, to take a half-truth like this and make it full truth. Graception teaches that all future sins are forgiven in advance. There is not one single Scripture that refers to future sins as forgiven. All sin is referred to as debt or past transactions. When we sin it creates debt, which needs to be paid. Jesus paid this debt for us. Colossians 2:13-14 (NASB) says, *"When you were dead in your transgressions and the uncircumcision of your flesh, He made you alive together with Him, having forgiven us all our transgressions, having canceled out the certificate of debt consisting of decrees against us, which was hostile to us; and He has taken it out of the way, having nailed it to the cross."*

At this writing, I have been in ministry for over fifteen years. I have ministered at more conferences, camps, and retreats than I can even remember. I have been a part of numerous services in which the pastor invited people down to the altar to write on a piece of paper sins with which they were struggling. The pastors then instructed those who responded to nail their papers to a cross displayed at the altar. These illustrated services were (and are) very impactful. That said, in fifteen years of ministry I've never witnessed anyone write down and nail to the cross a future sin. Predicted or premeditated sin? That would be silly. Jesus died in the past to forgive us in the future when we repent in the present. First John 1:8-10 (ESV) says, *"If we say that we have no sin, we are deceiving ourselves and the truth is not in us. If we confess our sins, He is faithful and righteous to forgive us our sins and to cleanse us from all unrighteousness. If we say that we have not sinned, we make Him a liar and His word is not in us."* Debt is cancelled at the moment of repentance.

In his book, *Hyper-Grace*, Dr. Michael Brown says: "The forgiveness of all of our sins have been prepaid, but that forgiveness hasn't been applied in advance. It's applied as needed." To discourage repentance is a dangerous deception. It sounds good, but is far from biblically accurate. In fact, we are taught the contrary. Jesus's very first message after fasting and praying for forty days was on repentance. Matthew 4:17 (NASB) says, *"From that time Jesus began to preach and say, 'Repent, for the kingdom of heaven is at hand.' "* In the Lord's Prayer, Jesus taught that when we pray daily we should repent and pray for forgiveness. Matthew 6:12 says, *"And forgive us our debts, as we also have forgiven our debtors."* Jesus taught repentance because our future sins are not under the blood until the moment we repent.

> "Jesus died in the past to forgive us in the future when we repent in the present."

Isn't It Under the Blood?

Vince was a young adult who struggled with SSA, but he also loved God with all his heart. He tried to distract himself from his hidden desires and the temptations of the flesh with clothes and other material items. It didn't work. Vince felt empty inside and needed more of God. He found a Spirit-filled church and got involved in the music department and young adult ministry. God moved in his life and he experienced joy and peace like never before. Vince formed strong friendships and found a purpose bigger than himself.

Another church volunteer who held an important public position in the church befriended Vince and the two developed a friendship. The man was about fifteen years older than him, and Vince admired and looked up to him. The man gained Vince's trust and then began to subtly come on to him. Vince liked the attention, but didn't think a man from the church would make a sexual advance toward him. Vince's SSA was stirred whenever he was around the man. Finally, the man's subtle flirtation became a series of strong invitations. He began to ask Vince directly if he would perform oral sex on him.

Vince didn't know what to do. He reached out to a mentor and asked for advice. His mentor told Vince to go with the pastor of the church to confront the man, saying the pastor had to know what the high profile volunteer was doing. Finally, Vince's mentor told him to follow Matthew 18 on biblical confrontation, and to take a trusted friend with him as a witness when he confronted the man.

Vince attempted to schedule a meeting with his pastor, but he had to go through the assistant pastor, and he was extremely effeminate and struggled himself with SSA, though privately. The assistant pastor refused to schedule the meeting until Vince told him what the meeting was about. Vince finally told him what had been going on, so the assistant pastor set up a time to meet with the sexually deviant volunteer and Vince.

Vince showed up for the meeting accompanied by a friend, but the assistant pastor refused to let the friend in. He then used intimidation to pressure Vince to handle the situation discreetly. Vince reluctantly sat down with the assistant pastor and the older volunteer who had come onto him.

As Vince began to share the story of what happened he was so nervous he couldn't stop shaking his foot. He felt like it was them against him. Halfway through, the assistant pastor interrupted him and said, "Vince, I know you're really upset, but isn't this all under the blood?" Vince was incredulous that he had referred to the blood of Jesus that way. How could it be under the blood when the man refused to repent of it? The meeting lasted five minutes. Nothing came of the meeting, and the assistant pastor covered it all up. The older volunteer continued to serve at the church even as he served his same-sex sexual desires. Vince left the church absolutely crushed by the demonic situation.

The Fear of the Lord

When people accept grace without truth they lose the fear of the Lord. You are under graception when you lose the fear of the Lord. When you lose the fear of the Lord, you lose all wisdom and discernment for life. You become spiritually numb. When people lose the fear of the Lord the deception causes them to lie to themselves and to God. That's what happened to Ananias and his wife, Sapphira. Acts 5:1-5 says:

1 Now a man named Ananias, together with his wife Sapphira, also sold a piece of property. 2 With his wife's full knowledge he kept back part of the money for himself, but brought the rest and put it at the apostles' feet. 3 Then Peter said, 'Ananias, how is it that Satan has so filled your heart that you have lied to the Holy Spirit and have kept for yourself some of the money you received for the land? 4 Didn't it belong to you before it was sold? And after it was sold, wasn't the money at your disposal? What made you think of doing such a thing? You have not lied just to human beings but to God." 5 When Ananias heard this, he fell down and died.

It's interesting that this story is from the book of Acts. This is in the New Testament . . . under grace. These individuals were a part of the church. But they lied to the Holy Spirit and God killed them.

After this took place, the fear of the Lord it had lost came back to the church. Acts 5:11 says, *"Great fear seized the whole church and all who heard about these events."* The fear of the Lord returned and the church began to grow. The fear of the Lord will keep you in right standing with God and in His true grace. When you remain in healthy fear of the Lord, your relationship with God continues to grow and mature.

"You are under graception when you lose the fear of the Lord."

Grace and Truth Is Freedom from Sin

When you truly encounter Jesus and the grace of God, it produces life change in you. If you merely continue a sinful life, the Bible teaches that you never truly encountered Jesus. First John 3:4-10 says:

4 Everyone who sins breaks the law; in fact, sin is lawlessness. 5 But you know that he appeared so that he might take away our sins. And in him is no sin. 6 No one who lives in him keeps on sinning. No one who continues to sin has either seen him or known him.7 Dear children, do not let anyone lead you astray. The one who does what is right is righteous, just as he is righteous. 8 The one who does what is sinful is of the devil, because the devil has been sinning from the beginning. The reason the Son of God appeared was to destroy the devil's work. 9 No one who is born of God will continue to sin, because God's seed remains in them; they cannot go on sinning, because they have been born of God. 10 This is how we know who the children of God are and who the children of the devil are: Anyone who does not do what is right is not God's child, nor is anyone who does not love their brother and sister.

Wow! What a heavy passage. If we continue in unrepented sin, it means we never truly encountered Jesus and His grace.

Grace isn't a license to sin when it's taught with truth. First John 2:6 says, *"Whoever claims to live in him must live as Jesus did."* Jesus wasn't gay. He wasn't immoral. He wasn't carnal. He lived a holy life. When someone encounters true grace, they no longer live a life of sin, but of freedom in Christ Jesus. Romans 6:14 says, *"For sin shall no longer be your master, because you are not under the law, but under grace."*

"Grace isn't a license to sin when it's taught with truth."

Most people embrace graception because they don't like hearing truth. Truth can be convicting. Truth can be uncomfortable. People love to hear the grace messages about how Jesus healed the man at the pool of Bethesda in John 5, but they don't like to hear the truth when Jesus said in John 5:14, *"See, you are well again. Stop sinning or something worse may happen to you."* We love the story of grace with the woman caught in adultery, but Jesus told her the truth when he said, *"Go now and leave your life of sin"* (John 8:11).

Pride Rejects Truth

Many people reject God's truth even though it brings freedom. John 8:32 says, *"Then you will know the truth, and the truth will set you free."* Pride won't let people repent. That's why pride is the greatest sin. Pride rejects repentance. Pride hates repentance. By refusing to admit we need to repent, we reject biblical truth. Pride gets angry and becomes violent when people speak truth. It's similar to the way the crowd responded to the martyr Stephen in Acts 6:8-10: *"Now Stephen, a man full of God's grace and power, performed great wonders and signs among the people. Opposition arose, however, from members of the Synagogue of the Freedmen (as it was called)—Jews of Cyrene and Alexandria as well as the provinces of Cilicia and Asia— who began to argue with Stephen. But they could not stand up against the wisdom the Spirit gave him as he spoke."* Stephen was full of grace and declared the truth of God. Stephen's audience didn't want to hear it. Acts 7:57-58 says, *"At this they covered their ears and, yelling at the top of their voices, they all rushed at him, dragged him out of the city and began to stone him."*

The way the crowd became angry and hostile to Stephen, full of grace but speaking truth, is the way that the world responds to the truth of purity and morality of sexual relationships that can only be established in monogamous, married, heterosexual relationships. If you stand up for biblical marriage and biblical relationships, the world will call you hateful, ignorant, intolerant, and judgmental. They don't want to hear it. Their pride makes them spiritually deaf and they don't have spiritual ears to hear. Jesus said there is a side of truth we must stand on as Christ-followers. See this in a dialogue between Pilate and Jesus in John 18:37: *" 'You are a king, then!' said Pilate. Jesus answered, 'You say that I am a king. In fact, the reason I was born and came into the world is to testify to the truth. Everyone on the side of truth listens to me.' "*

The Side of Truth

Many have exchanged the truth of God for the lie of graception (Romans 1:25). The side of truth listens to the teachings of Jesus who was and is the Word of God. The side of truth lives according the truth.

Proverb 23:23 says, *"Buy the truth and don't sell it."* When you have the truth of God, don't sell it for anything. Don't compromise that truth for anyone. Be assured that the truth of God will outlast any lie. Whatever you do, do not trade the truth of God for a lie. Don't trade the grace of God for graception.

The greatest deception of graception (extremely unbiblical grace) is that there is no sin you can commit that could cause you to lose your salvation. Let's look at this concept for a moment from a biblical perspective. Hebrews 10:26-29 (ESV) says:

> *26 For if we go on sinning willfully after receiving the knowledge of the truth, there no longer remains a sacrifice for sins, 27 but a terrifying expectation of judgment and THE FURY OF A FIRE WHICH WILL CONSUME THE ADVERSARIES. 28 Anyone who has set aside the Law of Moses dies without mercy on the testimony of two or three witnesses. 29 How much severer punishment do you think he will deserve who has trampled under foot the Son of God, and has regarded as unclean the blood of the covenant by which he was sanctified, and has insulted (grieved) the Spirit of grace?*

"...the truth of God will outlast any lie."

In this passage, the writer of Hebrews warns of the judgment of God that is at hand for the believer who continues to sin after encountering the grace and truth of Jesus. The apostle warns there is no sacrifice for sin left because such ones have grieved the Spirit of Jesus, the Spirit of Grace. I want to point out the word "willfully" in verse 26. *Grace is grieved* if we knowingly, willfully, continually choose to sin and reject Jesus by our actions. Some people might say, "Are you serious? All sin is willful!" What does the Bible mean by willful sin? In Psalm 19:13 David prayed, *"Keep your servant also from willful sins; may they not rule over me. Then I will be blameless, innocent of great transgression."* Willful sin is unrepentant sin. We must repent for our sin.

The body of Christ has embraced graception as it has embraced the homosexual lifestyle. The body of Christ has lost the fear of the Lord. You must choose to fear the Lord. Proverbs 1:29 (ESV) says, *"Because they hated knowledge and did not choose the fear of the LORD."* Jesus is full of grace and truth, and the truth is that He is the righteous judge and we will all stand before Him and be judged. Judgment isn't to be feared by Christ-followers, but embraced when we know His truth and receive God's amazing grace.

DON'T JUDGE ME

Judgment is a part of grace. And when you experience true grace with repentance you don't have to fear biblical judgment. "Don't judge me," has to be the most often used response when it comes to Christianity and any behavior the Bible refers to as sinful. I have jokingly said, "Don't judge me, is the Facebook Christian's favorite verse to partially quote." Most people don't understand Jesus, grace, or judgment, so they end up patching together their partial understandings to create their own version of the truth. It is true the Bible warns of the dangers of judging. Matthew 7:1 says, *"Do not judge, or you too will be judged."* But you can't stop there; you must continue to read the teaching of Jesus. Matthew 7:2 says, *"For in the same way you judge others, you will be judged, and with the measure you use, it will be measured to you."* Jesus is instructing us to not judge impartially or hypocritically, but too many believers have interpreted this to mean don't judge at all.

In the book of Jonah, God sent a prophet named Jonah to the wicked city of Nineveh. Like Sodom, the sin of Nineveh had reached the heavens, so God sent Jonah to the city to warn the people of the wrath and judgment that was coming to them. *"The LORD gave this message to Jonah son of Amittai:"Get up and go to the great city of Nineveh. Announce my judgment (preach against it, cry out) against it because I have seen how wicked its people are"* (Jonah 1:1–2, NLT).

God instructed Jonah to cry out, to preach against and warn the people of the judgment of God that was coming to them. If this happened today, many Christians on social media would tell Jonah to stop judging people. They would tell Jonah to be more loving. They would tell Jonah, "He who is without sin, cast the first stone."

The mature Christian understands that judgment is a reality for all mankind, and God had His servants, prophets, apostles, disciples, and even Jesus preach repentance and judgment. God did this not because He desires judgment, but because He desires mercy and grace. Jonah 3:10 says, *"When God saw what they did and how they turned from their evil ways, he relented and did not bring on them the destruction he had threatened."* God had Jonah preach judgment because He intended grace. God intends grace and mercy for us. Psalm 103:8 says, *"The Lord is compassionate and gracious, slow to anger, abounding in love."*

"God had Jonah preach judgment because He intended grace."

The Government of Judges

We don't need to fear judgment when we have the fear of the Lord. We need to seek to understand judgment and why God set up His government with judges. Originally, God set up His government to be run through His chosen people (the Israelites), particularly through judges and priests. After Moses and Joshua led the children of Israel out of slavery and into the Promised Land and established their nation, the people quickly fell away from God. Judges 2:10 says, *"After that whole generation had been gathered to their ancestors, another generation grew up who knew neither the Lord nor what he had done for Israel."*

The new generation didn't know God or follow Him. They began to compromise and live sinful lives, and were soon overcome by grief and trouble. Judges 2:14-15 (NIV1984) says, *"In his anger against Israel the Lord handed them over to raiders who plundered them. He sold them to their enemies all around, whom they were no longer able to resist. Whenever Israel went out to fight, the hand of the Lord was against them to defeat them, just as he had sworn to them. They were in great distress."* This was a period of anarchy and confusion for the Israelites.

Originally, God had the priests and judges govern and lead His chosen people. The priests instructed Israel on worship and keeping the law. The judges were to turn the hearts of the people wholeheartedly to God. The judges saved Israel from the consequences of their sin. Even the word "judge" in the Hebrew is "šōpᵉṭîm," from which it derives its name, one who "saved."

> ## "We don't need to fear judgment when we have the fear of the Lord."

Rejecting Judges

In the book of Judges, whenever a judge died, the people compromised with sin and sexuality and abandoned their spiritual calling to adopt the customs and behavior of those around them. The people grew tired of being judged. They didn't care for God's system of priests and judges, and they wanted a king. First Samuel 8:5-9 says:

> 5"Look," they told him, "you are now old, and your sons are not like you. Give us a king to judge us like all the other nations have." 6 Samuel was displeased with their request and went to the LORD for guidance. 7 "Do everything they say to you," the LORD replied, "for it is me they are rejecting, not you. They don't want me to be their king any longer. 8 Ever since I brought them from Egypt they have continually abandoned me and followed other gods. And now they are giving you the same treatment. 9 Do as they ask, but solemnly warn them about the way a king will reign over them."

Samuel, with words from God, went on to warn the children of Israel of all the hardships and consequences they would face as a result of their refusal to be judged. Solomon gave them a stern warning, but they refused to listen. They didn't want to be judged. They wanted a king to rule over them. The Lord spoke to my spirit as I read these Bible verses. He said, "If you won't be judged, you will be ruled." How true has that become? Today, Christians reject godly judging, reject accountability, and reject instructions. Like the children of Israel, we want to do what we think is right in our own eyes and ignore the Word of God, which was written according to what is right in His eyes. Let's learn from the mistakes of the children of Israel, embrace the fear of the Lord, and seek to understand the purpose of judgment and what the Bible teaches on judging.

> ## "If you won't be judged, you will be ruled."

Planks and Specks

The Bible is clear that we must judge correctly, with biblical clarity. You are in no place to help examine someone else's life when you can't see clearly because of sin in your own life. Matthew 7:3-5 says, *"Why do you look at the speck of sawdust in your brother's eye and pay no attention to the plank in your own eye? How can you say to your brother, 'Let me take the speck out of your eye,' when all the time there is a plank in your own eye? You hypocrite, first take the plank out of your own eye, and then you will see clearly to remove the speck from your brother's eye."* Jesus used the word "hypocrite" to describe someone who professes to be what he or she is not. It's like someone playing a part, like an actor, but his or her personal character is nothing like the character he or she is playing.

This passage is not saying we are not to help remove the speck from our brother's eye. We just need to be able to see clearly and justly first. I love what the theologian Albert Barnes said about this verse:

> By first amending our own faults, or casting the beam out of our eye, we can "consistently" advance to correct the faults of others. There will then be no hypocrisy in our conduct. We shall also "see clearly" to do it. The beam, the thing that obscured our sight, will be removed, and we shall more clearly discern the "small" object that obscures the sight of our brother. The sentiment is, that the readiest way to judge of the im

perfections of others is to be free from greater ones ourselves. This qualifies us for judging, makes us candid and consistent [17] ...

No one could serve as a judge if it required us to be sinless or perfect in all our ways. We are to manage our own lives first, and then help others. Galatians 6:1-2 says, *"Brothers and sisters, if someone is caught in a sin, you who live by the Spirit should restore that person gently. But watch yourselves, or you also may be tempted. Carry each other's burdens, and in this way you will fulfill the law of Christ."*

Judge Correctly

The key is to judge correctly by judging biblically. John 7:24 says, *"Stop judging by mere appearances, but instead judge correctly."* We start judging correctly by judging ourselves first. First Corinthians 11:31 (ESV) says, *"But if we judged ourselves truly, we would not be judged."* After judging ourselves using the Bible as the blueprint, we can help others live biblical lives and follow Jesus.

The Bible speaks of more than just judging people. In 1 Corinthians 14:29 we are taught to judge prophecy: *"Let two or three prophets speak, and let the others weigh what is said."* In Chapter 10 I listed a number of Bible verses that teach us to judge false teaching. We are even told we will judge angels one day. First Corinthians 6:3 says, *"Do you not know that we will judge angels? How much more the things of this life!"*

It's very important to understand that the Word of God tells us the only people we are to judge and help hold accountable are Christians. We are not to judge the lost unbelievers of the world. First Corinthians 5:12–13 says, *"What business is it of mine to judge those outside the church? Are you not to judge those inside? God will judge those outside. Expel the wicked man from among you."* We are not to judge the world. God will do that. He will judge us all.

I want to make this emphatically clear. As Christ-followers we are not supposed to judge those in the gay community who live a gay lifestyle but don't know Jesus. To go and hold signs at gay parades that spew hate and tell lost individuals they are "going to hell" isn't effective for reaching people. I wrote this chapter (and this book) for brothers and sisters who love God, but deal with SSA or identify as gay Christians.

Many individuals don't think it's their responsibility to keep their brothers or sisters in Christ accountable as followers of Jesus. It can be uncomfortable and awkward. It can strain and even end relationships. But how can iron sharpen iron unless they come together in honesty? Genesis 4:9 says, *"Then the LORD said to Cain, 'Where is your brother Abel?' 'I don't know,' he replied. 'Am I my brother's keeper?' "* God asked Cain, "Where is your brother Abel?" because it *was* Cain's responsibility to look out for his brother. We are our brother's keeper and our sister's keeper. From beginning to end, the Word of God challenges us to help our fellow Christ-followers stay on the narrow path God has called us to walk, and do what we can to help each other stay free from sin and bondage. How can you love people and allow them to compromise in a life of sexual sin, unchallenged? You can't!

In the book of Judges, God instructed all Israel to confront their brothers in the tribe of Benjamin (Benjamites) who had engaged in evil sexual sin. See the Bible account below.

22 While they were enjoying themselves, some of the wicked men of the city surrounded the house. Pounding on the door, they shouted to the old man who owned the house, "Bring out the man who came to your house so we can have sex with him." 23 The owner of the house went outside and said to them, "No, my friends, don't be so vile. Since this man is my guest, don't do this outrageous thing. 24 Look, here is my virgin daughter, and his concubine. I will bring them out to you now, and you can use them and do to them whatever you wish. But as for this man, don't do such an outrageous thing." 25 But the men would not listen to him. So the man took his concubine and sent her outside to them, and they raped her and abused her throughout the night, and at dawn they let her go. 26 At daybreak the woman went back to the house where her master was staying, fell down at the door and lay there until daylight. 27 When her master got up in the morning and opened the door of the house and stepped out to continue on his way, there lay his concubine, fallen in the doorway of the house, with her hands on the threshold. 28 He said to her, "Get up; let's go." But there was no answer. Then the man put her on his donkey and set out for home.
(Judges 19:22-28)

Similar to Sodom, the men of Gibeah (Benjamites) wanted to have sex with men from Levi. This demonic lust resulted in the rape and death of a concubine. After this sin, all of Israel rose up against the Benjamites to judge this awful sin and demand their repentance. The Benjamites refused to repent, so all Israel went to war against them. Judges 20:33-36 says, *"All the men of Israel moved from their places and took up positions at Baal Tamar, and the Israelite ambush charged out of its place on the west of Gibeah. Then ten thousand of Israel's able young men made a frontal attack on Gibeah. The fighting was so heavy that the Benjamites did not realize how near disaster was. The Lord defeated Benjamin before Israel, and on that day the Israelites struck down 25,100 Benjamites, all armed with swords. Then the Benjamites saw that they were beaten."* Israel knew they couldn't allow their brothers to continue to live sexually immoral and destructives lives and remain brothers. They couldn't live their lives in sin against their God and remain in the blessing of God.

> **"How can you love people and allow them to compromise in a life of sexual sin, unchallenged? You can't!"**

We must love everyone and be kind to everyone. But we must keep our friends in Christ accountable to a life that reflects Jesus and pleases the Lord. The key is to do this with the wisdom of God. Solomon prayed that God would give him wisdom to judge wisely. 1 Kings 3:9 says, *"So give your servant a discerning heart to govern your people and to distinguish between right and wrong. For who is able to govern this great people of yours?"*

Season of Repentance

I'm asked on a regular basis, "Should gay people be allowed to come to the church?" That is such a silly question! Of course gay people should be welcome in the church. Everyone should be welcome who desires to know more about Jesus. The better question is, "How long should they go to your church?" If yours is a full gospel, Spirit-filled church, the spirit of conviction should be strong there. The Holy Spirit will always convict the spirit of man. People can respond to the conviction with repentance, or they can respond by hardening their hearts. If their hearts become hard, they will not bear fruit and will become unhealthy to the church body and the community within it. Jesus said to remove the branches (people) that refuse to repent and produce fruit. Luke 13:6-9 says:

> 6 Then he told this parable: "A man had a fig tree growing in his vineyard, and he went to look for fruit on it but did not find any. 7 So he said to the man who took care of the vineyard, 'For three years now I've been coming to look for fruit on this fig tree and haven't found any. Cut it down! Why should it use up the soil?' 8 'Sir,' the man replied, 'leave it alone for one more year, and I'll dig around it and fertilize it. 9 If it bears fruit next year, fine! If not, then cut it down.' "

A close pastor friend of mine called me one day, very upset. He began to share with me that a gay man in his church had just called him to say he had left the church. I asked him why he left and he recounted the following conversation:

"Pastor, I just want you to know I've never been at a more loving church in my life! I love your church! It's the best church I've ever been to. I've never grown so much in my life."

Confused, the pastor replied, "I don't understand. What's the problem then?"

"Pastor, as you know, I'm gay. Well, my boyfriend and none of my gay friends will go to a church that isn't gay-affirming."

My pastor friend then asked me if he had done anything wrong. I encouraged him that he had done everything right! The man felt unconditionally loved and never once felt judged. But he knew that my friend's church was unwavering in their biblical stance. He was given time to soften his heart and lean into the truth of God, or harden his heart and pull away. He chose to leave the church and attend a church that would support his sexual preference above all.

Jesus told us in His revelation to John that there is a season or window of repentance. Revelation 2:20-23 says:

> *20 Nevertheless, I have this against you: You tolerate that woman Jezebel, who calls herself a prophet. By her teaching she misleads my servants into sexual immorality and the eating of food sacrificed to idols. 21 I have given her time to repent of her immorality, but she is unwilling. 22 So I will cast her on a bed of suffering, and I will make those who commit adultery with her suffer intensely, unless they repent of her ways. 23 I will strike her children dead. Then all the churches will know that I am he who searches hearts and minds, and I will repay each of you according to your deeds.*

The church that followed the Jezebel spirit and all her sexual immorality was given a season of time to repent, but they were unwilling. The result was death and destruction. Jesus said in warning of the tree that only produced bad fruit, *"I tell you, no! But unless you repent, you too will all perish"* (Luke 13:3). When is the time to repent? The time is always right now!

Sabrina's Story

Sabrina grew up in a very dysfunctional and broken home. Her father was in prison until she was five, and her mom was forced to provide for Sabrina and her brothers and sisters. Sabrina's home ended up having twenty people living in it at one point. Aunts, uncles, and cousins variously lived under one roof. Sabrina's earliest memory of her dad was when he molested her, which started when she was five, just after he got out of prison. This sexual abuse continued until Sabrina was eleven years old. During that same period of time, Sabrina's brothers and cousins (both boys and girls) also molested her. Sabrina remembers that at the time she was unsure if she was supposed to let boys and girls do this to her, or both.

At school they taught Sabrina and the other students to protect themselves and tell their parents if anyone attempted to do or did certain things to them. That way, their parents could protect them, the teachers asserted. Sabrina could trust no one to protect her at home or anywhere else. This began a time when Sabrina would go through a tremendous amount of confusion, both emotionally and sexually. Sabrina's older sister was openly gay. Her sister and her girlfriend lived at the house with everyone else. No one seemed to mind. Sabrina's sister modeled this relationship and she seemed happy.

When Sabrina was twelve years old, her life came crashing down. Her mother died. Her mom was the only good in her life. She was the only person with whom Sabrina felt safe, and she was the only person Sabrina believed loved her. With her mom gone, Sabrina recounts that she desired the love of a woman. She started acting like a boy at age fourteen. She decided she was ready to come out as gay, and didn't care what anyone thought about it.

One day, she found herself at the lunch table with all her friends, and they were all talking about which boys they liked. Thinking it was the perfect moment to come out, Sabrina decided to make the announcement. She told her friends that she didn't like any boys, and that she liked girls and she was gay.

News of this quickly circulated all around school. The gossip was that she had a girlfriend at school. Everyone was talking about Sabrina. Everyone thought she was so cool and brave, and she suddenly became very popular. She became "Instagram famous" and acquired over 14,000 followers in just a few weeks. Sabrina attracted attention from thousands of people beyond her school. She became sexually active, and engaged in sexual activity just about every weekend.

In her junior year, Sabrina made plans for prom. She decided to run for prom prince. She applied at the school office to run for prom prince. She wanted to prove to everyone she could win. The school denied her entry, saying only boys could run for prom prince. Sabrina refused to let the school deny or judge her. She started a petition to allow her to run, and got thousands of students to sign it. Sabrina got human rights organizations legally involved, including True Colors, the Gay-Straight Alliance, and others. A lawyer worked on her behalf and threatened the school administration and county with discrimination lawsuits to legally force them to let her run for prince. The school backed down. Sabrina won by a landslide. She was the first girl prom prince in the state.

Sabrina felt like she should have felt on top of the world. After all, she was popular and powerful. But she was empty and very lonely. Though Sabrina had not grown up in church, during that season of her life, she felt what she could only describe as God tugging at her heart.

Sabrina decided to go to a church, though she was terrified judgmental church people would reject her. She chose to try a downtown inner city church, and started to go regularly. At one service, a little old lady walked up to Sabrina and started giving her a word of knowledge, describing her entire childhood. As the lady spoke, Sabrina felt the warmth of the presence of God. She got more and more involved in church until every time the doors were open, she was there. Sabrina gave her life to Jesus and started to fall in love with Him.

It wasn't easy. Sabrina had major bondages in her life. She was severely addicted to pornography, and was sexually promiscuous. Sabrina learned about an internship opportunity at a church in San Francisco (of all places), and felt God leading her to go. As soon as she got to the internship, they began forty days of fasting and prayer. It was intense! In the middle of this time of prayer and fasting, the pastor called her out in a prayer service. As he began to pray over her, she felt a fire in her stomach. It was the fire of God, and it began to burn away all the impurity, lust, and shame of her past. In that moment, God delivered her.

Sabrina now sets major boundaries in her life. She guards her eyes, thoughts, and relationships. "I encountered the love of God," she says. "God's love produces passion. Passion produces fire. And fire produces holiness." Sabrina finished the internship in San Francisco and is still serving God to this day. Sabrina has been on mission trips all over the world, and is now in college finishing her degree.

Sabrina was afraid that Christians would judge her. They never judged her, but they did confront her. Sabrina told me, "God used that internship and that pastor to save my life." She never once felt judged by anyone there, but she said everyone there confronted her as necessary (as she did them).

We don't have to fear the judgment of God when we live in right standing with Him. Jesus was the prime example of this. He was willing to stand before men and be judged: *"Now Jesus was standing before*

Pilate, the Roman governor. 'Are you the king of the Jews?' the governor asked him. Jesus replied, 'You have said it.' But when the leading priests and the elders made their accusations against him, Jesus remained silent. 'Don't you hear all these charges they are bringing against you?' Pilate demanded. But Jesus made no response to any of the charges, much to the governor's surprise" (Matthew 27:11-14 NASB). Jesus was innocent of sin, but convicted as guilty. We are guilty and declared innocent through Jesus. Jesus allowed Himself to stand in the judgment seat because He is the righteous judge who will judge all mankind. Second Corinthians 5:9-10 (NASB) says, *"Therefore we also have as our ambition, whether at home or absent, to be pleasing to Him. For we must all appear before the judgment seat of Christ, so that each one may be recompensed for his deeds in the body, according to what he has done, whether good or bad."* We are all guilty and deserve the consequences of our sin, but Jesus died that we might be forgiven and live for Him.

The Rainbow Is the Sign of a Covenant

Over the years, it has grieved me that the gay community has adopted the rainbow as their emblem. This was the sign of the people of God that He would never again destroy the earth with a flood. Genesis 9:13 says, *"I have set my rainbow in the clouds, and it will be the sign of the covenant between me and the earth."* The interesting part is the relationship between the rainbow on the banner of the gay community and a sign of the promise of God related to God's judgment on the world. The people who don't want to be judged chose the sign of God's promise against the backdrop of God's judgment of the world.

I began to pray and ask God to speak to me concerning why the gay community chose the rainbow as their own. One day, in the middle of my daily Bible reading, I came across the reason. Revelation 4:3 says, *"And the one who sat there had the appearance of jasper and ruby. A rainbow that shone like an emerald encircled the throne."* Follow me on this. In Revelation 4, God was showing the disciple John a vision of heaven and the throne room of God. John puts into words what he saw in the presence of God, and describes it and all of its colors, like a rainbow. I believe the gay community chose the rainbow as their banner because they desire the presence of God without passing through the judgment of God. The flood of judgment came first. The rainbow of the presence of God followed.

Judgment Is the Price of Admission

Only Satan encourages men not to worry about judgment. Genesis 3:4-5 says, " 'You will not certainly die,' the serpent said to the woman. 'For God knows that when you eat from it your eyes will be opened, and you will be like God, knowing good and evil.' " Satan lied to Eve and told her there would be no judgment or consequences for disobeying God. We don't access heaven without passing through judgment. It's the process of admission.

> "...the gay community chose the rainbow as their banner because they desire the presence of God without passing through the judgment of God."

Jesus is the ultimate judge. He decides who enters through heaven's doors. Jesus warns us of what this might look like for many people who think they know God. Matthew 7:21-23 says, *"Not everyone who says to me, 'Lord, Lord,' will enter the kingdom of heaven, but only the one who does the will of my Father who is in heaven. Many will say to me on that day, 'Lord, Lord, did we not prophesy in your name and in your name drive out demons and in your name perform many miracles?' Then I will tell them plainly, 'I never knew you. Away from me, you evildoers!' "* This is what judgment looks like.

When you say, "don't judge me," you are resisting the judgment that is to come. Confident Christians who know God and His Word know that judgment is not to be feared, but embraced. I encourage you to welcome godly, biblical judgment. Lean into healthy accountability and use God's Word to judge your own life before Jesus uses His Word to judge your life.

BORN LIKE THIS

Why are some people gay? Why do they experience SSA? Everyone seems to have answers for these questions. The world has unified with their response. From celebrities to pop stars to politicians, they all have the same answer: You were born that way! This response can't be supported by any reputable scientific evidence, but offers many absolutes in the minds of those who accept it. Why would anyone choose to be gay? Why would anyone risk losing family and close relationships with friends? Why would anyone want to lose community within their churches? Why would anyone subject themselves to all the hardships that come with a gay lifestyle? They wouldn't. So they must be born that way. If they are born gay, the choice is out of their control and they must accept who they really are, gay. If homosexuality isn't a choice, the homosexual can't be held responsible for the way they were born.

Do these philosophies and opinions align with the Bible? They do not. And we are going to explore the truth that we were all born in sin, and that all of us, despite how we were born, must be born again.

If people aren't born gay, then why are they gay? Dr. Joe Dallas describes it as "the perfect storm." Dr. Dallas lived a gay lifestyle for many years, and played a part in starting the nationwide gay Christian movement. He explains that it is not any one thing but a number of things the enemy might use to get people to come into agreement with the lie that they were born gay.

Some homosexuals were sexually and emotionally abused, while others were effeminate from a young age. Some got involved in the arts and were pressured by society to be gay. Some were separated from one parent, so were drawn to imitate the gender of that gender. Others were rejected or abandoned by a parent, so in response, reject all people of that gender. There is no one reason that causes people to become gay. It would be easy to deal with if there was only one easily identifiable reason. If there was only one reason, the enemy would lose his control on mankind.

There is no gay gene, only a sin gene and we all carry it! The truth is the reason people are gay or participate in any sinful lifestyle or behavior is that we were all born that way—of sin. Psalm 51:5 says, *"Surely I was sinful at birth, sinful from the time my mother conceived me."* We were all born of sin, whether homosexual or heterosexual now. We all need to be born again.

Friends have told me, "Landon, I really feel like I was born like this. I have experienced same-sex attraction since as far back as I can remember! I was never molested, never abused, but always had SSA." I believe them. I believe that people can have those desires from the time they are old enough to realize it.

I also know that the devil tried to kill Jesus when He was only a baby. Matthew 2:16 says, *"When Herod realized that he had been outwitted by the Magi, he was furious, and he gave orders to kill all the boys in Bethlehem and its vicinity who were two years old and under, in accordance with the time he had learned from the Magi."* The Bible clearly warns us that the enemy comes to steal, kill, and destroy (John 10:10), but doesn't say when his attacks start. He can start attacking us even as children. Just think of how many babies are murdered in the womb through abortion each year. The devil's attacks on people in the womb result in millions of murders a year. The enemy will attack you as early as he can, and many of you are still dealing with the impact of spiritual attacks on your lives as children.

The truth is, it doesn't matter what temptations you were born with. Some of us are born tempted to lie and cheat. A lot of guys are born naturally perverted. Some of us are born violent. It doesn't matter what disposition you were born with, all of us must be born again! John 3:6-8 (ESV) says, *"That which is born of the flesh is flesh, and that which is born of the Spirit is spirit. Do not be amazed that I said to you,*

'You must be born again.' The wind blows where it wishes and you hear the sound of it, but do not know where it comes from and where it is going; so is everyone who is born of the Spirit."

The difference between the homosexual birth in sin and the heterosexual birth in sin is the homosexual wants his or her identity to be based in sexuality. My spiritual father, John Paul Jackson, used to tell me, *"The biggest war you will fight is the way you perceive you."* Homosexuals and individuals struggling with SSA tend to identify themselves through their sexuality instead of who they are biblically. Homosexuality has become an identity, but not an identity from Jesus. God fully knows who we truly are and who we He calls us to be. Jeremiah 29:11 says, *" 'For I know the plans I have for you,' declares the Lord, 'plans to prosper you and not to harm you, plans to give you hope and a future.' "* God has always had a plan for your life, and sexual perversion and homosexual practice are not part of that plan. I tell my friends that struggle with SSA to read their Bible. There isn't one Bible verse that suggests SSA is God's plan for anyone's life.

> **"Homosexuals and individuals struggling with SSA tend to identify themselves through their sexuality instead of who they are biblically."**

Kyle's Story

When Kyle was very young, his parents divorced. Kyle's mom became his best friend, but his father was never really around as he grew up. When his father was around he was severely abusive verbally, emotionally, physically, and at times, sexually. He said it was his way of teaching Kyle how to be a real man.

Kyle's grandmother introduced him to God at a very young age. He always believed in God and believed he loved God, but was not a true follower of Jesus. Kyle loved going to visit his grandma because she would take him to church where he could learn about God.

Kyle's childhood was difficult because he wasn't as masculine as other boys. He was badly bullied throughout his school years because he wasn't tough enough. As a result, Kyle hated school. He hated going so much that he would often hide in his room or go to the bus stop, but then run away and skip school. Sometimes he would hide in the dumpster across the street from the school so no one could bully him. He was first called a "faggot" in the first grade—a name he would be called thousands of times after that. For years to follow, this informed his identity.

Kyle hated that he was so effeminate. He tried to be more masculine. He played sports and even wore biker clothes, but no one bought it. Kyle tried "everything" to fit in but it didn't work. He was a very lonely boy, with no friends.

Kyle was so very confused about his sexuality that he would pray every night that he would die in his sleep so he would not have to tell his family he was gay. When Kyle was in the ninth grade, he finally made a friend. They had a lot in common. They hung out at school and slept over at each other's houses. Kyle was so excited to finally have a friend. One night, Kyle's friend invited him out to the woods near his house. Kyle had no idea what his agenda was, but he went anyway. They went into the woods and his friend put a rag over Kyle's face with an inhalant, knocked him out, and proceeded to rape him.

Kyle knew what happened, and that it wasn't right, but he didn't know what to do about it. He continued to be friends with the boy because he didn't know how to tell anyone what had taken place, and he didn't want to lose the only friend he ever had.

Kyle then began having same-sex attraction. He came out of the closet and told his family he was gay. In his mind, his only options were to come out or commit suicide, but he couldn't continue to live his life in a state of confusion. When he came out of the closet, it was amazing! Suddenly, he had a lot of friends and was considered a cool kid for the first time in his life. He finally felt normal, and that he fit in somewhere. He loved all the attention he received.

Kyle decided to take it to the next level and started dressing in drag. It started out on Halloween for fun, but everyone said he looked beautiful, so he kept doing it. The attention dressing in drag drew to him became addictive. In drag, his femininity was an asset, and he used it to his advantage. Little did he know that this was the beginning of living a gay lifestyle for the next twenty years.

Kyle continued dressing in drag all through the rest of his teenage years. He started working in gay nightclubs as a drag entertainer as soon as he was old enough to get in. Soon after, he started working in the adult industry as a transsexual prostitute. Kyle began doing it as a temporary thing, but he began making so much money that he continued to do it. He made around $1,000 a day, and became addicted to money. It helped to support his now heavy drinking habit and lavish lifestyle. Kyle couldn't do drag or prostitute himself without being drunk.

Kyle lived his life as a female for years because he felt accepted that way. To most people, his outer appearance was that of a very happy person, but inside he still felt hollow, empty, and sad.

Kyle began to realize that this lifestyle was very unhealthy. Many of his friends were dying young, getting infected with HIV, or ruining their lives with drug and alcohol addiction. He was just sick and tired of being sick and tired. He would always ask himself, "What would happen if I die?" It caused him great anxiety and fear. All he remembered from what he learned at church was that gay people were going to hell, and that was their punishment from God.

One of Kyle's friends invited him to go to church on Easter Sunday, and he agreed to go, but just to be kind. In that service, he saw a modern drama of the resurrection of Jesus Christ played out on stage. He began to cry as he saw all that Jesus had done for him, and realized the lifestyle he was living was not honoring to Him. The preacher asked all who were ready to accept Christ to raise their hands and pray a prayer. Kyle accepted Jesus that day.

When Kyle's gay friends learned about his faith, they immediately began to ridicule him and call him crazy. Suddenly, he was no longer popular. He lost all his friends. The desire to do drag, party, or go to gay clubs became less and less appealing. God began speaking to Kyle, and he got rid of all his female clothing and accessories.

Kyle planted himself in a healthy, Bible-based, Spirit-filled church. The pastors accepted Kyle as a person and helped him develop his true identity in Christ. He learned how a person might "think" he is born gay, but how God's design didn't include homosexuality. Kyle's favorite verse at the start was 2 Corinthians 5:17, "Therefore, if anyone is in Christ, the new creation has come: The old has gone, the new is here!"

Kyle graduated Bible college and is now involved in full-time ministry making Jesus famous!

A New Creation

Kyle became a new creation in Christ Jesus. The new creation means the past life, past behavior, and past thoughts are crucified with Jesus, and the new life, new behavior, new thoughts, and new desires are resurrected with Him. Ephesians 4:22-24 (NASB) says, *"That, in reference to your former manner of life, you lay aside the old self, which is being corrupted in accordance with the lusts of deceit, and that you be renewed in the spirit of your mind, and put on the new self, which in the likeness of God has been created in righteousness and holiness of the truth."* We can become a new creation because we lay our old lifestyle and sinful nature on Jesus. Then our past no longer matters. We are made completely new! Galatians 6:15 says, *"Neither circumcision nor uncircumcision means anything; what counts is the new creation."*

The new creation in Christ isn't gay. The new creation doesn't identify with homosexuality. The new creation begins to look, act, and think like Jesus. The new creation allows the Holy Spirit to take them through the process of transformation. *"Having lost all sensitivity, they have given themselves over to sensuality so as to indulge in every kind of impurity, and they are full of greed . . . . You were taught, with regard to your former way of life, to put off your old self, which is being corrupted by its deceitful desires; to be made new in and to put on the new self, created to be like God in true righteousness and holiness"* (Ephesians 4:19, 22-24).

Why does the gay Christian not become new? Why does the gay Christian not supernaturally change like the rest of Christ's followers? What makes their sin so special that they don't have to pick up their cross and deny their flesh? Matthew 16:24-25 (NASB) says, *"Then Jesus said to His disciples, 'If anyone wishes to come after Me, he must deny himself, and take up his cross and follow Me. For whoever wishes to save his life will lose it; but whoever loses his life for My sake will find it.'"* When we pick up our cross and deny our flesh, it means we daily crucify the desires of our sinful flesh. Colossians 3:5 says, *"Put to death, therefore, whatever belongs to your earthly nature: sexual immorality, impurity, lust, evil desires and greed, which is idolatry."* When we belong to Christ we don't *accept* our flesh, we *crucify* it with Christ. Galatians 5:24 says, "Those who belong to Christ Jesus have crucified the flesh with its passions and desires."

Over and over the Bible warns us that discipleship means to daily put off our old self, old man, and old desires. See a few Bible passages about this below.

19 and they, having become callous, have given themselves over to sensuality for the practice of every kind of impurity with greediness. 20 But you did not learn Christ in this way, 21 if indeed you have heard Him and have been taught in Him, just as truth is in Jesus, 22 that, in reference to your former manner of life, you lay aside the old self, which is being corrupted in accordance with the lusts of deceit, 23 and that you be renewed in the spirit of your mind, 24 and put on the new self, which in the likeness of God has been created in righteousness and holiness of the truth. (Ephesians 4:19-24 NASB)

He saved us, not because of righteous things we had done, but because of his mercy. He saved us through the washing of rebirth and renewal by the Holy Spirit. (Titus 3:5)

And we all, who with unveiled faces contemplate the Lord's glory, are being transformed into his image with ever-increasing glory, which comes from the Lord, who is the Spirit. (2 Corinthians 3:18)

Identity

In the Greek, the word for "transformed" is "metamorphóō." We get our English word, "metamorphosis," from this. It means, "transformed after being with." The change referred to here is of the essential form or nature of something. Spiritually, such change occurs when we spend time with the Lord. Like all of the real-life stories you have read in this book illustrate, the more time you spend with Jesus, the more you change. The more time you spend in His Word and in worship, the more you transform into the new creation that reflects His righteousness, His obedience, and His holiness.

As you have heard me say over and over, nowhere in the Bible does God, Jesus, the Holy Spirit, or any Holy Spirit-inspired writer promote homosexuality or homosexual practice. Nowhere does the Bible endorse homosexuality as one's identity. If you cannot separate your sexuality from your identity, you will never see your true identity. The only identity the Bible gives us over and over again is "child of God!" Romans 8:14-16 says, *"For those who are led by the Spirit of God are the children of God. The Spirit you received does not make you slaves, so that you live in fear again; rather, the Spirit you received brought about your adoption to sonship. And by him we cry, 'Abba, Father.' The Spirit himself testifies with our spirit that we are God's children."*

> **"If you cannot separate your sexuality from your identity, you will never see your true identity."**

The devil will try to keep you confused about your identity by keeping you focused on the old self and not as a born-again child of God. He will never stop using this strategy. He wants you to question your relationship with God. Satan did this with Jesus. He tried to get Jesus to question His Sonship. Matthew 4:6 says, " 'If you are the Son of God,' he said, 'throw yourself down. For it is written: ' "He will command his angels concerning you, and they will lift you up in their hands, so that you will not strike your foot against a stone." ' " Jesus knew who He was, and He knew who His Father was. Knowing His identity and knowing His Father gave Him the strength to say to the devil, "Away from me!" I think the enemy has confused the children of God long enough. Like Jesus, we need to respond with the Word of God and tell the enemy that we are not our temptations! We don't identify through the lens of our sexuality, but we identify through the lens of the Word of God. We are sons and daughters of God. We are loved by our Father in heaven.

THE HEART OF THE FATHER

All gay people and everyone who struggles with SSA are unique individuals. All people have distinct personalities and characteristics exclusive to them. Like any person, no gay person is exactly the same as another. Despite their differences, there are two common themes I've heard more frequently than any others over years of interacting with and hearing the stories of gay people, the gay community, and my gay friends.

Those common themes are abuse and the lack of relationship with one's father.

I have not met one individual who self-describes as gay or struggles with SSA who hasn't been sexually abused or had an absent/distant/strained/abusive relationship with his or her father. This cannot be ignored.

Righteousness Revealed

In late 2013, as I spent some beautiful time with the Lord on a prayer walk, I heard the Holy Spirit speak to my spirit and say, "2014 is the year of righteousness!" I was instantly excited! I have been saved just about all my life. My parents were pastors, and I was raised in the house of God. I gave my life to the Lord at age three. I remember doing it. I got a prize out of a wooden treasure chest afterward.

At age twelve I got baptized in the Holy Spirit after a small youth gathering, and received my prayer language. At age fourteen I preached my first sermon in India. I preached on the power of God! I started ministering full time at age sixteen, and was ordained at age eighteen. I later went on to get my degree in theology, but essentially, I've served the Lord all my life. In fact, my wife and I have always been described by others as "young people who pursue righteousness." So when the Holy Spirit said, "righteousness," I was thrilled, as I was very familiar with the subject.

I quickly realized one can be familiar with a subject but not have the full revelation of it. As I studied righteousness I noticed that it was everywhere in the Bible. Nearly 1,000 verses reference righteousness or the righteous. I began to highlight them all in my Bible in green. When I was done, my Bible looked like an army camouflage edition. One thing that stood out was that just after I read in the Word of a righteous man or woman I highlighted, I would see an account of the power and presence of God.

In Genesis 6:9 the Bible mentions Noah was righteous. There was no one like him in his generation. God chose to reestablish humanity through righteousness. In Romans 4:3 we learn that Abraham was righteous, and God used him to establish the children of Israel. In the book of Job we learn that Job was a righteous man who shunned evil. Satan never even mentioned Job's name—God did! Job 1:8 says, "Then the Lord said to Satan, 'Have you considered my servant Job? There is no one on earth like him; he is blameless and upright, a man who fears God and shuns evil.' " Job's righteousness introduced him to the devil over whom he had authority. Those who walked in righteousness were always victorious over the devil and his demons.

Not only did I find righteousness all over the Scriptures, but I found them in plain sight in Bible verses we use on a daily basis. I noticed that though people regularly quote these verses, they rarely quote them entirely—with righteousness. I'll show you what I mean.

Matthew 6:33 (NASB) says, *"But seek first the kingdom of God and His righteousness, and all these things shall be added to you."* Usually, when people quote this, pray it, or recite it in a sermon they say it like this: "But seek first the kingdom of God . . . and all these things shall be added to you." Have you heard it communicated the same way?

Here's another one. James 5:16 (NASB) says, *"Confess your trespasses to one another, and pray for one another, that you may be* healed. The effective, fervent prayer of a righteous man avails much." But when I hear it quoted most often I just hear people say, "fervent prayer avails much."

Proverbs 24:16 (NASB) says, *"For a righteous man may fall seven times and rise again, but the wicked shall fall by calamity."* But when people quote this verse they usually say, "Though you may fall seven times, the Lord will pick you back up!" That's not true! We all know people who fell down and stayed down. God doesn't pick up everyone. He picks up His righteous.

Proverbs 13:22 says, *"a sinner's wealth is stored up for the righteous."* Believers love to declare, "The sinner's wealth is stored up for me!" That may or not be true. Are you living righteously?

Here's the last one (though I could easily come up with many more). No verse is quoted or sung more in times of hardship than Isaiah 54:17 (NASB). It says, *" 'No weapon formed against you shall prosper, and every tongue which rises against you in judgment you shall condemn. This is the heritage of the servants of the Lord, and their righteousness is from Me,' says the Lord."* No weapon will prosper against the *righteous*! Not just anyone, but those who live righteously.

Righteousness, the Matter of Heaven

I found it interesting that with so many Scriptures on righteousness, why do we so rarely hear teaching on it? The Bible teaches us to pursue righteousness (2 Timothy 2:22) and no Scripture ever tells us to stop! I asked the Lord in prayer one day, "Why have we taken righteousness out of all these scriptures when we reference or quote them?" I heard the Holy Spirit speak to my spirit and say, "Because they have taken righteousness out of their lives!" The body of Christ must begin to pursue Jesus and His righteousness once again. Matthew 6:33 tells us to seek the kingdom through righteousness first. The very thing God told us to seek first—righteousness—we seek last, if at all.

My spiritual father, John Paul Jackson, used to tell me righteousness is the system of heaven. It makes everything in heaven work. I look at righteousness as the matter of heaven. Matter is the substance of the universe, and matter is the substance of the kingdom of God. (Romans 14:17 NASB) says, *"The kingdom of God is not eating and drinking, but righteousness and peace and joy in the Holy Spirit."* My

personal definition of righteousness, gleaned from all my time studying and praying into the subject, is this: "The intention to be, live, and
do right in God's eyes." (Not to do right in our own eyes—in God's
eyes!)

> ## "The very thing God told us to seek first—
> ## righteousness—we seek last, if at all."

♥

In 2014, I received the assignment from the Lord to minister on
His righteousness. I traveled around the nation and world preaching
and teaching on righteousness. That's all I did. Our ministry didn't
host any national conferences. We didn't record any TV shows. I didn't
write any books. I just ministered on righteousness. I taught twen-
ty-seven different messages on righteousness. I called it "Revelation
on Righteousness." It was the greatest year of ministry and the greatest year of my life. I credit it all to righteousness.

As I spent a few years preparing to write this book, I spent countless hours in study and preparation. I asked my personal intercessory
prayer team to stand in faith with me as I prepared to write this book.
My specific prayer was that the Lord would give me the heart of the
Father and the mind of Christ as I wrote this book. I prayed this prayer
every day with my prayer team for over a year.

One day toward the end of 2014, I was on the treadmill at the
gym, praying. (I lived in Phoenix at the time and running outside
wasn't an option.) As I ran, I prayed through my daily prayer list until I
got to the part where I prayed over this book. I started praying my normal prayer, asking for the heart of the Father, when I heard the Holy
Spirit interrupt me and say, "I already gave it to you!" I was surprised
to hear the Lord interrupt me. However, over the years I had learned
that when He speaks to me when I do not expect it, it is particularly
powerful. As soon as I thought about what the Holy Spirit said ("I already gave it to you") He showed me a vision. I saw the breastplate of
righteousness cover a chest (heart). I began to cry. I had been asking
the Lord for a year to give me His heart for this book, and He gave it to
me before I even asked for it. His heart is righteousness.

Romans 3:10 (NKJV) says, *"As it is written: 'There is none righteous, no, not one.' "* This means that no one is righteous on their own account, by their own deeds. We are only made righteous through Jesus. Romans 3:23-26 goes on to say, *"For all have sinned and fall short of the glory of God, and all are justified freely by his grace through the redemption that came by Christ Jesus. God presented Christ as a sacrifice of atonement, through the shedding of his blood—to be received by faith. He did this to demonstrate his righteousness, because in his forbearance he had left the sins committed beforehand unpunished— he did it to demonstrate his righteousness at the present time, so as to be just and the one who justifies those who have faith in Jesus."* Jesus is the only righteous one, but He became unrighteousness so that we could become the righteousness of Christ when we put our faith in Him. This is so powerful! Jesus trades us His righteousness for our unrighteousness.

"The intention to be, live, and do right in God's eyes."

Part of the purpose of Jesus and His righteousness was to reconcile us back to the Father. Second Corinthians 5:14-21 says:

14 For Christ's love compels us, because we are convinced that one died for all, and therefore all died. 15 And he died for all, that those who live should no longer live for themselves but for him who died for them and was raised again. 16 So from now on we regard no one from a worldly point of view. Though we once regarded Christ in this way, we do so no longer. 17 Therefore, if anyone is in Christ, the new creation has come: The old has gone, the new is here! 18 All this is from God, who reconciled us to himself through Christ and gave us the ministry of reconciliation: 19 that God was reconciling the world to himself in Christ, not counting people's sins against them. And he has committed to us the message of reconciliation. 20 We are therefore Christ's ambassadors, as though God were making his appeal through us. We implore you on Christ's behalf: Be reconciled to God. 21 God made him who had no sin to be sin for us, so that in him we might become the righteousness of God.

When Adam and Eve sinned, their sin created separation between God and man. This distance sin formed became a veil of separation. When Jesus died on the cross, the veil of separation was removed. Matthew 27:51 says, *"At that moment the curtain of the temple was torn in two from top to bottom. The earth shook, the rocks split."* This curtain was the separation from the outer court to the inner court. The high priest was the only individual allowed into the inner court, or the Holy of Holies. This was the place where God's presence was. Jesus removed the veil/curtain and gave us reconciliation to relationship with our Father God.

Enrique's Story

Enrique was born in Cuba, but fled the country with his mother and baby sister. Enrique had no dad. He had never met his biological father. He only knew that he was in Cuba somewhere. Enrique was an effeminate little boy, and drawn to the arts. He loved reading, dance, and art. Enrique had a hard time fitting in at school. His mother didn't speak English, so he was just beginning to learn the language. The language barrier made it hard for him to fit in with American kids. Affluent Cuban kids referred to him as "escoria marielit," a derogatory name for a refugee that means "a piece of scum" or, "a piece of driftwood floating ashore."

Enrique's mom remarried. Enrique and his stepdad did not get along at all. Enrique's stepdad was emotionally abusive. He made it clear he wasn't going to have a gay stepson. His stepdad took it upon himself to make Enrique a masculine, tough boy at any cost.

When Enrique was ten years old a family member molested him. Enrique didn't tell anyone because he was "already always being yelled at constantly," and "couldn't handle being yelled at for one more thing."

When Enrique was twelve years old, his stepdad went to prison. Shortly after this he got a letter from his biological father. He couldn't believe it! His dad was coming to America and wanted to meet him.

This was what Enrique had waited and longed for all his life. He could move in with his dad and be free from all the pain and abuse he called home.

The day finally came for Enrique to meet his biological father. Right when they met, Enrique noticed his father was tall and handsome just as he had imagined. They spent the entire afternoon together. It was the best day of Enrique's life.

Finally, Enrique's father told him he had to go. Enrique was confused. He thought his dad had come to get him. Enrique begged his dad to stay, telling him, "I want to go with you!" His dad told him, "I'm sorry, you can't, son." He went on to explain that he had a family back in Cuba. His family didn't know about Enrique, and it would bring shame upon the family if people found out about him. Enrique was heartbroken. With that, his father walked out the door. Enrique never saw him again.

With his stepfather's abusive words playing over and over in his head, and no hope to be saved by his real dad, Enrique started down a destructive path. Enrique continued to feel drawn toward homosexuality and everything the lifestyle had to offer. He became heavily addicted to pornography, and then began to seek out experiences about which he had only fantasized. Enrique soon fully immersed himself in the gay lifestyle. He found acceptance in the gay community.

Enrique's stepdad got out of prison and returned home. He and Enrique warred against each other. Enrique was older and no pushover. He and his stepdad's arguments blew up and steadily grew more and more violent. Finally, Enrique left home once and for all. After that, Enrique's mother and sister would only see him every other year or so.

Over time, his family became Christians and started attending church regularly. They prayed for Enrique to come to Jesus, but they were too ashamed of his lifestyle to ask their church to stand in faith with them for his deliverance. They would later deeply regret that decision.

On one of Enrique's few trips home, he and his sister had a long heart-to-heart talk. His sister pleaded with Enrique to come home and get right with God. She shared Jesus with Enrique and told him how much God loved him. Enrique admitted he wasn't happy, and that his lifestyle was becoming destructive, but he couldn't bring himself to be around his stepdad. Every time they were in the same room together, it was like World War III. Enrique just wasn't ready yet.

The next trip home for Enrique was life-changing for everyone. Enrique had contracted AIDS, and was getting very sick. He got to the point where he wasn't able to take care of himself. Enrique moved back home to let his family help take care of him. He and his sister had many long conversations about how Jesus died on the cross to forgive us of all our sins, but requires us to give forgiveness in return. Enrique desired forgiveness from Jesus, but wasn't ready to forgive his father or stepfather.

Enrique's condition deteriorated rapidly, and his family had to hospitalize him. It was there in his hospital room with his sister that he cried out to God. He prayed to his Heavenly Father, though his earthly fathers had rejected him. Enrique asked Jesus to forgive him of all of his sins and made Jesus Lord of his life.

Enrique had one more relationship to reconcile. He asked his sister to bring his stepfather to see him. Enrique's stepfather had given his life to the Lord some time before, but he and Enrique had never made peace. In his hospital room, Enrique and his stepfather repented to one another. They held each other and cried as they forgave one another. The love of God, Abba Father, healed both Enrique and his stepfather's hearts that day.

Shortly after, Enrique died. He is now in heaven with his Heavenly Father.

Enrique is just one of the millions of individuals who suffered broken relationships with their earthly fathers. Nothing damages the soul more than abuse and rejection from a father. God the Father is the total opposite of the abusive earthly father. He truly is a good Father who desires relationship with you. Like the prodigal son's father, he is waiting for you to come home. Luke 15:17-24 says:

17 When he came to his senses, he said, "How many of my father's hired servants have food to spare, and here I am starving to death! 18 I will set out and go back to my father and say to him: Father, I have sinned against heaven and against you. 19 I am no longer worthy to be called your son; make me like one of your hired servants." 20 So he got up and went to his father. But while he was still a long way off, his father saw him and was filled with compassion for him; he ran to his son, threw his arms around him and kissed him. 21 The son said to him, "Father, I have sinned against heaven and against you. I am no longer worthy to be called your son." 22 But the father said to his servants, "Quick! Bring the best robe and put it on him. Put a ring on his finger and sandals on his feet. 23 Bring the fattened calf and kill it. Let's have a feast and celebrate. 24 For this son of mine was dead and is alive again; he was lost and is found." So they began to celebrate.

God the Father is like the father in the parable. He is waiting for you to come home. When He sees you in the distance, He will run to you with a fierce love. Nothing can stand in His way. Did you hear me? Nothing! Romans 8:38-39 says, *"For I am convinced that neither death nor life, neither angels nor demons, neither the present nor the future, nor any powers, neither height nor depth, nor anything else in all creation, will be able to separate us from the love of God that is in Christ Jesus our Lord."* This very moment, God the Father seeks after you. I can feel it as I write. His love is all around you. He wants to heal you in this very moment. He wants you to know the love of your Father.

My Story

I know what it's like to be rejected and cursed by your father. I know the pain caused by wounds from your father. But I also know that God will send men and women into your life to fulfill the duties of a natural father and mother at the times you need that most.

I was on a prayer run when I heard the Holy Spirit speak to my spirit. He said, *You need John Paul Jackson in your life to accomplish your life's assignment.* I called his office that day and told his administrative assistant what the Lord had spoken to me. She told me, "Landon, I feel the Holy Spirit on this phone." She put me in touch with John Paul, and an initial forty-five-minute phone conversation turned into a five-hour face-to-face meeting that changed my life.

At the end of that meeting I was in great pain from the rejection I had experienced in the past, and the spiritual attacks of the enemy. John Paul said to me, "Landon, before you got here, the Lord spoke to me in a dream. He told me to stand with you and defend you." That's what fathers do! He prayed the simplest prayer over my wife and I, and as I described in my *Jezebel* book, the snowball of healing began to roll. That meeting began what became a weekly discipleship session during which we talked about everything. We met just about every week for years.

John Paul got sick a few years later. I got a phone call from his office one morning and they said, "You need to come quickly!" I jumped in my car and drove four hours to Dallas. I felt as if I was moving in slow motion. I couldn't figure out why the Lord would lead me to John Paul only to take him so soon. He couldn't die. I still needed him! When I got to his house his spiritual sons and daughters surrounded him. John Paul wasn't able to speak, but saw me. We held hands and I spent a wonderful time in prayer and worship with my spiritual father one last time. God did supernatural things in the next few hours together.

John Paul went to be with Jesus that day. I was brokenhearted. I was so grateful for my time with him, but longed for more. I was disappointed about one thing: he wasn't physically able to bless me. He was too weak to talk by the time I arrived, but I desired the father's blessing. To my surprise, when I got to his memorial service they played a video of John Paul. He gave a father's blessing. I couldn't believe it. I sat in that service and wept and wept. I'm crying again right now as I write this.

I want to give you a gift. I want to give you the blessing my spiritual father gave me. Many of you have never had a blessing from your father or spiritual father. Today, that changes. Open your heart and receive a father's blessing from John Paul Jackson.

The Father's Blessing
John Paul Jackson

Some of you did not have great father figures. Some of you have fathers who passed away before they could give you a blessing. Others of you, for one reason or another, are unable to receive a blessing from your father. To you, I want to offer the blessings of the Heavenly Father, through myself, an earthly father. This type of blessing is seen in Numbers 6, as God blessed the children of Israel under the pronouncement of Moses. It goes on to say that upon blessing the people, God would place His name and bless those who heard it. That means you!

Therefore, may the Lord bless you and keep you.
The Lord make His face shine upon you and be gracious to you.
The Lord lift up His countenance upon you and give you peace.

And from me, from my heart as a father and a grandfather,
I would like to bless you in this way.

May you reach the purpose for which you were created.
May you have courage above your peers.
May you have more passion for the things of God than others think is necessary.
May you dream more than others think is practical.
May you expect more than others think is possible.
May you choose wisely without earthly bias.

You have people to influence who you have not yet met.
You have lives to change that are waiting for your arrival.
You are strategically placed wherever God takes you by His grand design, just so you can become everything He made you to be.
That place is the place you can grow best.
That place is the place where you can be most fruitful.
The place where the future is changed because of your presence.
May you see vistas that others don't even know exist.
May you see God in every petal of every flower and every blade of grass, for each of them are designed by His hand.
May you bless your children and may they become giants in the faith under the mighty hand of God.
You won't fail!
You were made by God to be here, for such a time as this.

The Lord was right. I needed John Paul Jackson in my life to fulfill my life's assignment. I believe this book is a part of my life's assignment.

John Paul introduced me to righteousness and the heart of the Father, not just the topic, but the lifestyle. John Paul always talked about righteousness and now, so am I. Righteousness brings you into right standing with God. Righteousness gives you access to the throne room of God, where you may stand blameless before the Father, washed in the blood of Jesus, and made holy in His sight. Today is the day to pursue righteousness and never stop!

> **"May you choose wisely without earthly bias."**

♥

Let's read one more passage on righteousness. Second Peter 2:7-9 (NASB) says, *"and if He rescued righteous Lot, oppressed by the sensual conduct of unprincipled men (for by what he saw and heard that righteous man, while living among them, felt his righteous soul tormented day after day by their lawless deeds), then the Lord knows how to rescue the godly from temptation, and to keep the unrighteous under punishment for the day of judgment."* Out of every scripture on righteousness, this one took me most by surprise. If Lot chose to go live in Sodom, and was surrounded by homosexuality and immorality, how was he righteous? I wondered. Lot remained righteous in an unrighteous world. Lot teaches us that you can struggle with homosexuality and not give into it! You can remain righteous. You just need to put on the mind of Christ!

THE MIND OF CHRIST

As I said before, the two things I daily asked the Lord for when praying into this book were the heart of the Father and the mind of Christ. After you give your heart to the Lord, the next step is to give Him your mind. Your mind means your thoughts, views, and understanding. Isaiah 55:8-9 says, " 'For my thoughts are not your thoughts, neither are your ways my ways,' declares the Lord. 'As the heavens are higher than the earth, so are my ways higher than your ways and my thoughts than your thoughts.' " Jesus came down from heaven to teach us the mind of God and give us His thoughts.

I asked the Lord, "How do I get your mind?" I heard the Holy Spirit speak to my spirit and say, "Give me your thoughts and I'll give you mine." Proverbs 1:23 says, *"Repent at my rebuke! Then I will pour out my thoughts to you, I will make known to you my teachings."* The mind of Christ is so important for our spiritual health and identity. Spiritually healthy people know God because they know God's Word. When you know God's Word, you know what God thinks about you. We must daily put on the mind of Christ. First Corinthians 2:16 says, *"Who has known the mind of the Lord so as to instruct him? But we have the mind of Christ."* We learn the thoughts of Jesus and the mind of Christ by daily reading the Bible and by maintaining a fervent prayer life.

I am outspoken on the topic of biblical sexuality and purity. Sometimes I get very interesting comments and responses on social media. One time someone commented on one of my posts about homosexuality and said, "If Jesus came down from heaven on a white horse and said it was OK to be gay, would you accept homosexuality?" I thought this comment was very humorous, but a poor attempt at defending a position. To answer the question, I said I would, but also contended Jesus had not done this. God sent Him to the earth to save sinners from their sin, not to embrace or affirm their sin. Let's look at a few encounters with Jesus to better understand His mind through His words.

People love to quote Jesus when He said, in John 8:7, *"He who is without sin, cast the first stone."* After they use this quote they feel assured they cannot be judged, and are free to go on and live life as they please. The problem with that response is Jesus said it to a group of evil religious leaders who hated Him and constantly tried to trap him in His words. They were the ones who put Jesus on the cross.

> ## "Give me your thoughts and I'll give you mine."

♥

That quote is from the Gospel of John, in Chapter 8. The religious leaders who hated Jesus caught a woman in the very act of adultery, and were about to make a public spectacle of her by stoning her. Jesus wasn't talking to the woman when He said, *"He who is without sin, cast the first stone."* What was His mind toward her? What were his thoughts? John 8:10-11 says, *"Jesus straightened up and asked her, 'Woman, where are they? Has no one condemned you?' 'No one, sir,' she said. 'Then neither do I condemn you,' Jesus declared. 'Go now and leave your life of sin.'"* Jesus's mind was for a woman who was living in sexual sin to not feel condemned by men, but to encounter the grace of God, respond in righteousness, and leave her life of sin. That was the mind of Christ.

There is no biblical account in which Jesus encounters a homosexual, but we can see how He responded to a woman in heterosexual sin. He told her to leave the life of sin and renew her mind.

The apostle Paul encountered the topic of homosexuality and addressed it firmly in Romans 1, as we covered. In Romans he went on to warn the church (true followers of Jesus) that continuing to live in sexual sin—including homosexual practice—came with intense consequences. He warned of deception, and that if they affirmed false teaching over a period of time, it would corrupt their way of thinking and cause what he described as a "depraved mind." Romans 1:28-32 says:

> *28 Furthermore, just as they did not think it worthwhile to retain the knowledge of God, so God gave them over to a depraved mind, so that they do what ought not to be done. 29 They have become filled with every kind of wickedness, evil, greed and depravity. They are full of envy, murder, strife, deceit and malice. They are gossips, 30 slanderers, God-haters, insolent, arrogant and boastful; they invent ways of doing evil; they disobey their parents; 31 they have no understanding, no fidelity, no love, no mercy. 32 Although they know God's righteous decree that those who do such things deserve death, they not only continue to do these very things but also approve of those who practice them.*

The Depraved Mind

The depraved mind (also referred to as the "debased mind" or "reprobate mind" in other translations) is a mind that is undiscerning. The depraved mind can no longer judge right from wrong. The depraved mind refuses to submit to God. The depraved mind refuses to listen to godly counsel. The depraved mind refuses to listen to sound doctrine based on clear scripture. The depraved mind is determined to forget the righteousness of God and live in sexual sin. The *Geneva Study Bible* describes a depraved mind as, "a corrupt and perverse mind, by which it comes to pass that the conscience, having been removed by them, and they having almost no more remorse for sin, run headlong into all types of evil."[18] These are the same people who lose their sensitivity to the Holy Spirit and stop resisting sin (as the Bible defines it) and indulge in it. Ephesians 4:19 says, *"Having lost all sensitivity, they have given themselves over to sensuality so as to indulge in every kind of impurity, and they are full of greed."*

This is the mind of the individual who continues to allow the lies of the enemy, deceiving spirits, and the lusts of the world to dominate his or her thought life. This is the mind of the carnal believer who wants to reject righteousness and live in sexual impurity.

If followers of Jesus remain carnal and do not renew their minds, they will become as lost as the rest of the world. Second Corinthians 10:5 says, *"We demolish arguments and every pretension that sets itself up against the knowledge of God, and we take captive every thought to make it obedient to Christ."* Putting on the mind of Christ is the process of making an enemy of every thought that is contrary to biblical teaching and the Word of God itself. You imprison such thoughts and refuse to allow them to remain free in your thought life. It's the process of making sure everything you believe has support in Scripture.

Throughout this book we have taken the deceiving thoughts the devil has given us and compared them with the truth of God's Word. This is part of the process of renewing one's mind. Don't believe everything others tell you about faith and sexuality. Make sure it aligns with Scripture and the mind of Christ before you affirm it. That is how you renew your mind. Romans 12:2 says, *"Do not conform to the pattern of this world, but be transformed by the renewing of your mind. Then you will be able to test and approve what God's will is—his good, pleasing and perfect will."*

Armando's Story

Armando grew up in a strong Latin family. His mother was loving and affectionate, and they had a strong relationship. Though his father lived in the home and was part of Armando's life, their relationship was disconnected (as is the case with most individuals who struggle with homosexuality and SSA). Though Armando never suffered sexual abuse, as a child he always felt different from other boys. He grew up loving what was commonly thought of as "girl stuff." He played with dolls. He was into fashion. He would do his mom's hair and makeup. He loved to make her look pretty. Armando was very creative, but he had a slight perversion on his creativity. Armando truly believed he was born gay.

Homosexuality was unusually common in his family. He had five gay family members in his immediate family. His gay heritage extended back five generations. But that wasn't all. Many in his family practiced witchcraft. His grandmother's brother was a transgender warlock. (He was a man who lived life as a woman, and was also a witch.)

The family rejected his transgender life, so he was known to cast spells on them. Two of the curses he cast on the family (that they knew of) were divorce and death. The family witch declared women in the family wouldn't live past fifty, and none of the marriages in their bloodline would last. The demonic power was real. Three female family members died before age fifty, and four of five marriages ended in divorce. One of Armando's aunts was married six times!

Armando was always attracted to both guys and girls, but mainly to guys. Still, he always wanted a family and pictured himself with a woman as his wife. Yet even in elementary school, he flirted with boys and had more girls as friends than boys. It was obvious he was different from other boys, and they all let him know he was different. In fact, Armando was bullied at school. Other kids made fun of his big eyes and what he thought to be his "awkward smile." Kids called him gay, but someone always defended him. He was strong on the outside, but hurt deeply on the inside.

At age twelve, Armando started looking at porn. It hit him like a flood, overwhelming him. He had a computer in his room, which opened up to him a private world of sexuality. Armando couldn't believe it was all free! But he didn't read the fine print to see what it would cost him one day.

He started going to church with his mom at about the same time he discovered porn. He never told anyone at church about his struggles. The church kicked out people with sin issues, so he just kept it a secret. As Armando continued his life of sin over his teenage years, a secret shame began to grow in him. Condemnation became his best friend. Armando continued to embrace his SSA. He thought it was better to "live happy and go to hell than to be miserable and go to heaven." Homosexuality was becoming Armando's identity. He began taking on a gay persona and all the characteristics.

One day, as he viewed pornography on his computer, his computer caught a virus. Suddenly, all the gay pornographic videos he had ever watched started popping up on his computer—by the thousands. It seemed like millions of videos rushed at him at once. His mom walked into his room as his computer brought up video after video of gay porn.

Armando saw her and began to cry. He thought he should tell her, but couldn't bring himself to do it. He thought that if he came out as

*gay no one would love him. Then his mom said, "If you're gay, I'm here
for you." They sat and held each other and cried. After several minutes, fear gripped Armando and he told her, "Please don't tell dad!"
His mom agreed not to tell. Armando's mom had just begun following
Jesus and had experienced God's grace, but was still learning the truth
and wisdom of God. After his mom accepted his gay lifestyle without
hesitation, Armando ran into it full speed.*

*He started working at a theme park that encouraged the gay life-
style. This theme park was full of homosexuals. His boss at work was
a homosexual ten years older than Armando, and he began to pursue
him. He frequently complimented Armando on his "pretty" eyes and
"captivating" smile. He made Armando feel pretty. But mostly, he gave
Armando attention, which he craved.*

*One night after work, his boss invited Armando back to his house
and Armando had his first sexual encounter—a homosexual encounter. Years of gay pornography had prepared him for the moment. So
there he was. Armando was willing to go as far as someone else would
take him. He was gay and his virginity was gone. The best part about
it was, he felt no conviction! "No anger, God?" he thought to himself.
"No wrath? No getting struck by lightning? This must be OK. See you
later, God!" he reasoned. Armando continued his sexual relationship
with his boss for another six months, until his boss ended it before
others at work found out.*

*Armando was crushed that the relationship was suddenly over,
but he quickly found out that other men would give him the same attention. He even met "Christian gays" and noticed they were strongly
attracted to other Christian gays. Armando had many flings and a lot
of sex, but no meaningful relationships. Despite the lack of a long-
term relationship, Armando was happy. He finally felt comfortable in
his own skin. He was in college and had friends, and was a confident
atheist. God wasn't real, he reasoned, because he never felt anything
when it came to God. He believed he didn't need God to be a good
person, and he felt like a very good person.*

*One day, his college art instructor showed a sculpture of a wom-
an being touched by the Holy Spirit. Then she read a poem she had
written about it. This had a great impact on Armando. It reminded him
of how he used to feel when he was a kid in church. As Armando drove
home, he couldn't stop thinking about it. "God if you're real, prove it*

to me in an unexplainable way!" he blurted out as he drove. Nothing happened, and that was that.

On a random day a few months later, as he lay in bed at home and was about to fall asleep, he heard the door squeak and the floor crack under the feet of someone walking into his room. Armando just lay on his side facing the wall, but then felt a person sit on the bed and lie down next to him—close. He suddenly felt amazing warmth and comfort. He loved it! But who was it? He decided to just play along, like a kid pretending to be asleep when his parents come to check on him. In that moment, Armando felt a deep love and purity he had never felt in a bed before. He began giggling and elbowed the person in bed with him . . . but no one was there. Armando heard a voice whisper in his ear and say, "I'm no longer with you."

Armando jumped out of bed and turned on all the lights. He started investigating if anyone else was in his house, but his parents were asleep and no one else was there. Armando freaked out. It had been so real, but he didn't know what to make of it. First thing the next morning, Armando told his mom what happened. "It was God," she said without hesitation. Armando became so mad that he rushed out the door for class.

In art class, he recounted what happened to a pretty girl he sat next every day in art class. She said the exact same thing his mom had: "It was God!" Armando couldn't believe what he had just heard. He had already come to terms with being gay and rejecting God, and now it seemed a God he didn't even believe in might be complicating his life. The pretty girl invited him to a Bible study that night. Armando wasn't sure why, but he agreed to go.

Armando got through the Bible study part just fine. Everyone seemed to be nice. But it didn't really impact him or speak to him. Then at the very end, the leader of the group opened it up for questions. Armando just sat back and listened as different people asked questions. Five questions were asked, and every single one perfectly outlined Armando's life. He couldn't believe all the coincidences in one day! Finally, at the end of the study Armando said, "I just wanted you all to know that I'm an atheist, but I like you guys." He was trying to be friendly. At that moment, half the people in the room began weeping, which shook Armando to his core.

As Armando drove home, he became angry with God. He seriously considered driving his car into oncoming traffic. If God was real, he believed he would have to go "back into a box" and wouldn't be happy. To him, the only things attached to God were depression and judgment. "Why did you show up?" Armando yelled at God at the top of his lungs. He heard the same voice in that moment that he had heard in his bed say, "You don't know me or you." Armando began to weep. Finally, he responded to God, "If you want me, God, you get me gay!" Armando heard the voice speak to him again, saying, "Believe me, you'll love me."

For the next six months, Armando did everything he could that he believed would make God not love him or want him. He looked at a lot of porn and tried to flirt with and hook up with guys, but the desires were all going away. Armando saw a picture of himself as a child trying to hit a "father," but the father held him so tightly he could not hit him. He finally just fell into the father's arms.

One day, as Armando prepared for his day he looked at himself in the mirror and blurted out, "I love you." In that moment, everything he hated about himself was gone. He suddenly felt deep love for himself, and deep love for God. From that moment on Armando pursued God with everything in him.

The moment he stopped trying to be gay, most of his physically effeminate characteristics started changing without him even trying. As he fell in love with God, he forgot he struggled with homosexuality. He no longer identified himself as a homosexual.

Armando began to read his Bible and dedicated himself to discipleship. Every other love in his life faded away. He "became madly in love with Jesus." Day by day and step by step, God continued to heal and deliver Armando in every area of his life. He let go of everything and started over from scratch. He quit school, his job—everything. He gave everything he owned away, and let God renew his mind and his life.

He continued attending the Bible study, which became a church, and he got involved with an evangelistic creative arts ministry. He painted and ministered through creative arts in his city, and even in other nations.

Three years later, God spoke to Armando and said, "I have a wife for you." Armando wasn't sure that was a good idea, but he trusted

God. He had never dated a girl, and was not sure if he could ever be sexual with one. He heard God say again, *"If I made you fall in love with me, I can make you fall in love with her."* The Lord drew Armando's attention to consider the women in his life he honored, but knew the one God was talking about. She was a girl in his ministry who was very special to him. She had also come out of a lifestyle of homosexuality, and God had renewed and restored her life and identity as well. The attraction just came.

Armando started falling in love with everything about her. For over a year, Armando fell in love with this girl without going on one date. Finally, after getting the green light from God in his heart, and approval from his pastor, Armando invited her on a date. Armando held nothing back. He told her everything God had spoken to him about her, and what had taken place in his heart over the previous year. To Armando's shock, she said the exact same thing. God had been speaking to her about Armando at the same time. It was God! Nine months later, they were married. They are madly in love and continue to minister together to this day.

Armando's mom and dad both serve the Lord. The demonic curses spoken over his mother were broken off by the blood of Jesus. Armando has a strong relationship with his father. (Armando wanted me to let you know the wedding night was great!)

Jesus taught that the greatest commandment was to *"love the Lord your God with all your heart and with all your soul and with all your mind"* (Matthew 22:37). You actually love God by putting on the mind of Christ and renewing your mind. You love Him by making unbiblical, disobedient thoughts obedient to the Word of God. You love Him by choosing to think about things that please God. Philippians 4:8 says, *"Finally, brothers and sisters, whatever is true, whatever is noble, whatever is right, whatever is pure, whatever is lovely, whatever is admirable—if anything is excellent or praisewor*thy—think about such things."

In the book of James, we are taught that the double-minded man is unstable in all he does (James 1:8). An unstable mind creates an unstable life. You can't go on undecided. You either stand on the Lord's side and agree with biblical clarity on sexuality that reflects God's Word and the divine nature of creation, or you stand on the side of the world, the church of Satan, and homosexual practice. Make the choice today. Choose intimacy with the Father and the mind of Christ. Choose deliverance!

THE REVELATION OF DELIVERANCE

Deliverance, true freedom found only in Jesus, is available to you to-day. This is not the partial freedom some people experience, but complete freedom and victory. I'm not talking about freedom you merely sing songs about, or have heard about in some poetic sermon. I'm talking about true healing power that completely sets one free. This deliverance is already paid for through Jesus.

Is anything impossible for God—anything at all? No. God can do anything. So why do you believe (if you do) that He can't set you free from same-sex attraction (SSA)? The Bible says nothing is impossible for Him. You must take captive the lies of the devil and believe God's Word. Here is what Jesus said when His disciples had a hard time be-lieving: *"Jesus looked at them and said, 'With man this is impossible, but with God all things are possible' "* (Matthew 19:26). Deliverance is here for you today; you just need to believe.

The Deliverance Story

It was the fall of 2014, and the year was coming to an end. It had been the best year of my life and ministry and I didn't want it to end. I ac-credit all this to the revelation of righteousness I wrote about earlier. I felt like Joshua, and asked God not to let the sun set on 2014. I knew I needed to begin to lean into 2015 and ask the Lord to speak to me about my assignment and message from Him to the people of God.

On a Saturday morning during my monthly prayer call with my intercessory prayer team, I asked the Lord for the first time, "Speak to me about 2015." It was a simple prayer, but I meant it.

That night, I jumped on a plane to minister on Sunday morning at an amazing church in Michigan. On Sunday morning I ministered on the authority we have in the righteousness of Jesus, with Job 1 as the backdrop. (When we know God, He will introduce us to the demons over which we have authority.) It was a powerful service.

The minute I finished ministering and sat down on the front row, I heard the Holy Spirit speak to my spirit and say, "This is a year of deliverance!" *Wow!* I thought. Immediately, I thought about this book and my wife's book, *Unscarred,* her story of supernatural deliverance after a severe drug overdose. I thought of the prophetic conference I planned to do in San Francisco at the end of the year. The Lord knows that city needs deliverance. I was so excited about what God had in store.

I flew home to Heather and the kids, and Monday morning, I was back on the treadmill at the gym, doing my prayer and Bible reading. I happened to be in Psalm 31 that day in my daily reading plan. I couldn't believe the first verse I read: "I have taken refuge; let me never be put to shame; deliver me in your righteousness" (Psalm 31:1). The Holy Spirit spoke to my spirit immediately and said, "Righteousness is the setup for deliverance." I was amazed. The Lord led me to dedicate my life to the study, preaching, and teaching of righteousness for a year to prepare me to minister to His people on deliverance.

To be honest, I was frustrated it took me so long to finish this book. I wanted it out before the Supreme Court ruling on gay marriage, and I missed deadline after deadline. Between my commitments to traveling ministry and quality family time, it was a challenge to dedicate time to writing. Then it hit me. This was a divine delay from the Lord. What would a book on homosexuality be if it didn't have the power of deliverance? For over two years, the Lord's still small voice led me to this moment, right now—for your deliverance!

True Deliverance

Modern translations use the word, "deliverance," 397 times, and the word, "deliver," eighty-six times (according to BibleHub.com). Throughout the Word of God we see a variety of situations in which God delivers His people. We see deliverance from enemies, demons, demonic forces, sickness, and abusive behavior and lifestyles. The Greek word for deliverance is "sotayree'ah," which means, "salvation"! The God who saves us, by the same power, delivers us. Somewhere down the line many have come to believe they can be saved but not experience true deliverance.

Deliverance is a recurring theme throughout the Bible. Everywhere Jesus went, he cast out demonic spirits, healed people, and ministered deliverance. In His famous Sermon on the Mount, Jesus taught His followers how to pray. In that prayer, Jesus instructs us to pray for deliverance. Matthew 6:9-13 says, *"This, then, is how you should pray: 'Our Father in heaven, hallowed be your name, your kingdom come, your will be done, on earth as it is in heaven. Give us today our daily bread. And forgive us our debts, as we also have forgiven our debtors. And lead us not into temptation, but deliver us from the evil one.' "*

"The God who saves us, by the same power, delivers us."

I have heard ministers say, "You don't need to keep coming down to the altar over and over to get saved." Maybe they're not coming to get saved. Maybe they still need deliverance! I'm reminded of the story in Mark 9 of a man who asked the disciples of Jesus to cast the demon out of his son.

14 When they returned to the other disciples, they saw a large crowd surrounding them, and some teachers of religious law were arguing with them. 15 When the crowd saw Jesus, they were overwhelmed with awe, and they ran to greet him.
16 "What is all this arguing about?" Jesus asked. 17 One of the men in the crowd spoke up and said, "Teacher, I brought my son so you could heal him. He is possessed by an evil spirit that won't let him talk. 18 And whenever this spirit seizes him, it throws him violently to the ground. Then he foams at the mouth

and grinds his teeth and becomes rigid. So I asked your disciples to cast out the evil spirit, but they couldn't do it." 19 Jesus said to them, "You faithless people! How long must I be with you? How long must I put up with you? Bring the boy to me." 20 So they brought the boy. But when the evil spirit saw Jesus, it threw the child into a violent convulsion, and he fell to the ground, writhing and foaming at the mouth. 21 "How long has this been happening?" Jesus asked the boy's father. He replied, "Since he was a little boy. 22 The spirit often throws him into the fire or into water, trying to kill him. Have mercy on us and help us, if you can." 23 "What do you mean, 'If I can'?" Jesus asked. "Anything is possible if a person believes." 24 The father instantly cried out, "I do believe, but help me overcome my unbelief!" 25 When Jesus saw that the crowd of onlookers was growing, he rebuked the evil spirit. "Listen, you spirit that makes this boy unable to hear and speak," he said. "I command you to come out of this child and never enter him again!" 26 Then the spirit screamed and threw the boy into another violent convulsion and left him. The boy appeared to be dead. A murmur ran through the crowd as people said, "He's dead." 27 But Jesus took him by the hand and helped him to his feet, and he stood up. 28 Afterward, when Jesus was alone in the house with his disciples, they asked him, "Why couldn't we cast out that evil spirit?" 29 Jesus replied, "This kind can be cast out only by prayer" (Mark 9:14-29, NLT).

This is the state of the American church. Are there no demons in America? Why don't we see deliverance in the American church? Countless people in our world are asking the church (followers of Jesus) to help them find deliverance from their demonic afflictions, but followers of Jesus lack the power of the Holy Spirit to help them. So instead of casting out demonic spirits and ministering deliverance, we leave people to embrace their temptations, same-sex attractions, and demonic afflictions. Jesus rebuked everyone in Mark 9, cast the evil spirit out of the boy, and brought the healing power of the Holy Spirit to all. Disciples of Jesus need to stop embracing and affirming demonic temptations, and instead, take authority in righteousness and minister deliverance to a lost and hurting world.

Similar Feeling, Different Spirit

Before I begin to share on deliverance, I want to caution you about what the devil will try to do after you experience supernatural deliverance in just a few moments. The enemy will tell you that because you feel a similar SSA temptation or homosexual desire, that you are not delivered. This is not true! This is a strategy of the enemy to keep you discouraged so you won't fight or resist him. There is not just one spirit of homosexuality, SSA, immorality, perversion, and more. No person knows how many. But we can give a biblical guess that there are tens of thousands, possibly millions. There are a lot. So when you have the similar temptations or feelings, the devil immediately says, "See, you're not really delivered. You're still gay. You'll always be gay." The truth is, you were delivered. You defeated that demonic spirit and temptation.

When David defeated Goliath, he did two specific things. First Samuel 17:51 says, *"David ran and stood over him. He took hold of the Philistine's sword and drew it from the sheath. After he killed him, he cut off his head with the sword. When the Philistines saw that their hero was dead, they turned and ran."* David took Goliath's sword and cut off his head! Why? Because Goliath had brothers that looked, walked, and talked just like him. David wanted to be able to grab that detached head, look Goliath in the face, and know God had already delivered him from one giant, so could deliver him from any other giant.

There isn't just one spirit of same-sex temptation or of lust. There are many. The devil wants you to be discouraged by your feelings of temptation when you should be encouraged. God delivered you from the previous temptation. He will deliver you from the next temptation. Remember, temptation is not a sin. The enemy will always encourage you to give in because you already feel bad about the temptation. That is his strategy. Don't give in. Press into deliverance!

The Revelation of Deliverance

I continued reading Psalm 31:1 after the Lord spoke to me about the relationship between righteousness and deliverance. I made my way down to verse 5, and it jumped off the page at me: *"Into your hands I commit my spirit; Lord, my faithful God"* (Psalm 31:5). This is a psalm of David. King David prays here the prayer that Jesus would also pray: *"Jesus called out with a loud voice, 'Father, into your hands I commit my spirit.' When he had said this, he breathed his last"* (Luke 23:46). I had never noticed that before. I had read at least one psalm practically every day for years, and never noticed the last prayer Jesus prayed before He died on the cross for our sins was a prayer David prayed first.

My spiritual discernment went crazy! I knew there was a revelation there, so I began to ask the Holy Spirit to show it to me. *What's the difference between Jesus praying it and David praying it?* I asked myself. Then it came to me. Jesus is all Spirit all the time. He was always led by the Spirit of God. He was born of the Spirit but became flesh (Matthew 1:18; John 1:14). Jesus was led by the Spirit alone. Matthew 4:1 says, *"Then Jesus was led by the Spirit into the wilderness to be tempted by the devil."* Jesus was never led by the flesh. Jesus was born of the Spirit and became flesh. Man is born of the flesh and must be born again of the Spirit. John 3:1-3 says, *"Now there was a Pharisee, a man named Nicodemus who was a member of the Jewish ruling council. He came to Jesus at night and said, 'Rabbi, we know that you are a teacher who has come from God. For no one could perform the signs you are doing if God were not with him.' Jesus replied, 'Very truly I tell you, no one can see the kingdom of God unless they are born again.'"*

Jesus was led by the Spirit all the time. David was led by the Spirit some of the time, but also by his flesh. David slayed giants when he was led by the Spirit. David slayed at least one innocent husband when he was led by his flesh. When he was led by the Spirit, he took on lions and bears. When he was led by the flesh, he numbered the children of Israel in disobedience to God. As I considered all this, I heard the Holy Spirit speak to my spirit and say, "Deliverance is when your flesh follows your spirit." You remain in deliverance when you remain in the Spirit of God. You will remain in bondage when you allow your flesh to lead you.

We don't negotiate with our flesh; we crucify it. When David and Jesus prayed, "I commit to you my spirit," they were crucifying their flesh and giving God the Father their spirits. *"Now the Lord is the Spir-*

it, and where the Spirit of the Lord is, there is freedom" (2 Corinthians 3:17).

If you allow the Holy Spirit to lead you, your spirit will defeat your flesh, and you will continually walk in supernatural deliverance. King David experienced supernatural personal deliverance when he fought a lion and a bear, and this gave him confidence to take on the giant that cursed his nation and God. First Samuel 17:37 (ESV) says, *"And David said, 'The LORD who delivered me from the paw of the lion and from the paw of the bear will deliver me from the hand of this Philistine.' And Saul said to David, 'Go, and the LORD be with you!' "* You experience personal deliverance first, and then you help lead your family, friends, community, and nation into deliverance. You can't help deliver anyone from anything in which you are currently bound.

> ## "Deliverance is when your flesh follows your spirit."

We have heard from the heart of the Father. We have seen the mind of Christ. His desire is to not only save us from our sins by grace, but to deliver us from our sins through faith. Let's take a moment and pray a prayer of deliverance. I have prayed this simple prayer with people all over the world, and seen the supernatural power of God heal and transform lives. This is your season of deliverance. This is the moment you have been waiting for. Deliverance is now! I want you to say this prayer with me. Let's ask God to do what He does best; deliver His children from bondage.

Prayer of Deliverance

Father, once again I declare you are holy, holy, holy. Jesus, you are holy, holy, holy. Spirit of the living God, you are holy, holy, holy. Father, I pray to you in the name of Jesus. As we come in agreement with your Word, I ask in faith that you deliver me in your righteousness! (Say it again, louder.) JESUS, DELIVER ME IN YOUR RIGHTEOUSNESS! (Now, just take a moment and let the Holy Spirit minister to you.)

Five Elements of Deliverance

A mentor of mine, Pastor Zane Anderson, says, "Deliverance without discipleship is a pattern." If you walk the same pattern long enough, it will become a rut. It's time to get out of your rut and on the path of righteousness to experience the blessing of the Lord, the peace of God, and to fulfill the call of God on your life! I want to give you five elements of deliverance. These are five practical responses to use when the enemy attacks and tempts you. I'm going to teach you how to physically respond when you feel same-sex attraction. I'm going to teach you how to make your flesh follow your spirit. These five elements will change your life.

1. Pray in the Holy Spirit (Speaking in Tongues)

When you speak in tongues, your physical flesh follows your spirit. Jude 1:20 says, *"But you, dear friends, by building yourselves up in your most holy faith and praying in the Holy Spirit."* Speaking in tongues strengthens your spirit. In 1 Corinthians 14:4, the apostle Paul adds, *"Anyone who speaks in a tongue edifies themselves, but the one who prophesies edifies the church."* This is how you strengthen your spirit. However, the enemy doesn't want you strong because you would resist him.

There is strategic, demonic resistance to speaking in tongues. It's not coincidental. The devil knows disciples filled with the Spirit are stronger than he is. Recall Mark 9, when the disciples couldn't cast the demon out of the boy. They asked Jesus why they couldn't, and Jesus told them: *"This kind can come out only by prayer"* (Mark 9:29). He didn't specify what kind of prayer.

Later, the disciples received the baptism of the Holy Spirit, and the gift of speaking in tongues. *"When the day of Pentecost came, they were all together in one place. Suddenly a sound like the blowing of a violent wind came from heaven and filled the whole house where they were sitting. They saw what seemed to be tongues of fire that separated and came to rest on each of them. All of them were filled with the Holy Spirit and began to speak in other tongues as the Spirit enabled them"* (Acts 2:1-4). Never again did the disciples of Jesus meet a demon they didn't have authority over, and cast out.

I recall ministering in an amazing church in which everyone spoke in tongues all at once. No one prophesied in tongues, but corporately they all used their personal prayer language (in order, but to themselves). As I prayed, I saw a vision. I saw demons hovering over the church. As the people prayed in their heavenly prayer languages, a blue glowing dome hovered over the church. I asked the Lord what it was. "That's the hedge of protection," He said. As the church began to press into prayer, I saw that blue glow explode off the church and every demon was gone. I believe the gift of tongues is one of the greatest weapons the Holy Spirit has given the church to respond to every attack of the enemy, including all temptation.

A few days later, a young man I mentor who struggles with SSA called me late at night. I answered the call and he began to share with me how frustrated he was, and how strong his temptation had been, lately. I told him to pull his car over. After he did so, I asked him, "When was the last time you spoke in tongues?"

He couldn't remember.

I told him my vision of the hedge of protection. He and I began to pray in the Spirit together, and as we did, God's amazing peaceful presence came upon me.

"Do you feel that?" I asked him.

"Wow, oh yeah!"

"Where is your temptation?" I asked.

"It's gone!"

As soon as you feel SSA temptation (or any temptation), begin to pray in the Holy Spirit. If you don't have the gift yet, ask God for it. He loves to give spiritual gifts to His children. Matthew 7:11 says, *"If you, then, though you are evil, know how to give good gifts to your children, how much more will your Father in heaven give good gifts to those who ask him!"*

2. Start a Fasting Lifestyle

Fasting is a spiritual discipline that causes your physical flesh to follow your spirit. It's a time of resisting physical needs to become more spiritually sensitive to the Holy Spirit. The Bible describes many different types of fasts. Over and over, fasting is used to prepare God's people for breakthroughs.

A fasting lifestyle is one that consistently denies the physical flesh and seeks to become spiritually strong and sensitive to the leading of the Lord. Matthew 4:1, 10 says, *"Then Jesus was led by the Spirit into the wilderness to be tempted by the devil. . . . Jesus said to him, 'Away from me, Satan! For it is written: "Worship the Lord your God, and serve him only." ' "* I love that Jesus commanded Satan to get away from Him after His season of fasting. Your spirit will become stronger when your flesh doesn't rule you.

In the book of Esther, Queen Esther called all Israel to fast and pray for the deliverance of their people. Esther 4:15-16 says, *"Then Esther sent this reply to Mordecai: 'Go, gather together all the Jews who are in Susa, and fast for me. Do not eat or drink for three days, night or day. I and my attendant will fast as you do. When this is done, I will go to the king, even though it is against the law. And if I perish, I perish.' "* Notice the Bible didn't exempt anyone in Israel from fasting.

If you need physical healing, start fasting. If you need direction in your life, start fasting. If you need deliverance, start fasting. I want to encourage you to not let fear keep you from a lifestyle of fasting. Learn the discipline of resisting your physical flesh. That's what disciples do! Matthew 9:15 says, *"Jesus answered, 'How can the guests of the bridegroom mourn while he is with them? The time will come when the bridegroom will be taken from them; then they will fast.' "*

3. Sing Songs of Deliverance (Worship)

When you physically worship the Lord, your flesh must follow your spirit. When you lift your hands or get on your knees, your flesh is following your spirit. King David learned how to fight lions, bears, and giants in the fields alone with God . . . in the same fields where he learned how to worship. Psalm 32:7 says, *"You are my hiding place; you will protect me from trouble and surround me with songs of deliverance."* As you worship the Lord, deliverance takes place. As you worship God, your flesh must submit to your spirit. It doesn't matter how you sound, only how you press into God. David was a worshiper, and that worship created the warrior in him. First Samuel 16:23 says, *"Whenever the spirit from God came on Saul, David would take up his lyre and play. Then relief would come to Saul; he would feel better, and the evil spirit would leave him."* It's very interesting that Saul had to have David fight his giant for him, because he first had him worship for him.

Your worship is warfare. If you are feeling intense temptation and same-sex attraction, worship constantly. I want to encourage you to play worship everywhere. Have it playing 24/7 in your house, car, and office space. Keep worship around you and remain in deliverance.

4. The Shabach Shout

The shabach shout was the shout of spiritual warfare the Israelites would give before battle. *"Cry out, (shabach) 'Save us, God our Savior; gather us and deliver us from the nations, that we may give thanks to your holy name, and glory in your praise' "* (1 Chronicles 16:35, parentheses added). Israel would cry out to God and warfare would start in the heavens before even one strike of the sword on earth.

> **"...Saul had to have David fight his giant for him, because he first had him worship for him."**

"Shabach" in Hebrew means, *"to address in a loud tone, i.e. (specifically) loud; figuratively, to pacify (as if by words)—commend, glory, keep in, praise, still, triumph."* The shout became a weapon of the people of God.

The shabach is very similar to the shofar. The shofar is an instrument of war made from a ram's horn. The Israelites blew the shofar and gave a shabach shout before the walls of Jericho fell.

The making of a shofar offers some interesting spiritual insights. First, they have to remove the horn from the flesh of the ram's head. Next, they have to set the horn aside and wait for the attached flesh to die. Only when the flesh dies can they use it as an instrument of war. When your flesh dies, your voice becomes an instrument of war. Only when your flesh is dead can your spirit lead you and your shout engage in spiritual warfare on your behalf. You might need to put this book down right now and let out the greatest shabach shout of your life. Get in a safe place, ask the Holy Spirit to display His glory, and then shout! Don't hold back. Watch what happens. Go ahead. Do it. Shout!

5. Give the Extravagant Gift

At one point, I was in a prayer room in the woods of Washington state to pray into this book. The Lord had already given me the previous four elements of deliverance. I felt like there was one more, a fifth. As I was prayed, I saw a vision of the woman with the alabaster box, and I heard the Holy Spirit speak to my spirit and say, "The fifth is the extravagant gift." We see the story of the woman in Mark 14:3-9.

> *3 While he was in Bethany, reclining at the table in the home of Simon the Leper, a woman came with an alabaster jar of very expensive perfume, made of pure nard. She broke the jar and poured the perfume on his head. 4 Some of those present were saying indignantly to one another, "Why this waste of perfume? 5 It could have been sold for more than a year's wages and the money given to the poor." And they rebuked her harshly. 6 "Leave her alone," said Jesus. "Why are you bothering her? She has done a beautiful thing to me. 7 The poor you will always have with you, and you can help them any time you want. But you will not always have me. 8 She did what she could. She poured perfume on my body beforehand to prepare for my burial. 9 Truly, I tell you, wherever the gospel is preached throughout the world, what she has done will also be told, in memory of her." (Mark 14:3-9)*

This woman gave a sacrificial, extravagant gift that not only broke the strongholds of the past, but also marked the start of her future ministry. Her ministry and destiny began that moment.

Giving is so powerful because it takes your spirit to do it (as your flesh never wants to give). When you give, the gift has to leave your flesh. This is one of the most challenging elements for most people. Your flesh never wants to give on its own, and every time you feel in your spirit you are supposed to give, your flesh resists. That's when you know it's the Holy Spirit leading your spirit—He leads you to give!

Speak to Me About Something Else, God!

In my late teenage years, I started my adventure with the Holy Spirit and asked Him to speak to me every day. Every day, over and over, I would ask Him to speak: "Speak, Lord, your servant is listening!" God began to speak to me, but the only thing He would talk to me about was money—not my tithe, but extravagant gifts. (You're not giving until you give beyond your tithe.) I started out giving away $100 to strangers, over and over.

Every time I questioned God about this, the Holy Spirit spoke to my spirit and said, "Do you want me to speak to you or not?" So I kept listening and kept giving as He told me to do. It went from giving $100, to giving $200, to giving $500, and finally, to giving thousands of dollars. This happened over and over, not just one time. After a while, I noticed that every time I gave money in response to God's leading, something supernatural followed.

Years into this adventure, I said to the Lord, "I want to sow the largest, most extravagant gift I've ever given you." I told the Lord, "I want to give $2,000." I then prayed, saying, "God, multiply my ministry and give me my network in my twenties!" (At age eighteen, I began believing God for a network to reach young people.) I heard the Holy Spirit speak to my spirit and say, "If you want me to multiply your ministry, multiply your offering!" I immediately drove to the bank, got the money out, and gave the extravagant gift in faith. I learned that day that you don't tell God what sacrifice is. He tells you. I was about to get married, yet I gave all I had, in faith.

> **"I learned that day that you don't tell God what sacrifice is. He tells you."**

Six years went by. I followed the leading of the Lord to the best of my ability. One day, as I climbed a mountain to pray, I heard the Holy Spirit speak to my spirit and say, "I'm not giving you a network!" I was shocked. *What about the extravagant gift I gave?* I thought. "OK," I said to God, "you need to tell me what I'm supposed to do with my life, now."

Two weeks later, I was in Florida at a conference. A minister there called me out and said, "Landon, I sense God wants to give you your own network!" When he said that, I laid facedown before the Lord. I heard the Holy Spirit speak to my spirit and say, "I tested you to see if you would give it back to me."

The Lord showed me a vision of how to launch the network. We launched it the following fall. I was twenty-nine years old. When I gave the extravagant gift in my early twenties, it gave birth to my dream and ministry for the rest of my life.

I want to encourage you to pray and ask the Lord what you are to give extravagantly. What is your alabaster box? Pray about the ministry into which you are to sow a gift. Jesus said the extravagant gift was "beautiful." Those who experience deliverance respond extravagantly. It's a beautiful thing.

A CALL TO HOLINESS

Dominick's Story

Dominick was a very outgoing young boy. Like most Native American boys on his reservation, he loved adventure. He was always outside playing, but lacked supervision.

Alcoholism was like an epidemic on his reservation, and his dad was one of its victims. As a result, his father was physically and emotionally absent throughout his childhood. Dominick interpreted his dad's absence as rejection, and came to hate his father because of it. He longed for male companionship.

Dominick first noticed his SSA at age five, at a school assembly. (He describes it now as his initial attack!) He was in first grade, and sat in the second row of the bleachers. There on stage he saw the principal present an award to a student. Dominick remembered feeling attracted to the student. The stage was far away, and he thought the student being awarded was a girl. When the principal called the student's name, Dominick realized it wasn't a girl, but a boy who looked like a girl. Just then, Dominick heard a voice speak to him and say, "You like boys!" Dominick was absolutely shocked, but unsure of what had just happened. Right then he had a massive anxiety attack. He was so completely overwhelmed; he couldn't breathe and had to fight to regain his composure. Though he never went to church and was never introduced to Jesus, he knew in his heart that boys weren't supposed to like other boys . . . not like a boyfriend. It wasn't what he wanted. Even at that young age he felt like his life was over.

The next year, Dominick attended an all-boys private school in which all elementary students lived in dormitories on campus. When he was just six years old, a few older boys sodomized Dominick. This was the most traumatic experience of his life. Dominick was so embarrassed and ashamed that he didn't tell anyone. He had always felt weaker than everyone else, and never felt he had the strength to resist the cruelty he suffered. The sexual abuse continued for years, and Dominick was unable to process what was happening to him and why, but he continued to keep the abuse a secret.

A few years later, Dominick began having health problems and had trouble going to the bathroom. His parents took him to the doctor, who quickly discovered signs of the abuse Dominick had suffered. When Dominick's parents learned what had happened to their son, they were mortified, but the damage had already been done.

Dominick began to experience strong attraction to men, and particularly drawn to those inclined to take advantage of him. Though for years Dominick had been the victim of sexual encounters, at some point his flesh began to desire the experience. He became willing to go along with his abusers. He justified his involvement if someone else initiated it. This opened the door for deep perversion to saturate Dominick's mind. He became consumed with pornography and masturbation. Lust burned freely within him throughout high school. The outgoing, energetic boy became more and more reclusive. He knew his same-sex encounters and lustful desires were wrong. A deep darkness descended on Dominick's mind and spirit. He constantly felt a sense of death hanging over him. He often contemplated suicide. He was lost.

Toward the end of high school, Dominick was invited to church for the first time. He sat in the back at a youth service, but he goofed off and paid little attention to what the pastor was talking about. As the pastor closed out the service, he made an invitation for anyone there to join him at the front to receive Jesus. Dominick felt he should go down to the front, and finally did. When he reached the front, an older man came up to him and asked if he knew what Jesus had done for him. Dominick said, "No." The man began to share the gospel with him. Dominick began to weep in the presence of God, and gave his life to the Lord that day. As he stood at the altar, Dominick had the overwhelming thought, "I'll do this one day," and immediately felt a call to ministry. But this thought confused him. He wondered, "How can I be a minister and still be attracted to guys?"

Dominick started to attend church regularly, and learned more and more about Jesus. Still, he felt very awkward because he was a Christian, but still had same-sex attraction. Dominick had no one to mentor and disciple him in the things of the Lord, so he decided to let the Bible disciple him. Dominick got serious about studying and reading God's Word. He began to discover his identity in Christ as a son of God. He studied the scriptures on sexuality and the boundaries of godly relationships, and made a decision he would live his life according to the standard of God's Word. Dominick decided to live a life of holiness.

Dominick's attraction and temptation didn't all go away, but He knew God's Word is clear about His standard of holiness. Dominick decided to be celibate until God gave him attraction for a wife to one day marry. He pursued a holy life to honor a holy God. He began to guard his mind and thoughts, and to resist the lust of the flesh and pornography. Dominick learned he wasn't free from temptation, but lived his life above temptation. The Holy Spirit showed Dominick how to live a life of purity, despite his temptations.

Today, Dominick works in the ministry! He is an amazing revivalist who ministers on reservations throughout North America, but his ministry has taken him all over the world. He is discipling a generation to answer the call of holiness. Dominick's parents both serve the Lord and support Dominick in his ministry. His relationship with his dad was fully restored. Dominick is excited to fall deeper in love with his wife, but is still waiting for God to bring her into his life. Dominick told me, "Landon, every temptation you face is an accusation against the person God intends you to be." Dominick knows who he's called to be—holy—like Jesus!

I have heard the frustration of those who love God and have SSA, when they talk about their future. "So my only option is celibacy," they say with irritation. But that isn't their only option. When celibacy isn't an option, holiness always is.

Holy is the only word in our language that even begins to describe our God. He is a holy God. It's the name God gave His own Spirit, the Holy Spirit. John 14:26 says, *"But the Advocate, the Holy Spirit, whom the Father will send in my name, will teach you all things and will remind you of everything I have said to you."* Even the demons described Jesus as holy: *"What do you want with us, Jesus of Nazareth?*

Have you come to destroy us? I know who you are—the Holy One of God!" (Mark 1:24). There is power in declaring the holiness of God.

I love using the word *"holy"* when worshiping, praying, or thinking about the Lord. I use it constantly. My favorite worship songs are those that declare God is holy. When I travel the nation and minister, I tell worship leaders, "When we get to the altar time, just play a song with 'holy' in it!" When I pray, I start off declaring the holiness of the Father, Jesus, and Holy Spirit. You might have noticed this in the prayers in this book. I do this for a few reasons. First, just declaring who God is draws the power and presence of God. Just sit in a room and start declaring over and over to God, "You are holy!" and watch the presence of God fall in that moment. I've literally experienced this more times than I can count.

> ## "When celibacy isn't an option, holiness always is."

♥

The angels in heaven cry, "Holy, holy, holy," continuously—without stopping—in the throne room where God sits. Revelation 4:8 says, *"And the four living creatures, each one of them having six wings, are full of eyes around and within; and day and night they do not cease to say, 'HOLY, HOLY, HOLY is THE LORD GOD, THE ALMIGHTY, WHO WAS AND WHO IS AND WHO IS TO COME.' "* When you declare the holiness of God, He takes you into the holy of holies. Even in the Lord's Prayer in Matthew 6:9 Jesus said, *"This, then, is how you should pray: 'Our Father in heaven, hallowed (holy) be your name' "* (parentheses added). Before I pray about anything I declare His holiness. It puts one in the place of intimacy with God.

The Bible doesn't call us to a heterosexual or homosexual life, but to a holy life. Homosexual practice has no place in holiness. Psalm 119:9 (ESV) says, *"How can a young man keep his way pure? By guarding it according to your word."* Only within the boundaries of heterosexuality can you participate in sexual relationships and remain in a life of holiness. Adam and Eve were naked in the Garden of Eden and felt no shame because they were living in holiness (Genesis 2:25).

A Call to Holiness

The apostle Peter charged us to live holy lives.

> *13 Therefore, with minds that are alert and fully sober, set your hope on the grace to be brought to you when Jesus Christ is revealed at his coming. 14 As obedient children, do not conform to the evil desires you had when you lived in ignorance. 15 But just as he who called you is holy, so be holy in all you do; 16 for it is written: "Be holy, because I am holy." 17 Since you call on a Father who judges each person's work impartially, live out your time as foreigners here in reverent fear. 18 For you know that it was not with perishable things such as silver or gold that you were redeemed from the empty way of life handed down to you from your ancestors, 19 but with the precious blood of Christ, a lamb without blemish or defect. 20 He was chosen before the creation of the world, but was revealed in these last times for your sake. 21 Through him you believe in God, who raised him from the dead and glorified him, and so your faith and hope are in God. 22 Now that you have purified yourselves by obeying the truth so that you have sincere love for each other, love one another deeply, from the heart. 23 For you have been born again, not of perishable seed, but of imperishable, through the living and enduring word of God. (1 Peter 1:13-23)*

> ## "The Bible doesn't call us to a heterosexual or homosexual life, but to a holy life."

Look closely at verse 16, *"It is written: 'Be holy, because I am holy.'"* What's very interesting about this is the apostle Peter again references the Old Testament and declares a call to holiness. Peter was the disciple closest to Jesus. No one had more intimate moments with Jesus than Peter. Peter is teaching us the secret of intimacy with Jesus: holiness! Holiness brings you into intimacy with God. Hebrews 12:14 says, *"Make every effort to live in peace with everyone and to*

be holy; without holiness no one will see the Lord." Holiness brings us into close proximity of intimacy so we can see the Lord, be with Him, and know Him.

Moses wrote Leviticus, which includes God's original declaration, *"Be holy, because I am holy"* (Leviticus 11:44). Moses wrote this because he knew God intimately. He saw God face to face. Deuteronomy 5:4 says, *"The Lord spoke to you face to face out of the fire on the mountain."* If you truly want to know God on an intimate level, it will require the pursuit of holiness. Holiness isn't under the law—it preceded the law. Holiness is under the blood of Jesus.

Intimacy with God comes from intimacy with God's Word. If we are to know God we must know His HOLY Word (the Bible). (This is why there are 406 scripture references in this book.) Knowing God will help you discern right and wrong, good and evil, moral and immoral, holy and common. Leviticus 10:10 (NLT) says, *"You must distinguish between the holy and the common, between the unclean and the clean."* The word used here for "holy," in Hebrew is "ko'-desh," which means, "dedicated, set apart, *the most holy*"! The word "common" in Hebrew is "khole," which means, "profaneness, commonness (what pertains to all, whatever was in general use)." To put it plainly, everything that isn't holy is common.

> ## "Intimacy with God comes from intimacy with God's Word."

♥

We can't give in to lifestyles that are common to our fleshly desires. We can't give in to the temptation of homosexual practice. First Corinthians 10:13 says, *"No temptation has overtaken you except what is common to mankind. And God is faithful; he will not let you be tempted beyond what you can bear. But when you are tempted, he will also provide a way out so that you can endure it."* All temptation is common to man, but holiness is common to God! When you know God intimately, you will know His strength intimately, and you will know when you are weak His holiness is very strong (2 Corinthians 12:10). Since He is holy, we can be holy through the blood of Jesus and the power of the Holy Spirit. Romans 15:16 (NLT) says, *"I am a special messenger from Christ Jesus to you Gentiles. I bring you the Good News so that I might present you as an acceptable offering to God, made holy by the Holy Spirit."* You don't have to fight this temptation. Jesus already did. You just have to die to it.

Will I Deal with This the Rest of My Life?

The question I get more than any other is, "Am I going to have to deal with this the rest of my life?" My answer is always the same: "Not if you die to it first!" You never drive by a graveyard and wonder with which temptations the bodies in the graves struggle. You never think that thought because dead men cannot be tempted. Being alive in Christ means you're dead to sin! Romans 6:11 says, *"In the same way, count yourselves dead to sin but alive to God in Christ Jesus."* You don't have to live with SSA for the rest of your life; you just have to daily die to the desires of the flesh. Galatians 2:20 says, *"I have been crucified with Christ and I no longer live, but Christ lives in me. The life I now live in the body, I live by faith in the Son of God, who loved me and gave himself for me."*

Hear me! You don't have to worry about this the rest of your life if you die to this daily and follow Jesus. In Matthew 6:34, Jesus taught, *"Therefore do not worry about tomorrow, for tomorrow will worry about itself. Each day has enough trouble of its own."*

> ## "...dead men cannot be tempted."

You don't have to worry about tomorrow, next week, or next year. Don't worry about the desires going away. Focus on passionately pursuing a life of discipleship, following Jesus. First Peter 4:1-2 (NASB) says, *"Therefore, since Christ has suffered in the flesh, arm yourselves also with the same purpose, because he who has suffered in the flesh has ceased from sin, so as to live the rest of the time in the flesh no longer for the lusts of men, but for the will of God."*

A life of holiness is lived one day at a time by daily offering one's life and choices to the Lord as a sacrifice to Him. Romans 12:1 says, *"Therefore, I urge you, brothers and sisters, in view of God's mercy, to offer your bodies as a living sacrifice, holy and pleasing to God— this is your true and proper worship."*

I want you to pray one more prayer over yourself, that you would know God intimately and reflect His holiness, that you would live a life that pleases Him and glorifies Him, and that you would live a life of holiness unto Him. Prayerfully read my prayer below. Then pray as God leads you.

"A life of holiness is lived one day at a time..."

Prayer of Holiness

Father, once again we declare you are holy, holy, holy. Jesus, Son of the living God, you are holy, holy, holy. Spirit of the living God, you are holy, holy, holy. We love you, God! We need you, Holy Spirit. We worship you, Jesus! There is none like you. We exalt your name, O holy God.

In the name of Jesus, I pray now for the power and presence of God to fall on my friends as they read. I pray the Holy Spirit, our comforter, will fall on them right now. I pray they feel the tangible presence of God to manifest over them now in Jesus's name.

Lord, we thank you that you make us holy through the blood of Jesus, so we ask for intimacy with you. We want to know you, Lord. Father, show my friends your glory, show them your presence, and make yourself intimately known to them.

Lord, I pray for my friends, that you would expose every lie of the enemy and deceptive thought at work in their lives. In Jesus's name, I rebuke the demons in hell that attack their minds, bodies, and spirits. I declare, the Lord rebuke you foul spirits that have harassed my friends. I pray complete freedom over their minds now, in Jesus's name.

I pray every demonic spirit sent to deceive them are rebuked in Jesus's name! I declare God's thoughts and the mind of Christ. I pray my friends will put on and keep on: the helmet of salvation to guide their minds and thoughts, the breastplate of righteousness to guard their hearts, and the shield of faith and the sword of the Spirit to stand their ground. I pray no more giving in to temptation! THEY ARE NOT THEIR TEMPTATION! THEY ARE SONS AND DAUGHTERS OF A HOLY GOD!

Reveal yourself as they continue to study and read the Bible. Father, give them the grace to respond to your call of holiness with holiness that reflects they know you. Jesus, be made famous in their lives. Bless their lives. Speak, Lord, your servants are listening. Speak to your servants, O holy God! You are holy, holy, holy! We love you, Lord. Amen.

LOVE LETTERS

To My Friends Struggling with Homosexuality and Same-Sex Attraction (SSA) . . .

I want you to know I'm proud of you for making it through this book. Every chapter I wrote, I prayed that you would have ears to hear the Spirit of God, a soft heart to receive God's Word, and a mind set on being renewed. The reason I put over 400 scriptures in this book is because it had to be Bible-based. You won't make it in the marathon of Christianity if you aren't in your Bible daily. It has to be the foundation of your life and the center of your relationship with God. We don't live by man's word; we live by God's Word! King David said, *"How can a young person stay on the path of purity? By living according to your word"* (Psalm 119:9). Now is the time to be in the Word of God daily, and in the presence of God. Now is the time to make the decision to deny your flesh, resist the sexual desires you have, and live a Bible-based life. Now is the time to pursue Jesus with everything you have. You are not your temptation; you are a child of God!

I felt in my spirit to tell you that you are like the disciple Peter, expressive and passionate. Jesus loved Peter and was very close to him. Peter was one of Jesus's favorites. You, too, are one of God's favorites! After Peter made a huge mistake and denied Jesus—not only with his words, but with actions—Jesus came back to Peter with love. Jesus asked Peter three times, "Do you love me?" Now I ask you, do you love Jesus? Do you love Him like crazy? I know you do! Are you willing to give up everything to live the way He taught us to live? Then put Jesus first in every area of your life. Put the Word of God first. Put it above your feelings, desires, and sexuality. Make it your daily passion to love Jesus more than anything else in life. I promise you, His grace will be sufficient for you.

Get plugged into a church that loves people unconditionally, and is unwavering on fundamental biblical standards for marriage and sexuality. Plant yourself in a healthy church to be around other Christians who will love you, stand with you, and keep you accountable. Be careful of those with whom you choose to spend a lot of time. Don't be around individuals who stir up your temptation or encourage a compromised lifestyle. Stay away from false teachers and individuals who teach a partial gospel and tell you what you want to hear. You will be drawn to them, so you need to be on guard.

Finally, implement the strategies in this book to live a victorious life on a daily basis. Read chapters again if you have to. Pray the prayers as many times as you need to. Keep standing, for God stands with you.

I encourage you to share this book with your friends who love God, but struggle with same-sex attraction. Let's believe God for freedom in this generation!

Friends and Family Members Who Struggle with Homosexuality and Same-Sex Attraction (SSA) . . .

You are in a very challenging position. You love God and you love someone who struggles with a very real, complex life issue and temptation; they experience SSA or practice homosexuality. You are caught in the middle. What do you do? You have heard me say over and over, "Love people unconditionally and remain unwavering in your loyalty to God's Word." Let them know where you stand and what the Bible says. Then continue to be kind, supportive, and loving, just as Christians are taught to be.

You must be strong and stand in faith. I want to remind you of the story of Anna in Chapter 6. Her mother never affirmed Anna's identity or behavior as a homosexual. She loved Anna and was kind to her lesbian girlfriend, but never embraced her lifestyle. Anna's mother is a perfect example of how we need to respond as friends and family of individuals who self-describe as LGBTQ.

Over the years, I have noticed the majority of people who begin to reject clear biblical understanding and embrace false teaching have a friend or family member who is LGBTQ. They watch their family member struggle in life. They watch them change their sexual orientation—and after a long battle—fully give in to homosexual practice. They cannot imagine their struggling loved one not being permitted in church, or even worse, not permitted in heaven. So they begin to adapt their beliefs and positions based on their very hard situation rather than stand on the Word of God, in faith that their loved one will experience complete freedom and deliverance.

You must stand firm! Don't affirm, endorse, or embrace any lifestyle of sin in any of your loved ones. You might be the last person on earth to stand in faith for their freedom. Don't acknowledge their identity in any way that doesn't align with what God's Word says about them. Don't call them "gay friend," "gay son," "gay daughter" or, "gay Christian." Choose your words wisely. Don't let the enemy discourage you. There are millions of people like you who are standing in the gap for their loved ones.

Finally, don't keep it a secret because you are embarrassed. Recall the story of Enrique in Chapter 14. His family was embarrassed and worried about what people at church would think about them if they knew Enrique practiced homosexuality. Don't make the same mistake. Tell people you can trust, who are living godly, righteous lives. Let them stand with you in prayer and faith. Remember, a three-cord strand isn't easily broken, and there is power in prayers of agreement.

You are in your loved one's lives for a reason. You may be the last aroma of Jesus in their lives, so be the salt and light of God in their lives. Shine bright and love much!

Pastors and Church Leaders . . .

I understand that this is a sensitive topic to address. There are many factors on the line when you step out and address homosexuality, but the greatest factor on the line is eternity. It's your job as a pastor, minister, and shepherd to protect the sheep (people). You must protect them from the wolves, themselves, and each other. You must do this with wisdom and discernment. We must be as wise as serpents and innocent as doves.

In Chapter 1 I addressed three mistakes the church typically makes in regard to homosexuality. They make it the greatest sin, ignore it, or affirm it. Don't make these mistakes as leaders of God's people. Don't make insensitive remarks like, "God created Adam and Eve, not Adam and Steve," which make light of the situation and degrade people. Homosexuality isn't the primary issue. There is always a greater hurt, wound, or fracture underneath it that needs healing.

Don't ignore the issue! Don't be afraid of what people will say or think of you. Don't use politically correct answers or PR directors to tell you how to publicly talk about issues from the pulpit every week.

The pulpit is no place for cowards. Don't run your church like King Saul. Afraid of the people.

This isn't my fight; this is our fight. Satan is coming after this generation with everything he has. You and I are to stand between this generation and the gates of hell. This battle is coming to your ministry. Watch laws pass that will take away your legal ability to preach Scripture. It will happen. If we can't resist affirming and embracing those who practice homosexuality, how are we going to prepare the people of God to resist the things of the world, including the mark of the beast?

You're not called to be popular! I want to say it again: YOU'RE NOT CALLED TO BE POPULAR! Jesus told us the opposite. If you do your job, some people will reject you, hate you, and persecute you simply because of God's Word and righteousness. At times, this is hard for me, too. I want to be liked. I want to fit in. But I realize it's not me they are rejecting. They are rejecting the Word of God, and Jesus. Remember, they are not rejecting you and your ministry, they are rejecting Jesus!

This generation of preachers is far too concerned with their following and reputation. Jesus lost followers on a regular basis. Jesus told us to "make ourselves of no reputation." Yes, standing on God's Word may cost you your reputation. However, one day in heaven, you will meet the people your ministry of grace and truth helped keep on the narrow road to life and the path of righteousness.

Don't let intimidation cause you to shrink back from addressing homosexual practice. Don't simply deflect by saying, "We believe what the Bible teaches." Many people believe some crazy things that false teachers say the Bible teaches. As spiritual leaders, it's your job to clearly teach how the Bible defines marriage between a man and a woman, and how not having sex outside that union is pure and blessed in the Lord's sight. Be loving and bold.

I will warn you, when you stand for righteousness and holiness in sexuality, you will face demonic opposition. Never in my life have I felt the warfare and intimidation I felt while writing this book. At times I felt like I was having a heart attack, the witchcraft of anxiety was so great. However, when I felt the demonic intimidation I knew I was on the right track. I would just recall David's words: "You come at me with weapons of intimidation, but I come at you with the name/Spirit of God!" Stand strong. It's worth it.

Minister to minister, I want to challenge you to be very careful what you say when it comes to people. If you use derogatory words (you know what I mean) toward LGBTQ people in private or behind closed doors, you will never have a public impact or effectively reach that community for Christ.

Finally, I want to encourage you to begin to pray and ask God to give you a heart for the gay community and people who are LGBTQ. Pray for them every day. Ask God to pour out His Spirit on their community. On a regular basis, go to the gay districts in your city and pray. Ask God to send the Holy Spirit to bring conviction and repentance. Let's believe God for a revival in the LGBTQ community, for the glory of God!

BONUS CHAPTER
Answering Hard Questions with Dr. Brown

Can you address hermaphrodites? How should they live and approach sexuality?

Hermaphrodites are people with dual genitalia, and it really is a handicap most of us can't relate to or understand. The gay/lesbian community is more acclimated to reach out to those who are marginalized. In many cases, people find acceptance in their midst because they are "different." As the church, we are to make everyone feel at home in the midst of struggles, issues, and problems. We need to do this for everyone, including the hermaphrodite.

In point of fact, a hermaphrodite is either male or female, and this is determined chromosomally, or in other ways. This is who he or she is, and the way he or she needs to identify. In some cases he or she has undergone surgical modifications. In some cases he or she has not or cannot undergo modification. What we need to do is help these people—and all people—find their identity in Jesus. They need to find wholeness as children of God, just as those who are blind, deaf, or crippled must find this, as their handicap is not their primary identity. The same is true for the hermaphrodite.

As they find wholeness as children of God, if they are able to have a sexual relationship in marriage with someone, wonderful. If they have a platonic relationship with someone who wants to marry them, that's wonderful as well. I've heard of marriages lik1`1   4513R3e that. But the key thing we need to realize is that not everyone fits easily into the distinctively normal male/female category.

There are exceptions, and this is where we need to have great compassion and say, "Come in with whatever issues, struggles, handicaps, or problems you have, and you can find wholeness in Jesus."

Can you address the Greek word "malakos/malakoi"? Was the apostle Paul really talking about homosexuals in 1 Corinthians chapter 6?

The word "malakos" (malakoi in the plural) is used in 1 Corinthians 6 in the list of sinful behaviors that exclude people from the Kingdom of God. In that list are things like fornication, adultery, and drunkenness. Then another key word is used, "arsenokoitai" (plural form), and it's the most important one. (Paul also uses it in 1 Timothy 1.) The word malakos by itself can have a varied meaning. For example, it means "soft" in Matthew 11 when Jesus speaks about people wearing soft clothing. Because of the soft meaning in a sinful context, the King James wrongly translated it as "effeminate," but it could refer to "soft men," meaning, men who act in a feminine way in order to have sex with other men. The key thing is that it is used side by side with arsenokoitai, a Greek word that was specifically coined by either Paul or another Jewish author of his day to communicate the idea of a man lying with a man.

Side by side, those two words definitely speak of homosexual practice, possibly even of both the so-called passive and active member in a homosexual act. If you look it up online you will see that even the Gay and Lesbian Encyclopedia online says that without question those two words together speak of male homosexual practice that Paul makes clear is strictly forbidden.

Can you address eunuchs in the Bible? Were these people God "made" gay?

In the Bible, the term "eunuch" most commonly refers to a castrated male. Castration was performed on males in captivity. These castrated males, or eunuchs, would then be put over harems because they had no interest in the women. They had no sexual drive, therefore, they could oversee king's harems with no risk they would sleep with any of the women. Some of these people became high court officials, but technically, a eunuch is someone who has been castrated.

However, in Matthew 19, Jesus speaks of three classes of eunuch: those born eunuchs (born without sex drive or the ability to have sex—lack sexual capacity), those made eunuchs by others (for example, the castrated male), and those who make themselves eunuchs for the Kingdom of Heaven (for example, the person who makes this commitment: "I will not have sex, I will not be married. I am just going to give myself totally and completely to the Kingdom of God"). This is the way Paul lived out his life as a believer; a single man devoted to the Lord.

There are gay activists who say, "But in the ancient culture, if you were a man attracted to other men, you could not be sexually active with them because this was taboo in the ancient Jewish world. You *would just have to abstain from sex and relationships with women. People would think such men were eunuchs because they were not sexually active with women. So when Jesus talked about eunuchs and said some were born that way, He was actually giving a wink and say- ing, 'I know you are gay. You are out there and you are included.' "*

Is this true? Well, if in fact gay men would have been viewed as eunuchs because they were not with women and weren't sexually ac- tive, such usage would be rare and not largely attested. Either way, it's clearly not what Jesus was addressing when He talked about people being born eunuchs. In context, He was talking about people without sexual capacity.

Now, for argument sake, let's say we accepted the gay argument that Jesus was including homosexuals in His teaching about eunuchs. What was His point? It was not that a gay man can marry another man, or have sex with another man. Instead, He was saying that such a person belonged exclusively to Him—no marriage and no sex—for the sake of the Kingdom of Heaven. To use it to justify homosexual relations would be the exact opposite of anything Jesus said.

If in Christ there is no male or female (Galatians 3:28), so why can't we choose our gender?

When Paul wrote that there is neither male nor female, he also wrote that there is neither slave nor free, Jew nor Gentile. But then in his letters he addresses slaves, masters, men, women, husbands, wives. He gives certain rules for men and certain rules for women. At certain points he also addresses Gentiles and speaks of himself as a Jew. But why would he do that if there was neither Jew or Gentile, slave or free, or male or female?

What he means is we have equal status in Jesus. What it means is equal standing. What it means is, there is no caste system or class sys- tem. Men and women, Jews and Gentiles, slaves and free have equal standing in God. Romans 10:12 says that the same Lord is Lord of all, and He richly blesses all who call upon Him. Jew, Gentile, male, female, slave, free—we are one in Jesus. We can all be used by God. God is our Father equally, and we are equal in status as brothers and sisters.

Yet in this world the simple fact is that no man can have a baby. In this world, only a woman can conceive and carry a baby. In this world, some people are slaves, some people are free, some people are

Jews, and some people are Gentiles. So this has nothing to do with choosing gender or saying some are gay or some are straight. It has nothing to do with behavior or sexual attraction. It has to do with our standing in God, that's all.

If a transgender person isn't gay, is it okay to live-out as transgender? *Most transgender individuals don't think of themselves as gay, but rather as men trapped in women's bodies or women trapped in men's bodies. Let's say a man is not even interested in sexual issues or romance, but wants to find wholeness in himself and believes the only way to do so is to become a woman: dress as a woman, take hormones to become a woman, and have sex-change surgery. The fact is, he is still not a woman. God did not make him as a woman. As believers, we need to help these people find wholeness from the inside out.*

I know these are deep strongholds. Some begin to struggle as young as age two. I know these are complex issues, but the fact is biology and chromosomes say you are who God designed you to be.

There are people who have what is called body identity integrity disorder (BIID). They are convinced that their mind map is telling them a certain thing that does not line up with their body, and they will go to great lengths to make the two line up. For example, if his mind tells him he should not be able to see, that something is wrong with his eyes or wrong with him in general, and that he should be blind, the man with BIID will blind himself. One woman with BIID had her psychologist pour cleaning fluid into her eyes to blind her. Some have become convinced they must remove a limb and sawed them off by themselves, or allowed trains to cut them off. Some become suicidal. Once they blind themselves, cut off their limbs, or take other drastic action, they report feeling happy. They are happy they are amputees or blind because their minds finally agree with their bodies.

That is a disorder. We don't celebrate it. We don't say, "I'm so glad you are blind. Let's have a parade for you." We say, "That is a tragedy. You took two healthy eyes and blinded them."

When a woman has sex-change surgery, she has perfectly normal, healthy breasts removed, or has her private parts mutilated to make them into something God didn't intend them to be. We need to have compassion on these people, not celebrate their actions. We need to keep trying to understand why some of these people do what they do, but always point them to wholeness in Jesus.

True wholeness does not come by identifying as something contrary to how God made us. We need to live out how God made us to be, and in the very rare cases of biological or chromosomal abnormalities, we need to do our best to determine who God intended the individual to be and bring his or her body and mind into harmony.

If an individual had sex-change surgery before becoming a Christian, how should he or she live now?

This question is becoming more and more common. Again, we need to wrestle deeply in prayer for these individuals and realize they may be very fragile. They may be more prone to suicide or depression. They may have gone through a lot of internal torment and rejection along the way. So we need to speak the truth, but in an embracing way. We need to be there for these people first and foremost. We need to incorporate them into our community with as much love and compassion as possible, but once again, the decision they made before they were saved was a terribly wrong one.

Let's say a man gets a tattoo on his forehead that says, "Satan Is Lord," and then he gets saved. Of course the Lord will forgive him completely, but he is desperate to go through the very painful and expensive process of having his tattoo removed so he can preach and be a witness for Christ. Out of love and compassion, your church might do whatever it can to help. It might raise funds to get the man's tattoo removed so he can preach and witness, as his new heart desires.

Sometimes we make terrible mistakes. For the most part, complete sex-change surgery is irreversible. The person might have irrevocably handicapped himself or herself. He or she might once have had normal, functioning private parts, and therefore, the potential to be involved in a sexual relationship with someone of the opposite sex. Most often, this is not possible after sex-change surgery.

This person might get surgery to reverse whatever he or she can, and then get off the hormones. This person might stop the unnatural things he or she is doing to try to be who God created him or her to be. This person might even be wise to choose a different church congregation and attend as brand new—as the person he or she originally was.

I heard of one person who attended church for a while as a man, but was actually a woman. One day, she went to the pastor and said, "This is not who I am. I've been living a lie. I need to do the right thing." In her case, probably the best thing for that church to do was bless her and send her to a new congregation where everyone would know her as a woman. Otherwise, it's too confusing. Kids might well say out loud for all to hear, "Oh, I thought he was a man, but now he's a lady."

I know one man who had sex-change surgery and realized he was still not at peace. That had not been the root cause of his problems. He came to genuinely know the Lord, repented of living as a woman, and today, is happily married, though not physically 100 percent whole because he could not reverse everything he had done surgically. He's a man speaking the truth and telling others there is a lot of regret. There is an answer. (His website is www.sexchangeregret.com, and many people write to him after sex-change surgery to share their regrets.)

My friend/family member is gay. How do I love this friend/family member without affirming his or her lifestyle?

We love them because they are people. We love them because they are our son/daughter/cousin/best friend. We love people because they are people. We need to say, "You can tell me whatever you want. You can tell me you're attracted to the same sex, or you can tell me you have no sexual attraction and you'll still be my son/daughter/cousin/friend."

I've told young people that if a church friend says, "I've got to tell you something that is very difficult, and I don't know what's going to happen," then let them tell it. After he or she shares, no matter what it was, simply say, "And? Is there anything else?" It's one thing if a friend confesses he or she is a mass murderer. In that case you go to the police together. But when someone tells you, "I'm attracted to people of the same sex as me," you say, "And? What else?" If he or she says, "I'm attracted to all genders and sex," you reply, "And? What else?" He or she is still your son/daughter/cousin/friend.

I tell parents to tell their kids that if they announce they are gay, tell them you realize how difficult this must be for them, especially in a Christian home. Tell them, "You know what we believe, and the Bible is very clear to us that homosexual practice is sin." Just tell them once, since they already know your views and this is already hanging over their heads and they probably already feel condemned enough. But then say, "Listen, you're our son/daughter, you're always going to be our son/daughter, and in this moment, sitting here with you, we probably feel more love for you than we have ever felt in our lives. We know how difficult this must be, and we are here for you. We love you. If you have a problem, we want to be the ones you call. If you're going through a struggle, we are always going to be here for you."

What if your son says, "Can I bring my boyfriend to Thanksgiving dinner?" Pray about it and if you feel it would be great, and an opportunity to reach out to that young man as well, then act accordingly.

Now, what if you if your son says, "Hey, can my boyfriend spend the night when we are here for Thanksgiving?" Well, you do the same thing as if he had a girlfriend with him. I would say, "There are two separate rooms down the hallway. If you spend the night you'll stay in separate rooms." Each family has to pray and realize that, for the most part, people are confused and lost. Some of our sons and daughters are in outright rebellion. No matter what, we need to be the stable voice. I have heard from so many parents and their kids that the persevering love of their parents got them through their time of confusion and rebellion.

Should Christians attend gay weddings?

In my view, Christians should not attend gay weddings. However, everyone has to get God's mind for himself/herself. By attending we participate in the celebration. By attending we are witnesses when they say, "We now pronounce you man and man/woman and woman/wife and wife/husband and husband, and you may now kiss each other." We are there as witnesses. We are there celebrating the event. We're going to give them a gift afterwards and greet them at their table. I could not do that. I could not sit there without walking out at some point, or saying something.

You say, "Why is that sin worse than other people doing all kinds of things?" But I'm not there celebrating it. I'm not there endorsing it. So I don't care how much they love each other and they really want to commit the rest of their lives to each other. That's not the issue. It's wrong and it's sinful. I'm grieved over it. I'm not celebrating it.

That said, I would do my best to reach out to them. I would do my best to have a meal with them before or after.

I can't tell others what to do. It may be that God will send some-one to a same-sex "wedding" to be a witness, and if so, that's God's business. But my own counsel, my own convictions are that, no, I could not go.

My church now affirms homosexual relationships. What should I do?
You should meet with the pastor and leadership team and ask them if they would carefully consider other arguments on the issue. They will probably tell you they have. Either way, ask: "Would you consider reading Professor Robert Gagnon's book, 'The Bible and Homosexual Practice'?" or, "Would you consider reading my book, 'Can You Be Gay and Christian'?" or, "Would you read Landon Schott's book, 'Gay Awareness,' or other books that are out there?" or, "Would you consider watching a debate or a video lecture?" If they say, "No thanks, we've already been through that," you leave (unless they called you there as a witness and the pastors are OK with you staying there after you tell them, "I disagree and will be working against this").

If they are willing to read the books or watch the videos, give them a little space and pray for them. Maybe they made a serious (but honest) mistake, and God will bring them to repentance. But I would be deeply concerned because this is not a light issue. For them to have gone that far that they affirm the gay lifestyle means they have quenched the Holy Spirit's conviction within them. They have twisted the meaning of Scripture already. They have taken a stand. I would say, barring divine intervention, it is highly unlikely they will turn back. Still, give them the benefit of the doubt and try. Be a witness. Present the truth to them so they are accountable, at least. If they are fine with you staying there, knowing you will work to undermine what they say and preach, you need to leave in a hurry. Then pray for them from the outside and get into a church that affirms Scripture.

When married, practicing homosexuals come to church, how do you respond when they want to go to marriage conferences, retreats, or get involved in ministry?
They are not married in God's sight. It's not marriage any more than if three men/women came together. It's not marriage. It's not marriage if a person "marries" his or her dog. It's not marriage if a man marries a man, or a woman marries a woman.

I understand these couples might have intimate relationships, be incredibly loving and caring toward one another, and find great emotional support in one another. But it's not marriage. It's not as God intended it to be. It's not marriage as law and society have defined it throughout history. The very relationship is sinful/ugly/wrong in God's sight.

We must say, "No, this is only for married couples. This is a church, and you are not married in God's sight. If you love the preaching here, enjoy the ministry here, and you are finding truth and hope, we welcome you to come and hear the Word, and to come to our Bible studies. But your relationship is not marriage in God's sight, and no matter what the Supreme Court says, we don't recognize it."

When do you encourage the biblical practice of excommunication with homosexual individuals?

Excommunication should be exercised with those practicing homosexuality the same as we exercise it concerning those committing adultery or other sins like that. This means we reach out to people with compassion and gentleness, and seek to restore them with a spirit of meekness, as Galatians 6:1 says, "Brothers, if someone is caught in a sin, you who are spiritual should restore him gently. But watch yourself, or you also may be tempted." We reach out. We appeal to them privately. We say, "This is sinful. This is wrong in God's sight. You need to break away from this."

Remember, all of this applies only to someone who claims to be a follower of Jesus, and refuses to repent, not to someone who is struggling, brand new in faith, just trying to figure out right from wrong, or who tries hard but keeps falling. This is talking about someone who says, "I am following Jesus and I'm living like this. I'm free. I have liberty. You're not going to condemn me" (or whatever his or her line is). If the person refuses to repent, you deal with him or her privately. You deal with him or her accompanied by several witnesses. If he or she still refuses to repent, the next step is excommunication.

The Bible does not give a specific timeline, but if you wait five years to do something, it's completely ineffective and sends no message. On the other hand, if you give someone thirty minutes, you haven't really been able to pray for the fear of the Lord to convict him or her. So, you might make this solemn decision over a couple days, weeks, or months. However, at the point the person refuses to repent of his or her sin but still claims to follow Jesus, you have to put him or her out of the fellowship.

Now, if the person has already left the fellowship, and churches in your area are tight-knit, you might put out the word that the person claims to follow Jesus but lives in sin, and that he or she might show up in their fellowship. It's the same if a couple is living in adultery. For example, say a man leaves his wife with no biblical grounds to do so, and goes to live with and have sex with another woman. He and the woman show up at church together, raise their hands together, praise the Lord together, and hold hands while they take Communion, though they're in sin and bringing destruction on their own lives. You are to mark them and excommunicate them if they refuse to repent. All the while, you pray for them. All the while, you look for the day when they will return to get whole.

Now, if the person says, "I'm hurting, I need help, I don't know how to get free," you put your arms around him or her, and you love on him or her. You help him or her. They say, "We want to do the right thing, but we feel bad," so you help them. You excommunicate the ones who refuse to repent.

Can you explain why we follow some of the laws of the Old Testament, but not others?

Some laws were given to ancient Israel for a certain time and a certain season. Many of them were designed to keep Israel from being like the rest of the nations, to keep them separate from other nations. Some of them were like the scaffolding on a building and brought the building to completion before the Messiah arrived.

How do we know which are which? Very simple. God gave some laws to Israel based on universal moral principles. For example, "Don't murder," is a universal moral principle for all people for all time. "Don't commit adultery," is a universal moral principle for all people for all time. What about the dietary laws? Those were given to Israel only, to teach them certain things and to keep them separate from other nations.

How do we distinguish laws based on universal moral principles for all people from those just given to Israel? In short, when God gives a law that is for all people, He will either say it's for all people and all times, or He will repeat it in the New Testament for all people.

When did laws against murder start? In Genesis 9, God made it a universal law that if you took the life of someone else, the penalty would be the forfeiture of your own life. Why? Because human beings are created in God's image, so our lives are sacred. Teachings earlier in Genesis show murder is wrong, and these are repeated in the New Testament. In one example, 1 John tells us no murderer has eternal life.

It's the same thing with adultery. God judges nations for their sins against one another—for being unfaithful to one another. This judgment against adultery is repeated in the New Testament: adulterers will not enter the Kingdom of Heaven.

What about homosexual practice? Homosexual practice is forbidden in Leviticus 18, in a chapter that is for all people. How do I know this? Because God told Israel not to do what the Egyptians did, for they were coming out of Egypt. He told them not to do what the Canaanites did, for they were going into Canaan. Because of these sins, the land vomited out their inhabitants. Because of these sins, God judged Egypt and Canaan. (God makes this all clear in Leviticus 18, so read it from beginning to end.) God told Israel, "Don't do these things: don't commit incest, don't sacrifice your children to these false deities, don't commit adultery, don't commit homosexual practice." Why? They are wrong for all people for all time, so don't do them. The prohibition against homosexual practice is repeated in the New Testament.

In contrast, God did give dietary laws to Israel. He never judged the surrounding nations for eating pork, shrimp, or lobster. And in the New Testament, it is very clear that these are not binding laws on the Gentiles in the church.

Some laws are based on universal moral principles, and are for all people for all time, either based on explicit portions of the Old Testament and/or by being repeated in the New Testament. Other laws given just to Israel were for a past time and season, but were not meant for all believers for all time.

The Bible says Jesus knew all sin or temptation in Hebrews 4:15. So did Jesus struggle with homosexuality?

We don't know that Jesus struggled with anything. The idea of Him struggling with sinful temptation is not what the text says. Rather, it says He was tempted as we are, so He knows the reality of the temptation, yet was without sin.

So did Jesus deal with temptation to be a serial killer? Atheist? Buddhist? Rapist? Pedophile? He did not necessarily have to deal with every specific temptation to be able to relate to us. It was more to understand what it feels like for us to be tempted in many different ways. So, we don't know for sure, but it's possible He was tempted in that way just as He would have been tempted to lust for a woman. It's also possible that in His category as a heterosexual male, He was tempted in every way that we are, and now we just relate because we are all tempted in our own situation, in our own lives. He can relate because He was tempted in like manner.

Is there a difference in men struggling with homosexuality and women struggling with homosexuality?

Psychologists and counselors have talked about different patterns, different mindsets, different things that may contribute to same-sex attraction and desires. Just as men and women are different, the dimensions of male homosexuality and female homosexuality may be different. For example: male homosexual relationships tend to be much more promiscuous than female relationships, but both are less stable compared to heterosexual relationships. There are aspects of male homosexual parenting that are different from female homosexual parenting because again, men are different from women.

That being said, there are similarities in the struggles they may go through as they grow up and develop. For example, "What's the matter with me? Why aren't I attracted to the opposite sex? Does God hate me? I'm not going to be able to marry someone of the opposite sex and have children naturally. I'm cast out by certain parts of society." Men and women who struggle with homosexuality go through this very similarly: if it's a girl, she's a tomboy; if it's a guy, he's a sissy. They are called names and share many parallel experiences, which is what brings the gay/lesbian community together. However, as you read more about homosexual relationships, the history, and expressions, there really are differences in the struggles gay men and gay women encounter, but the struggle itself is the same.

What do you say to the individual who thinks the word "homosexuality" is not found in the Bible—that it was never used in the original biblical languages?

This is an absolutely ridiculous argument that because the word wasn't invented until the 1800s or 1900s, it should not be in the Bible at all. There are plenty of words we use today that we didn't use fifty, 100, 200, or 500 years ago, but they are part of our vocabulary. If they are equivalent to something in the Bible, then great, we should use them. As our vocabulary expands, we can more accurately translate things in Scripture. To say "homosexuality" is not prohibited by the Bible because the word itself is "new" is utterly meaningless.

The question is, are the concepts there in the Bible? This is the second part of the answer. The Bible does not address the issue of same-sex attraction. The Bible addresses the issue of same-sex acts—a man being with a man and a woman being with a woman. That is what the Bible addresses and what the Bible categorically forbids. The concept of sexual orientation is, for the most part, a new concept. Through the centuries, homosexuals did not primarily have a complex concept of homosexual orientation as much as the relatively simple idea: "I'm a man who likes to have sex with other men; I'm a woman who likes to have sex with other women." Sexual orientation is a newer concept, and one with many faults and flaws.

So in that sense, does the Bible talk about homosexuality? No. Does the Bible talk about homosexual practice and homosexual acts? Absolutely, and it strictly forbids them. Does the Bible talk about homosexual relationships? There is not a single example—not a single reference anywhere in the Bible—to homosexual relationships in any positive way. There is not a single positive example. Some might point to Jonathan and David, but they need to study the text more carefully. They will find that Jonathan was married, with children, and David kept getting in trouble because of his lust for women. Neither of these applies to gay men.

So there is not a single positive example of a homosexual relationship in the Bible, and every reference to homosexual acts is categorically negative and strictly forbidden. In the Bible, every positive example of the marital relationship addressed in a law, teaching, parable, or story, is between a male and a female. The Bible is exclusively heterosexual in terms of relationships that it blesses. It presumes heterosexuality. "Husbands love your wives," "wives submit to your husbands," and "children, honor your father and mother." All of this is presumed. Every parable, every teaching, every example of marriage is heterosexual. It is really black and white and clear. So the ideas that the word shouldn't be used, and that the concept isn't there, are really a smoke screen for getting away from the main point.

Say you have two women with children who are married, living together, and going to a church. They get saved and give their lives to the Lord. If you're the pastor, what do you tell them?
The first thing I would tell them is that following Jesus costs all of us everything, and to really follow Him, they need to lay everything on the altar: relationships, future plans, their very lives. I would remind them Jesus says that unless we leave everything and follow Him, we cannot be His disciple. We all must deny ourselves, take up the cross, and follow Him.

Initially, they may not know anything except that He is the Savior who cares for them. But as soon as they can, they need to understand that everything belongs to Him—that He is Lord.

The first thing they would need to do is stop any type of sexual relationship. They might still reside in the same home, but they must separate physically.

I know of two lesbians who started going to church. One of them was seriously born again. Right away, she felt conviction for sleeping with her girlfriend. Next, she felt conviction for even sleeping in the same bed. Then she felt conviction for living in the same house with her.

This is going to be the new reality for them, and the kids who are not their natural children. Though the kids might be the biological children of either of the women, they are not of both. The children would ultimately go to live with their natural mothers as God works to bring them into healthy relationships. If God brings men into the women's lives, the kids will have the fathers they missed out on.

The kids might always share a special friendship with their stepsiblings because they were raised together and their mothers respected each other in the Lord. For their part, the mothers wouldn't want to get too close because there would be obvious potential to fall back into sin.

I know this is difficult, but the reality is that even people in our world today are getting their heads chopped off for merely following Jesus. Others are suffering torture and spending decades behind bars, or in solitary confinement for their faith.

In the case of these mothers facing separation for their faith, they are not facing torture. They are being offered a wonderful new life in Jesus—just as God intended. Remember, without some outside help, there would be no children between these women, so no unique offspring of the two of them.

If what I'm saying here seems too radical, remember the books of Ezra and Nehemiah. When the men of Israel married foreign wives and had children with them, this came to the attention of the leaders. The men actually had to separate from their wives and children in order to get right with God. The marriages were sinful, so God required them to break away.

So how does the church take stances on social and moral issues without driving people away?

The philosophy that I follow . . . the burden the Lord laid on my heart was, "Reach out and resist." We must reach out to people with compassion, but resist the agenda with courage. We need hearts of compassion and backbones of steel.

First, we need to pray for a real heart of love for those who identify as LGBT. Get past the rhetoric, extremism, and the activists, and get God's heart for people for whom Jesus died. These are people He loves dearly, and many of them are broken and hurting. Many of them have suffered a lot of rejection over the years, especially from the church. So we ask God for His heart, but also recognize we function as salt and light in the culture and society. To paraphrase Dr. Martin Luther King, Jr., it's up to us to be the moral conscience of society. It's up to us to shine light in dark places. It's up to us to expose darkness.

Therefore, we have to stand for marriage. We have to stand for family. We have to stand for sexual morality. Dietrich Bonhoeffer said that the ultimate test of a moral society is the kind of world it leaves to its children. So we need to ask ourselves what kind of world we are leaving to our children and grandchildren.

Gay activism has become the principle threat to freedom of religious speech and conscience in America. Yet it is our sacred responsibility to stand up, speak, and do what is right. At the same time, we must address social and moral issues and call our congregations to do what's right.

For example, let's say there's a transgender bathroom bill going through our local legislature which seeks to mandate that every public bathroom and locker room become gender neutral to accommodate those who identify as transgender. Whenever I speak on such things, I keep in mind the fact that sitting right there on the front row might be a fifteen-year-old boy who just came out as gay, and he wants to hear what the church has to say. He wonders if there is hope for him. There might be a couple in the back whose child just came out to them as gay, and they don't know what to do—they're struggling. A woman in the crowd might have a best friend who recently came out as gay, and she might want to see how the church addresses this because she loves her friend and doesn't want her church to be harsh and mean, and so on.

When I speak on an issue like gender-neutral bathrooms, I speak in such a way that I address it holistically, ever mindful that the primary role of the church is to make disciples, win the lost, and build people up. Our primary role is not social action, but it is an important part of what we do. It's been a major part of my calling, but this is not typical for the average pastor. We must be consistent in our purpose to love all. We must be intentional about building relationships with people in our communities. We must get involved with people where they are, in the midst of their needs, and show them the real love of Jesus. So then, when we stand for moral and cultural issues, they will know we are genuine people because we have proven it with our love, sacrifice, and compassionate involvement in their lives. These could be the very things that turn them around. We stand for what's right, but we reach out and build solid relationships.

Notes

1. http://abcnews.go.com/Primetime/story?id=132001

2. http://biblehub.com/dictionary/s/sin.htm

3. Alan Bullock, "Human Sexuality: A Christian Perspective," Christian Life Theological Seminary, 1.

4. http://dictionary.reference.com/browse/sodomy?s=t

5. https://www.opendoorsusa.org

6. http://biblehub.com/commentaries/gsb/genesis/2.htm

7. Pearlman, Myer, *Knowing the Doctrines of the Bible* (Springfield: Gospel Publishing House, 1937), 108.

8. Szandor, La Vey Anton, *The Satanic Bible* (New York: Avon, 1969), 67.

9. http://www.churchofsatan.com

10. Szandor and La Vey, *The Satanic Bible*, 66.

11. Szandor and La Vey, *The Satanic Bible*, 69.

12. Szandor and La Vey, *The Satanic Bible*, 70.

13. Szandor and La Vey, *The Satanic Bible*, 71.

14. Szandor and La Vey, *The Satanic Bible*, 75.

15. Szandor and La Vey, *The Satanic Bible*, 67.

16. Schott, Landon, *Jezebel: The Witch Is Back*, (Austin: Famous Publishing, 2011), 43.

17. http://biblehub.com/commentaries/barnes/matthew/7.htm

18. http://biblehub.com/commentaries/gsb/romans/1.htm

Recommended Reading

Brown, Michael. *A Queer Thing Happened to America: And what a Long, Strange Trip It's Been.* Lake Mary: Equaltime Books, 2011.

Brown, Michael. *Can You Be Gay and Christian? Responding With Love & Truth to Questions About Homosexuality.* Lake Mary: Front Line, Charisma Media/Charisma House Book Group, 2014.

Brown, Michael. *Hyper-Grace: Exposing The Dangers Of The Modern Grace Message.* Lake Mary: Charisma House, 2014.

Brown, Michael. *Outlasting the Gay Revolution: Where Homosexual Activism Is Really Going and How to Turn the Tide.* Lake Mary: Charisma House, 2015.

Dallas, Joe. *The Gay Gospel? How Pro-Gay Advocates Misread the Bible.* Eugene: Harvest House, 2007. (Revised and expanded edition of *Strong Delusion*.)

Nancy Heche, eds. *The Complete Christian Guide to Understanding Homosexuality: A Biblical and Compassionate Response to Same-Sex Attraction.* Eugene: Harvest House, 2010.

Davidson, Richard M. *Flame of Yahweh: Sexuality in the Old Testament.* Peabody: Hendrickson, 2007.

De Young, James B. *Homosexuality: Contemporary Claims Examined in Light of the Bible and Other Ancient Literature and Law.* Grand Rapids: Kregel, 2000.

DeYoung, Kevin. *What Does the Bible Really Teach about Homosexuality?* Wheaton: Crossway, 2015.

Fox, E. Earle and David W. Virtue. *Homosexuality: Good and Right in the Eyes of God?* Alexandria: Emmaus Ministries, 2003.

Gagnon, Robert A. J. *The Bible and Homosexual Practice: Texts and Hermeneutics.* Nashville: Abingdon, 2001.

George, Robert P. and Jean Bethke Elshtain, eds. *The Meaning of Marriage: Family, State, Market, and Morals.* Dallas: Spence Publishing, 2006.

Goldberg, Arthur. *Light in the Closet: Torah, Homosexuality and the Power to Change.* Beverly Hills: Red Heifer Press, 2008.

Heimbach, Daniel R. *True Sexual Morality: Recovering Biblical Standards for a Culture in Crisis.* Wheaton: Crossway, 2004.

Heyer, Walt. *Gender, Lies, and Suicide: A Whistleblower Speaks Out.* Create Space, 2013.

Jones, Stanton L. and Mark A. Yarhouse. *Ex-Gays: A Longitudinal Study of Religiously Mediated Change in Sexual Orientation.* Downers Grove: IVP Academic, 2007.

Lovelace, Richard F. *Homosexuality: How Should Christians Respond?* Eugene: Wipf and Stock, 2002.

O'Leary, Dale. *One Man, One Woman: A Catholic's Guide to Defending Marriage.* Manchester: Sophia Institute Press, 2007.

Orr-Ewing, Amy. *Is the Bible Intolerant? Sexist? Oppressive? Homophobic? Outdated? Irrelevant?* Downers Grove: InterVarsity, 2005.

Reisman, Judith A. *Sexual Sabotage: How One Mad Scientist Unleashed a Plague of Corruption and Contagion on America.* Nashville: WND Books, 2010.

Swartley, Willard M. *Homosexuality: Biblical Interpretation and Moral Discernment.* Scottdale: Herald Press, 2003.

Turek, Frank. *Correct, Not Politically Correct: How Same-Sex Marriage Hurts Everyone.* Charlotte: CrossExamined, 2008.

Via, Dan O. and Robert A. J. Gagnon. *Homosexuality and the Bible: Two Views.* Minneapolis: Fortress Press, 2003.

Webb, William J. *Slaves, Women and Homosexuals: Exploring the Hermeneutics of Cultural Analysis.* Downers Grove: InterVarsity, 2001.

White, James R. and Jeffrey D. Niell. *The Same Sex Controversy.* Minneapolis: Bethany House, 2003.

Whitehead, Briar. *Craving for Love: Relationship Addiction, Homosexuality, and the God Who Heals.* Grand Rapids: Monarch Books, 2003.

Worthen, Frank. *Destiny Bridge: A Journey Out of Homosexuality.* Winnipeg: Forever Books, 2011.

Yarhouse, Mark A. *Homosexuality and the Christian: A Guide for Parents, Pastors, and Friends.* Minneapolis: Bethany House, 2010.

Yuan, Christopher, and Angela Yuan. *Out of a Far Country: A Gay Son's Journey to God. A Broken Mother's Search for Hope.* Colorado Springs: Water Brook Press, 2011.

About the Author

Landon Schott, the top-selling author of *Jezebel: The Witch Is Back,* travels the world with his wife, Heather, as a prophetic voice, ministering to all generations at churches, conferences, and crusades. Landon and Heather founded The Rev Ministries in 2008, a media ministry that airs TV programs internationally. REVtv.com is a 24/7 online youth and young adult network dedicated to turning the heart of a generation to Jesus through Christ-centered media.

Landon and Heather have a daughter, Payton Olivia Lynn, and a son, Preston Noah Lee. They plan on growing their own family as they work hard to grow God's family. Their mission in life is simple: To make Jesus famous!

For booking or more information, go to:
Contact@therev.com
TheRev.com
REVtv.com

LANDON SCHOTT

Jezebel

THE WITCH IS BACK

FOREWORD BY
JOHN PAUL JACKSON

HEATHER SCHOTT

Unscarred

foreword by
JUDITH CRIST

Making Jesus famous one book at a time.

www.therev.com/ministries/famous-publishing